SOCIOLOGY, POLITICS AND CITIES

Editor: JAMES SIMMIE

PUBLISHED

Manuel Castells: CITY, CLASS AND POWER
Patrick Dunleavy: URBAN POLITICAL ANALYSIS
John Lambert, Chris Paris and Bob Blackaby: HOUSING POLICY AND THE STATE
James Simmie: POWER, PROPERTY AND CORPORATISM

FORTHCOMING

Brian Elliot and David McCrone: THE MODERN CITY
Alan Hooper: MARXIST VIEWS OF URBAN SOCIOLOGY
Valdo Pons and Ray Francis: SLUMS AND SHANTY TOWNS

Power, Property and Corporatism
The political sociology of planning

JAMES SIMMIE

B.Sc. (Econ.), M.Phil, Ph.D.

Lecturer in Sociology, University College London

© James Simmie 1981
All rights reserved. No part of this publication
may be reproduced or transmitted, in any form
or by any means, without permission.

First published 1981 by
THE MACMILLAN PRESS LTD
London and Basingstoke
Associated companies throughout the world

ISBN 978-0-333-32359-5   ISBN 978-1-349-16575-9 (eBook)
DOI 10.1007/978-1-349-16575-9

To Ken Hearn for his contributions
to this book and to rugby football

The paperback edition of this book is sold subject to the condition
that it shall not, by way of trade or otherwise, be lent, resold, hired
out, or otherwise circulated without the publisher's prior consent in
any form of binding or cover other than that in which it is published
and without a similar condition including this condition being
imposed on the subsequent purchaser.

Contents

List of Figures	vi
List of Maps	vii
List of Tables	viii
Acknowledgements	x
Foreword by David Donnison	xi

Part I — Introduction

1 Power in Cities	**3**
Introduction	3
Definitions	7
The study of power	17
Conclusions	28

Part II — Social Structure, Cities and the State

2 Social Class, Organisation and the City	**33**
Introduction	33
Social structure	34
The division of labour and organisations	43
Cities as the locations of distributional outcomes	49
Conclusions	56
3 Civil Society and the State	**60**
Introduction	60
Marxist theories	65
Economy	66
Society	78
State	85
Bureaucracy	93

    Corporatist theories   98
        Corporate economy   106
        Corporate polity   109
        The corporate state   114
        Conclusions   122

Part III — Aims and Methods of the Study

4 The Empirical Analysis of Power   131
    Introduction   131
    Aims   132
    Methods of study   133
    Conclusion   146

Part IV — Planning, Production and Consumption in Oxford, 1947–77

5 The Political History of the Planning of Development and Production   149
    Introduction   149
    Bureaucratic autonomy   165
    State production of roads, redevelopment and collective facilities   168
        Roads   169
        St Ebbe's   188
        Housing   197
        Collective facilities   202
    Profitability, externalities and public health   209
        Private and public profitability   210
        Externalities   214
    Conclusions   215

6 The Distribution and Consumption of New Physical Development   219
    Introduction   219
    Residence and social class   225
    The acquisition of new property rights   230
    Illustrations of the informal acquisition of property rights   240
    Who got what and where   251

New productive floorspaces	257
Housing	268
Public goods and services	281
Conclusions	282

Part V — Summary of Data and Relationships to Theory

7 Summary and Conclusions

Introduction	289
Context	290
Development planning	293
Development control	297
Theoretical conclusions	304

Appendices

1 Members of the Planning, Central Area Redevelopment and Housing Committees and their known connections, 1950/1 to 1973/4	309
2 First amendment to the Development Plan	316
3 Second amendment to the Development Plan	317
4 Latest plan for St Ebbe's (now substantially completed)	318
Bibliography	321
Name index	347
Subject index	349

List of Figures

4.1	Oxford wards, 1951	140
5.1	Oxford County Borough Council structure, 1946-7	153
5.2	City of Oxford Council structure, 1970-1	157
5.3	City Architect and Planning Officer's Department, April 1949	158
5.4	City Architect and Planning Officer's Department, 1970-1	159
5.5	Charles Street, 1962 and 1977	196
5.6	The Cuttleslowe Walls	208
6.1	Hockmore Street and Cowley Centre	262
6.2	Friars Wharf, 1959 and 1973	274
6.3	Gas Street, 1952 and 1976	275
6.4	The university and north Oxford	279

List of Maps

5.1	Oxford City Development Plan - town map and programme submitted 1953, approved 1955	163
5.2	Oxford City District - main roads, areas, landmarks and planning issue locations	164
5.3	Proposed outer bypasses	170
5.4	Private proposals for inner relief roads	172-3
5.5	General Purposes Committee proposed inner relief roads	175
5.6	Duncan Sandys' proposals	178
5.7	Council alternatives A and B	179
5.8	Council alternative eventually preferred in modified form	180
5.9	Preservation Trust scheme	181
5.10a	The routes of the relief roads favoured by the Minister of Housing and Local Government	182
5.10b	The 'Jellicoe Plan' for a sunken Meadow Road	183
5.11	Oxford roads: showing proposed modifications to town map amendment No. 2	186
5.12	Oxford City central area comprehensive development area: programme map submitted 1964, approved 1967	192
5.13	Charles Street	194
5.14	Oxford City green belt: submitted 1958, approved 1975	205
6.1	Site of University College expansion in north Oxford	242
6.2	Morris Motors' body-painting plant	248
6.3a	Westgate Centre: location	263
6.3b	Westgate Centre: plan	264
6.4	St Ebbe's redevelopment	277

List of Tables

2.1	An illustration of the Condorcet paradox	43
4.1	Principal component analysis of British towns	134
4.2	England and Wales, urban characteristics compared with those of Oxford	136-7
4.3	Index of residential segregation in Oxford, 1951	142
5.1	Oxford City Council political composition, 1953-73	150
5.2	Total planning applications for Cowley and Iffley, North and South wards, 1953-73	162
6.1	Number and type of applications	221
6.2	Residence and social class	226
6.3	Type of application by type of applicant	232
6.4	Type of application by type of applicant (B type applications)	233
6.5	Local decision by applicant (B type applications)	235
6.6	Local decision by ownership (B type applications)	236
6.7	Proposed main use by applicant (B type applications)	237
6.8	Proposed main use by applicant by ward (B type applications)	238-9
6.9	Main use by applicant (B type completed or started before 1977)	252
6.10	Main use by applicant by ward (B type completed or started before 1977)	253-4
6.11	Gross new productive floorspaces by type of applicant by ward (B type completed or started before 1977)	258
6.12	Multiples' rents and leases in Cowley Centre	260
6.13	Cowley Centre: expenditure and income	261
6.14	Westgate Centre: expenditure and income	265

6.15	Commercial property values (B type completed or started before 1977)	266
6.16	New accommodation units by type of applicant by ward (B type completed or started by 1977)	269
6.17	Length of residence in St Ebbe's since marriage	273
6.18	Industries and shops in St Ebbe's	276
6.19	Private dwellings and population in private households	278
6.20	Residential property values (B type completed or started before 1977)	280

Acknowledgements

The production of a work such as this is heavily dependent on the willing co-operation of a large number of different individuals and groups. Many people have provided this co-operation to the extent that the long individual effort of writing a study of this size has been relieved and often transformed into a real pleasure.

My greatest debt in this respect is owed to Derek Hale, who not only collected and processed the empirical data contained in Part IV but also arranged a continuous flow of darts and football matches which were both diverting and informative. Both of us are indebted to the Planning Committee, especially Mike Thomas and Jim Sharpe, and to the Planning Section, especially Peter Robottom, the late Ken Hearn and all the members of the Development Control Section of the City District of Oxford for permitting us to work with them for two years. Their co-operation and assistance were invaluable. This part of the study was financed by a small grant from the Social Science Research Council.

My thanks are extended to David Donnison for his customary friendly and encouraging readings and discussions of large volumes of manuscript. Graeme Duncan also helped to improve the final draft. I am also indebted to the *Oxford Mail* and *Times*, the City District of Oxford, the Oxford Preservation Trust, the Architectural Press, Faber & Faber, and Miss A. H. Spokes for their kind permission to reproduce the various figures and photographs attributed to them, their employees or relatives in the text.

I should also like to thank Hilary West for patiently typing and retyping the manuscript and Catherine Tranmer for the index.

Finally I must append the usual disclaimer that despite the best endeavours of friends and colleagues, the mistakes that remain are solely the responsibility of the author.

Foreword

It was during the 1960s that a new generation of social scientists emerging in the rapidly growing universities and polytechnics rediscovered the ideas of Karl Marx and his followers — ideas which most of their predecessors had been only dimly aware of. James Simmie made a contribution, widely read by students of urban sociology and planning, to the new and more critical social analysis of these years.

Since then some of those who played a part in this new wave have taken off into rarified theoretical controversies which mean less and less to ordinary people, whose plight is the central concern of true radicals. But others have got down to detailed empirical research, armed with a tool-kit of ideas sharpened by their study of the works of earlier social scientists, both Marxist and bourgeois. The best of them are now giving us a more interesting and complex account of urban, industrial societies and their power structure than earlier neo-Marxists provided.

In this book James Simmie makes one of the most revealing contributions to this literature. He describes how a city's power structure works by making a detailed study of the development of Oxford since the Second World War. He traces the decisions taken by investors and public authorities operating there, and shows who benefitted from them. He calls the pattern which emerges 'imperfect pluralism'. Its benefits are distributed unequally, in ways which reflect the influence of the city's larger and more lasting organisations — institutions of the labour movement, the state, and semi-feudal authorities such as Oxford's colleges, besides those of a capitalist economy. It is the 'small men' — the unorganised individuals in all social classes — whose interests tend to be neglected.

The reader will find here a revealing analysis and a lastingly valuable record of the workings of British society, and the ways in which the opportunities which that society confers are distributed.

October 1980   David Donnison

Part I

Introduction

Chapter I
Power in Cities

Introduction

This study of the political sociology of urban development is concerned with the theory and practice of power in cities. A theoretical analysis of the concept, structure and use of power is conducted. An empirical evaluation of the outcomes of its use, with respect to land-use planning in one city, is presented as an illustration of its general characteristics.

In Part I, alternative definitions of power and its related concepts, like authority and politics, are outlined. This provides the basis for the more specific analyses which are needed to examine its uses in urban development. Previous analyses of power, particularly in the context of local communities, are reviewed. These show both the importance of power as a determining factor in the nature of cities and the difficulties associated with trying to study it empirically.

The problems of studying power are specified. They include difficulties of definition; contradictory theories of society and the state, which form the context and vehicle for the use of power; problems of identification of significant participants or non-participants; differences arising from the lack of similarity between different communities and their historical development; methodological problems; standardisation of the interpretation of results; and finally, the necessity to measure the outcomes of power.

The conclusion reached in Chapter 1 is that the most significant indicator of the distribution of power in a given society or community is the distribution of the outcomes of political and economic decisions. This is why the empirical sections of the study seek to show what the immediate outcomes of planning decisions were on urban developments over a period of time.

Part II examines the structure of power in industrial urban society and the relationships between this structure and the state. Alternative theories of these structures and relationships are evaluated.

Chapter 2 compares and contrasts the urban evidence and concepts for its interpretation employed by Marx and Engels in the nineteenth century with the changed circumstances and understandings of the twentieth century. It is argued that the structures of power relationships, at least in Britain, have changed sufficiently since the Victorian era to warrant the use of theories developed since then by non-Marxist theorists rather than contemporary neo-Marxist interpretations. The structure of contemporary power relationships is outlined in the light of this argument.

Chapter 3 evaluates different theories of the national state as the vehicle for the exercise of political power at that level. Marxist and corporatist theories are examined. Each is shown to have deficiencies either in terms of their lack of consideration for the society in which political action takes place or because that society is said to have a determining influence on state action. Each is therefore said to present an unbalanced analysis of the relationships between society, the state and the use of power.

The original theoretical contribution of this study is an attempt to relate these three concepts using theories of industrial society, the idea of imperfect pluralism and an empirical study of political processes through time to illustrate their validity.

It is argued that all industrial societies have to face similar technical problems at comparable stages in their political and economic development. These lead to some important similarities in their social and power structures. Among these significant similarities are the division of society into distributional groupings based on different forms of power, and the accomplishment of tasks by the use of formal and informal organisations. The characteristics of these organisations are therefore said to exert a predominant influence in both the structure of power relationships and the outcomes of the use of power.

The structure and overt action of organisations in industrial societies may be understood in terms of modern neo-classical economics, particularly with respect to the ideas of perfect and imperfect competition. It is argued that many of the most significant uses of power take place in conditions akin to those of imperfect competition. In the political sphere this is termed imperfect pluralism.

This concept is designed to convey the idea that organisation is a prerequisite of effective political participation and the use of power. In political conflict, organisations may be the producers or consumers of goods and services. In either case, political abilities, size and degree of importance in the field in question will determine the outcomes of power struggles. There are also barriers preventing individuals or new organisations from entering effectively the political determination of significant outcomes.

Part III sets out the aims and methods for studying empirically these propositions. Chapter 4 advocates the use of the hypothetico-deductive method in the study of power. This means that hypotheses are proposed to explain the relationships between society, the state and the use of power. From these, various factual consequences or predictions are made about the use of power in cities during the processes of urban development. Observations are then taken of the evidence concerning these processes and their outcomes. It is then argued that this evidence generally substantiates the original hypotheses.

In practice, the methods employed in this study involve analysing the historical, political and output effects of development planning in the City District of Oxford over the post-war period. The study commences with the establishment of post-war town and country planning and ends with the re-organisation of local government in 1974 and an assessment of the effects of planning decisions taken before that date up to 1977.

Part IV presents the results of the empirical analysis. It examines the political history of development plans in the city, together with their implications for urban outcomes. It also analyses the immediate outcomes of development planning using development control and building regulation records for three wards.

Chapter 5 outlines the political history of town planning in Oxford from the Second World War up to 1974. First, the conflicts over the objectives set in the development plans are described. Second, the power of different individuals, groups and organisations to determine these objectives are analysed. It is concluded that larger organisations were more successful in establishing the inclusion of their objectives in development plans than private individuals or disorganised groups.

Chapter 6 evaluates the immediate outcomes of the new developments constructed between 1953 and 1977. It examines the distributions of properties to different groups and different areas over the period. This permits a precise analysis of the new distributional outcomes to organisations and areas, and some imputation of their distributions between different socio-economic combinations of individuals.

Part V draws the theories and empirical findings together with some conclusions. The use of grounded theory is advocated as a way of studying power in the urban context. The different distributions of power and urban outcomes may, in this way, be explained theoretically and illustrated empirically.

Chapter 7 draws the general conclusion that urban development, in industrial society, may be explained in terms of the relative distribution of power between groups and the objectives pursued by the organisations they form for the pursuit of their interests. In practice, this means that the most significant forms of urban development are constructed or acquired by the more powerful organisations. They exert considerable influence on the formal objectives of land uses as embodied in development plans. They are best placed to manipulate those objectives even after they have been established as statutory land-use policies.

Groups wishing to improve their allocation of physical resources, particularly those distributed through state-managed queues, must form organisations and alliances in order to alter current distributions in the future. This study concludes that organised labour has improved its share of physical resources since the Second World War in this way. Local chambers of trade, trade unions, the Trades Union Congress and the Labour Party have been the organisations through which power has been exercised by organised labour to effect this result.

Disorganised individuals and those groups largely dependent on the state for their incomes do not appear to have acquired a larger share of urban resources over the period of the study. In fact, a number of the gains accruing to the more powerful organisations, at least in Oxford, seem to have represented inadequately compensated losses to the poorest groups in the city.

The total pattern of urban development and its immediate distributional outcomes in this study were therefore characterised by large gains to industrial and commercial organisations, significant relative gains to organised labour and relatively uncompensated losses to disorganised and poorer groups. It is argued that these physical outcomes reflected the relative degrees of power held by the groups and their organisations.

Definitions

The main concept employed in this study is that of power. It is a slippery concept and is used in different ways by different theorists. It is therefore necessary to spend a little time examining its alternative definitions so that the conceptual framework of the ensuing analysis is made clear at the outset.

Three basic concepts must be distinguished in the study of power. First, there is power itself. This may be defined as a concept denoting the ability or capacity for producing effects. These effects can be produced in a number of different ways. Force and coercion produce them by overt and manifest compulsion. Dominance produces effects by a hegemonic, ascendant or commanding influence. Manipulation, on the other hand, produces them by 'unfair' or 'underhand' means. Finally, influence produces effects unobtrusively and sometimes by ascendancy. Power is therefore a complex concept denoting the ability to produce effects by means of force, coercion, dominance, manipulation or influence. These means represent a declining scale of visibility in the exercise of power and also of the vigour of action. They also represent an increasing scale of subtlety in use.

Second, there is authority. This is a concept which denotes essentially the rational and legal exercise of power. Authority is usually associated with particular offices or roles. Because of its rational, legal and formal characteristics, it provides legitimacy for control and government. In most cases these characteristics also lead to relatively willing compliance and obedience on the part of those subject to control. The main difference between power and authority is that the former is not necessarily rational, subject to formal constraints or willingly accepted by those subject to it. Authority, on the other hand, is generally supposed to be rational, subject to constraints and willingly complied with as long as it has those two characteristics.

The third concept which it is necessary to define in the study of power and authority is politics. In this context, politics is the collection of processes in which groups or individuals seek to exercise power with the object of gaining authority, control or compliance. Politics is therefore the process by which power, and the different forms of exercising it, is translated into the results required by groups and individuals with particular and contending interests. This can be done subtly by using influence, manipulation or even dominance to acquire authority for particular interests by translating them into apparently rational rules and regulations and then seeking control and compliance on the basis of these 'objective' rules. It can also be achieved by using force and coercion to achieve control and compliance in the face of opposition. In Western industrial societies the former procedures are normally employed so that the study of power is usually concerned with the ways in which individuals and groups use influence and manipulation to satisfy their interests by establishing authoritative systems to obtain the control and compliance of others. Politics is the process in which the balances of different interests are struck.

Some of the differences said to exist in power studies so far are the result of different or confused definitions of power. So, as Bachrach and Baratz argue,

> Among the obstacles to the development of . . . a theory is a good deal of confusion about the nature of power and of

the things that differentiate it from the equally important concepts of force, influence, and authority. These terms have different meanings and are of varying relevance; yet in nearly all studies of community decision-making published to date power and influence are used almost interchangeably, and force and authority are neglected. (Bachrach and Baratz, 1962b)

Nevertheless, this complaint itself illustrates the kind of confusions which still reign between power and the way it may be exercised on the one hand and authority on the other.

Much of this confusion may be traced back to the differences between Weber's individualistic definition of power as the probability of a command from one individual being obeyed by another individual and Marx's insistence on the class nature of power. Despite their avowed allegiance to these relatively incompatible starting positions, most students of power have in fact defined it in individualistic Weberian terms. Dahl, for example, says that 'My intuitive idea of power ... is something like this: A has power over B to the extent that he can get B to do something that B would not otherwise do' (Dahl, 1957). Bachrach and Baratz add that,

Of course power is exercised when A participates in the making of decisions that affect B. But power is also exercised when A devotes his energies to creating or reinforcing social and political values and institutional practices that limit the scope of the political process to public consideration of only those issues which are comparatively innocuous. (Bachrach and Baratz, 1962a)

More recently, Martin has broadened the individualistic definition still further to define power as 'any kind of influence exercised by objects, individuals or groups upon each other' (Martin, 1977, p. 35).

Such individualistic conceptions of power contain unargued implications about the way it is exercised and also a stimulus-response model of the relations between contending parties. The implications concerning the exercise of power are essentially that it is applied with the use of force, coercion or dominance. Few theorists make this explicit. Bachrach and Baratz do, however, point out that

> First, in order for a power relation to exist there must be a conflict of interests or values between two or more persons or groups. Such a divergence is a necessary condition of power because, as we have suggested, if A and B are in agreement as to ends, B will freely assent to A's preferred course of action; in which case the situation will involve authority rather than power. Second, a power relationship exists only if B actually bows to A's wishes. A conflict of interests is an insufficient condition, since A may not be able to prevail upon B to change his behaviour. And if B does not comply, A's policy will either become a dead letter or will be effectuated through the exercise of force rather than through power. Third, a power relation can exist only if one of the parties can threaten to invoke sanctions. (Bachrach and Baratz, 1962b)

This ignores the possibility that groups may use influence, manipulation and dominance to gain authority and so this may be indirectly a power relationship. It also makes an unsubstantiated distinction between force and power which is weakened by the third contention that power can only exist when one party can threaten the use of sanctions. If sanctions are imposed, this must entail the use of force or coercion and so these are not different from power, as Bachrach and Baratz argue.

The authors then go on to compound the confusion by arguing that manipulation is an aspect of force and not of power. But if force, as they say, is the achievement of ends in the face of non-compliance, then manipulation cannot be an aspect of force because by definition manipulated parties are not supposed to find out that they are being manipulated and so fail not to comply in their own interests. Conversely, Bachrach and Baratz argue that power is exercised when one party achieves another's compliance. In practice, if they wish to associate power with the threat of severe sanctions, then force, coercion and dominance seem to be the implied ways of exercising it. Indeed, in the same article the main distinction they appear to make between force and power is that the former applies severe sanctions while the latter only threatens them. Often the threat is as effective as the application.

As Fisher argues,

> This dominance view of power often contains implicit assumptions about the nature of man and society which stress the self-seeking, egocentric aspect of social behaviour. It suggests that some areas of social behaviour are dominated exclusively by motives of self-interest and that men employ strategy and subterfuge to attain and maintain positions of advantage. According to these assumptions, the only effective restraints are the strength of opposing forces. (Fisher, 1963)

This description, with one modification and together with the use of a relatively simple stimulus–response model, could equally well apply to the work of some French structuralists despite their protestations to the contrary. Castells, for example, defines power as 'the capacity of one social class to realise its specific objective interests at the expense of others' (Castells, see Pickvance, 1976, p. 148). The one main difference is, of course, that Castells talks of social classes rather than of individuals.

Both the traditional students of power and many of the contemporary French authors posit a unidirectional flow between powerful and powerless groups. As Dunleavy says,

> The assumption of unidirectional influence reduces the study of protest to a very simple stimulus–response model in both the pluralist and structuralist views, but there can be no theoretical basis for making such simplistic judgements about causality, particularly as both groups of writers freely interpret the causal links they posit in terms of power. (Dunleavy, 1977)

If power is to be analysed in terms of the abilities of different groups to influence, manipulate or dominate society through the processes of politics then a rather more sophisticated model is required.

Studies such as those by Dahl and Castells which see power in relational terms either involving individuals or social classes identify only one of the ways in which power may be exercised. Dahl, for example, has argued that power is a relation between people, that there must be a time lag between stimulus and response and that power cannot be exercised at a distance. Castells merely adds to this model that power relations are between social classes. Bachrach and Baratz point out, however, that

> power is also exercised when A devotes his energies to creating or reinforcing social and political values and institutional practices that limit the scope of the political process to public consideration of only those issues which are comparatively innocuous to A. To the extent that A succeeds in doing this B is prevented, for all practical purposes, from bringing to the fore any issues that might in their resolution be seriously detrimental to A's set of preferences. (Bachrach and Baratz, 1962a)

In this hypothesis, power is not a relational, chronological, stimulus–response concept but the ability to structure institutional arrangements in such a way that significant outcomes are the result of the 'rules of the game' rather than direct confrontations.

This view of power as the ability to set the acceptable parameters of action is expressed by Mills, Kaysen, Touraine and Westergaard. They say that 'Power has to do with whatever decisions men make about the arrangements under which they live' (Mills, in Pizzorno, 1971, p. 110); 'the scope of significant choice' (Kaysen in Pizzorno, 1971, p. 136); and that it 'is no longer an instrument of economic exploitation for the benefit of a minority but rather a structure of management, control and manipulation of all social life' (Touraine, in Pizzorno, 1971, p. 310). Westergaard argues that the locus of power is to be found in limits which are set to 'acceptable conflict and the consequently restricted range of alternative courses of action which can be considered by less powerful groups. The locus of power cannot be seen except from a standpoint outside the parameters of everyday conflict; for those parameters are barely visible from within' (Westergaard, in Rex, 1974, p. 30). The net result of these circumstances is that power is exercised by some groups who can manipulate the political environment in such a way that direct, frontal challenges by groups subject to such manipulation is relatively unthinkable.

Marxists tend to regard this as the more important aspect of power. They link it to the idea of dominance whereby one part of a social structure can set 'limits to the independence of other levels, and [define] the looseness of the degree of fit between the elements of the structure' (Glucksmann, in Rex, 1974, p. 238). Whether any group is dominant or relies on manipulation and influence to structure the parameters of political action is a matter of degree and interpretation. There is no doubt that such action is an important aspect of power. Equally, power studies have tended to show that a limited variety of groups have exercised such power over time. Even avowedly Marxist studies, however, have argued either that the dominant group has changed over time, for example from manufacturing to finance capital, or disputed which group is dominant at a particular point in time, for example the bureaucracy or the representatives of the proletariat.

Such disputes illustrate the Marxist difficulty of arguing that one group is either always dominant or dominant at a particular point in time. Such a view has been challenged in different ways by non-Marxists. Mosca, for example, maintained that although elites normally ruled they also tended to be different at different times. Some pluralists have echoed this view and argued that power structures are not stable over time. Parsons also takes a characteristically opposed stance. He contends that the dominance view of power only considers its distributive aspects and neglects its productive characteristics. He defines power as total community resources. It is therefore exercised when members of society act together as a whole to maximise its productive potential. While it is true that a society has to produce before there is anything to share among its members, it is also clear that differences in original and potential distributions of the social product are a more important stimulus to the nature and types of production than a general social commitment to produce. If a commitment to produce was all that was required to turn aspirations into reality, no doubt some of the 'underdeveloped' countries of the world would have more to share among their members.

A further difficulty with the definition of power as the ability to produce effects by force, coercion, dominance, manipulation or influence is the distinction of interests. This is particularly critical if power is said to be exercised by subtle dominance, manipulation or influence. If it is to be argued that one group is more successful in establishing its interests either by setting goals or in daily confrontations, then its interests must be defined as opposed to those of other groups in order to show that that is in fact the case.

One way to define interests is to accept the definitions given by specific groups of how they perceive their own long-term interests. The problem with this is that those perceptions can themselves be heavily contingent upon the perceived power structure. An alternative is to define interests as 'possibilities - potential objectives if action - that are inherent in structured positions irrespective of whether and how the incumbents happen to see them at any given time' (Westergaard, in Rex, 1974, p. 30). The trouble with this is that it merely substitutes the analyst's definitions of interests based on a prior and debatable analysis of the structure of society for those of the participants themselves.

A more satisfactory definition would depend on a careful analysis of what is at stake in any goal-setting or confrontational exercise. The stakes of issues could vary considerably but would not necessarily correspond either to those subjectively perceived by protagonists because if, for example, one group was being manipulated it would not perceive the stakes correctly, or with some predefinition of what they ought to be regardless of the specific groups or issues involved. The relationship between interests and stakes is that the latter indicate what particular groups will tend to gain or lose with the resolution of particular sets of circumstances and it is assumed that the former involve distributions and a preference for gaining rather than losing. Thus the interests of a particular group will be defined as gaining or not losing a particular phenomenon.

Where real interests conflict, the processes of politics are employed to resolve such conflicts. Again the actual constituents of these processes have been in dispute. A simple view is propounded by Rossi, who says that

> On the one hand, there is a set of governmental institutions manned by officials and employees with defined functions and spheres of authority and competence. On the other hand, there is the electorate, the body of citizens with voting rights, organised to some degree into political parties. (Rossi, 1960)

This is the formal view which sees political power and authority as unproblematically linked through representative government to the rational and overt exercise of authority through administrative bureaucracies. These kinds of political processes and authority are only the visible tip of a large iceberg of power. They are not the primary concern of this study.

More apposite is Schattschneider's proposition that

> the forms of political organisation have a bias in favour of the exploitation of some kinds of conflict and the suppression of others because organisation is the mobilisation of bias. Some issues are organised into politics while others are organised out. (Schattschneider, 1960, p. 71)

The net result of this process is, in Laswell's famous phrase, to decide 'who gets what, when and how'. The reason that this is such a critical process is the dominant political fact that scarcity prevails with respect to most valued goods and services.

Both Marxists and other kinds of political scientists have recognised the centrality of political processes in the mobilisation of power. The latter have again tended to conceive it in individualistic and psychological terms. Marxists, in contrast, have seen it in structural and class terms. Castells, for example, says that

> The political refers to the structure by which a society exercises control over the different instances which constitute it, thereby assuring the domination of a particular social

class . . . Politics refers to the system of power relations. The theoretical location of the concept of power is that of class relations. By power we mean the capacity of one social class to realise its specific objective interests at the expense of others. By objective interests we mean the predominance of the structural elements which, in combination, define a class over the other elements which are in a contradictory relation with them. (Castells, see Pickvance, 1976, p. 148)

Here the distinction between the simple, formal definition of politics and the processes of which it is really composed is made by differentiating the former as 'the political' and the latter as 'politics'. Politics is then defined as power relations between social classes based on their different interests which are defined by the contradictory structural elements which define the social classes themselves. This illustrates the difficulty of breaking away from the pluralist stimulus-response model without substituting an entirely circular argument which cannot explain both the maintenance of the *status quo* and political change. There is no internal source in Castells's model for altering the structural position of social classes and hence their interests and the power to realise them. His is essentially an equilibrium concept of politics albeit held in that state by tensions or contradictions. This is why he has to resort to attempts by voluntary groups or social movements to alter structures to account for change.

Clearly the definitions of power and politics play an important part in what analysts subsequently choose to study, the kind of processes they regard as important and the way they interpret their findings. Two conceptual fields have been identified, however, which need to be explored. One is the establishment of the parameters or structures within which 'acceptable' political disputes can take place. The other is the analysis of particular disputes and the operation of the informal or formal rules established at other levels. According to the definitions propounded above this will involve studying how different social groups produce effects on institutional arrangements or goals by dominance, manipulation and influence, how they use those same techniques in everyday conflicts and locating this study in the field of politics.

The first is examined in Part II, where theories of industrial society and the state are evaluated. The second is analysed in Part IV, where the workings and outcomes of power and politics with respect to development planning in Oxford are presented.

The study of power

It is one thing to define the concept of power and how it ought to be analysed, it is another to find ways of studying it empirically. As a result the empirical analysis of power is largely a twentieth-century phenomenon starting with the second study of Muncie, Indiana, published by the Lynds in 1937. It is also largely confined within the administrative boundaries of local communities.

The results of these studies have varied considerably. They range from the discovery of pyramidal power structures through factional and coalitional to the amorphous absence of any persistent pattern of power. A number of reasons have been assumed for this variation. These include the implicit theoretical stance of investigators, the differing contexts of their studies and the different methods they have adopted to ascertain the nature of the power structure in particular communities. Even if all these factors could be controlled it is still doubtful whether past studies provide sufficient insights to predict the distribution of power in future analyses. One of the main reasons for this is the almost complete neglect of the possibility that distributions of power actually do change over time.

Most power studies have ignored historical change altogether. They have neglected to consider whether changes in the nature of society and consequently in the nature of its political institutions and processes might not lead to genuine changes in the distribution of power. Thus, for example, one of the main differences between the analyses of Marx and Engels and the study of contemporary industrial society found in Chapter 2 is historical difference of over a century in the societies under discussion.

Genuine historical change or stage of economic, political and social development may therefore account for some of the differences in power study results. Some of these changes may have taken place during the last few decades. In practice, most of the early studies of American cities which concluded that they were dominated by small, unelected and wealthy groups of individuals were conducted around the second quarter of this century, while more of the studies showing a factional or coalitional structure were conducted around the third quarter of the twentieth century.

This may give some support to Dahl (1961), who does include a historical dimension in his study. He argues that the history of political power in New Haven has been one of a shift from oligarchy to pluralism based on dispersed inequalities. Over time, members of the most powerful groups have changed from patricians to entrepreneurs to ex-plebians.

There may be genuine reasons, therefore, why pyramidal power structures do not appear so often in the later power study literature. These are related to changes in the forces operating in modern industrial cities which are marked by:

1. The increasing heterogeneity of interests within the business section.
2. The rise of new power structures.
3. The growing specialisation, professionalisation, autonomy, and heterogeneity of interests in all institutional sectors (see Fisher's 1963 summary of Miller).

These observations are, to some extent, in accord with those of Weber, Mannheim and Schumpeter. They tended to see politicians in this context as balancers of interests. The politics in which they engaged were essentially regulated procedures for the acclamation of factions or elites alternately appointed to exercise power.

The results of power studies are therefore best seen in the light of historical changes in the nature of particular societies and the consequent characteristics of their national states and political processes. Within the theoretical frameworks developed in this study it should be possible to predict the general form that the empirical data will take both in this and in other analyses of power. In very broad terms it should be possible to discern some relationships between the growth of private and public organisations in industrial society, their acquisition of power, a related decline in personal, private entrepreneurial power, as free markets are superseded by oligopolies, and a consequent and growing necessity to develop formal or voluntary organisations in order to participate in the significant exercise of power at all. This latter symptom has indeed appeared in a number of other empirical studies.

Pizzorno, for example, has summarised his understanding of some modern political systems. He says that 'parties and pressure groups, mechanisms of the political system, parallel the function of oligopolies, the equivalent mechanism in an economic system of imperfect competition' (Pizzorno, 1971, p. 189). Some bases for this judgement are given by Banfield, Beer, Castells, Harvey, Miller and Mills. Banfield (1961) concluded that influence in community affairs varies with the issue, and that issues tend to rise out of the maintenance and enhancement needs of large formal organisations. Castells says that 'everything depends on the prevailing power relations, these being largely a function of the linking of the urban demand focused organisations with the political process' (Castells, 1978, p. 121). Harvey makes the same point, saying that 'Most of the decisions made on the physical planning of the urban system are likely to be made or strongly influenced by small and powerful oligopolistic groups' (Harvey, 1971). Miller (1970) also pointed to the importance of organisations in the power structures of Seattle, Bristol, Lima and Cordova. There is therefore something to be said for Mills's contention that 'The history of modern society may readily be understood as the story of the enlargement and the centralisation of the means of power - in economic, in political and in military institutions' (Mills, see Pizzorno, 1971, p. 112).

Three further points follow from these analyses. The first is that large, amorphous or disorganised groups are not likely to wield much power if organisation is a prerequisite of its possession. It is difficult to see, therefore, how social classes as such can exercise power in some modern conditions without first forming organisations like trade unions, political parties or confederations of employers.

The second point is that groups without homogeneous class-base connections must also form voluntary organisations or social movements if they are to have any impact on the outcomes of power struggles. Both Beer and Castells have made this point. Beer, for example, 'shows that the system of pressure groups corresponds to an oligopolistic market. The large groups are the focus of most of the power, and through a process of negotiation with one another, make all the decisions in which they have an interest' (Pizzorno, 1971, p. 14). Castells is also well known for the view that 'urban social movements, and not the planning institutions . . . are the true source of change and innovation within the city' (Castells, 1973, p. 4).

Third, organisations will seek to produce effects which are in accord with their interests or the political stakes as they see them. Where these interests are predominantly economic, the organisations involved will seek to satisfy economic interests. In societies where economic organisations are large and powerful their interests will predominate in that society as a whole. There are organisations in industrial societies whose interests are not predominantly economic and who engage in power struggles to substitute objectives and results other than primarily economic ones. Voluntary associations are one each set of organisations. The state can be partially another. Insofar as state agencies enter power struggles by virtue of being large organisations themselves, or become relatively independent of one set of interests as a result of being subjected to pressure by others, or follow independent professional codes, to that extent they can follow not primarily economic interests.

The results of power studies also show that in addition to wielding power by action, organisations can also maintain their interests by their presence and inaction. Crenson (1971) studied two neighbouring cities in Indiana. Both suffered from air pollution and both were similar types of community. East Chicago took measures to clear its pollution in 1949; Gary did nothing until 1962. Crenson attributed the difference to the fact that Gary is a one-company town dominated by United States Steel and a strong party organisation. East Chicago, on the other hand, contained a number of different steel companies and no strong party organisation at the time it passed its legislation to control air pollution. The mixture of organisations, action and inaction in different locations is another factor accounting for some of the differences in the results of power studies so far.

The ideas of Bachrach and Baratz and their empirical application by themselves (1970) and Crenson (1971) mark a new and important departure in the study of power. Until the late 1960s, power had nearly always been studied as if it were possessed and actively wielded by specific individuals or groups. This was one of the reasons which largely confined its analysis to particular local communities. It was thought that this was a level at which the intricacies of connections and relationships could be unravelled technically and power directly attributed to particular people. These people were then said to be the power elite and their relationships to constitute the power structure.

The late 1960s, however, saw the emergence of the idea that organisations rather than specific individuals could influence or manipulate the structure of power and hence the objectives of different groups. Furthermore, this type of power did not have to be wielded actively but could be employed by political presence and the maintenance of some general frames of reference or values. This idea, if accepted, tended to invalidate the already heavily criticised methods previously employed for studying power. As a result, a number of analysts turned to the outcomes of power struggles as the main indicators of the relative power of different groups and organisations.

It is argued here that the analysis of the outcomes of the use of power is the most effective form of political analysis. It has the advantage that a relatively specific empirical analysis may be conducted which does not depend on such unsure foundations as political rhetoric, reputations and the arbitrary identification of key decisions. It also focuses on the main objective of political action, namely to ensure continuing or more favourable distributions of scarce and desired goods and services. It is therefore a method for examining the relationships between the objectives of different groups and organisations, their relative power and their abilities to achieve their objectives. It avoids the pitfalls of taking political disputes at their face value and devoting too much attention to verbal and administrative disputes which may have little or no significant outcomes.

The study of the outcomes of the distribution of power and political processes has had its own methodological problems. These are the familiar ones of what to measure and how to measure it. At the present there is some agreement on the former. It is generally reckoned that the incidence of income effects is probably the most important output result of power struggles. The concept of income is often derived from Titmuss. Harvey, for example, quotes the following passage with approval:

> No concept of income can be really equitable that stops short of the comprehensive definition which embraces all receipts which increase an individual's command over the use of a society's scarce resources – in other words his net accretion of economic power between two points of time ... Hence income is the algebraic sum of:
>
> 1. the market value of rights exercised in consumption
> 2. the change in the value of the store of property rights between the beginning and the end of the period in question. (Titmuss, in Harvey, 1973, p. 53)

This study focuses on the change in the new property rights and their value over a twenty-one year period. It is not therefore a study of the incidence of total income effects but a significant part of them.

As the output effects of political action generally emanate from the state and its various agencies because they are the focus of that action, most studies have looked at the ways in which state action produces effects on various aspects of income. Again this normally involves examining changes in the distribution of income between different groups over a period of time. The distributions of money incomes, financial and tangible wealth have been extensively studied and now appear regularly in government annual statistics. The distributions of goods normally provided by the state, which either cannot be charged directly to consumers (called pure public goods) or which cannot be charged wholly at market rates (called impure public goods), are not so well documented. The distributions resulting from the allocation of land-use rights are hardly understood at all. For that reason and because they form one of the most important outcomes of the use of power in urban developments, they form the main subject of investigation in this study.

As with the study of power, so most of the studies of urban outcomes are American. One of the earliest was conducted by Benson and Lund (1969) in Berkeley. They examined participation rates in health, police, inspection, library, recreational and school services in three neighbourhoods of Berkeley. The neighbourhoods were chosen according to their social-class composition so that the use of and payment for services could be related indirectly to social class.

The services were combined into poverty-related services and personal developmental services. The poorer area had the highest rate of participation in the former while the richer area had the highest rates of participation in the latter. Each social group had to pay for services which they did not use so much as other social groups. This resulted in distributions from rich to poor and vice versa. Richer groups were able to minimise these costs by moving out of the tax districts incurring heavy expenditures on poverty-related services. The flight to the suburbs was therefore one way of redistributing the costs of impure public goods.

Levy, Meltsner and Wildavsky (1974) studied the distributions of local services in Oakland. In particular, they examined the service areas of schools, streets and sewers. They concluded that

> There is an adage that the rich get richer and the poor get poorer but in our work we found a distribution pattern that favoured both extremes. Some mechanisms were biased toward the rich. Other mechanisms favoured the poor. We discovered no mechanisms that favour the middle. (Levy et al., in Lineberry, 1977, p. 16)

Lineberry, himself, sought to test five conventional hypotheses in San Antonio. They were:

1. That the quantity and/or quality of urban services are positively related to the proportion of Anglos in a neighbourhood population (the race preference hypothesis);

2. That the quantity and/or quality of urban services are positively related to the proportion of the neighbourhood population which is of higher socioeconomic status (the class preference hypothesis);
3. That the quantity and/or quality of urban services are positively related to the proportion of the neighbourhood population occupying positions of power in urban government (the power elite hypothesis);
4. That the quantity and/or quality of urban services are functions of ecological aspects of urban neighbourhoods, including but not limited to their age, density, geographical character, and residential-commercial mix (the ecological hypothesis); and
5. That the quantity and/or quality of urban services are primarily functions of bureaucratic decision-rules made to simplify complex allocations of administrative time and resources (the decision-rule hypothesis). (Lineberry, 1977, p. 66)

Although he found that political inequality between neighbourhoods, as exemplified by residence of formal and informal political office holders, was sharp, this was not reflected in differences between the location of the costs and benefits of public services. Although there were variations in their locations they were not significantly correlated with race, class, elite residence or ecological characteristics. Lineberry summarises the results of his study as follows:

1. The distribution of urban public services in San Antonio can be characterised as one of 'unpatterned inequality'.
2. Neither neighbourhood ethnicity, nor political power, nor socio-economic status are very satisfactory predictors of service allocations, casting doubt upon the underclass hypothesis.
3. To the degree that any attributes of neighbourhoods are related to service delivery, their ecology (specifically, their population density and age of housing) is more closely related than any other attribute.
4. Older, denser neighbourhoods are more proximate to public service facilities, and the quality of services there

is roughly equivalent to other neighbourhoods; hence, more service 'discrimination' is suffered by residents of peripheral areas, beyond the present outreach of municipal service networks.
5. The pattern of tax assessment is also better explained by ecological than by underclass hypothesis, with homes whose assessments most closely approximate their 'true value' (by our admittedly crude estimates) located in newer, less densely settled (hence peripheral) areas . . .
6. Urban public bureaucracies, through their discretion both to make delivery rules and to fit a particularistic claim to one of several rules, probably have more to do with the allocation of services than does the distribution of political power. (Lineberry, 1977, p. 183)

The results of these three studies do not therefore show that the distribution of public services, in these particular cities, is directly correlated with differences in the social class of local residents. What they do show is that, within given total levels of provision, the decision rules adopted by local bureaucrats in public organisations are more significant than any other single factor in the distribution of the outputs of local public services. Lineberry (1977) also argues that these rules and their interpretation are the relatively autonomous preserve of the bureaucrats. Electoral reprisals against local politicians and, indeed, those politicians themselves are not thought to be particularly effective in altering either the rules or their interpretations. Accordingly, Lineberry is 'more impressed by the limits to the power of the power structure than by its presumed omnipotence' (Lineberry, 1977, p. 159). Even allowing for the differences between American and British cities, findings such as these do not appear to offer much encouragement for further studies based on the premise that differences in class power will have a linear relationship with the distribution of the outputs of local government agencies.

However, these findings may be as much a characteristic of the studies themselves as a reflection of the relative power of different groups. In the first place, they only study public services used by all members of local populations. Schools, libraries, parks, roads and sewage systems are all used at some time or another by local families. Local agencies are charged with providing them to everybody. It would therefore be relatively difficult, within a given city, for a political agency to have rules for the provision of these services or actually to provide them in a significantly unequal way without the mobilisation of political power to change these rules or provision. The desegregation of schools would provide a case in point. There, given sufficient time and political energy, rules for the provision of education have been changed.

In the second place, it is very difficult to distinguish in measurable ways between the quality of public services. Two areas may have similar numbers of school places but this is by no means the same as providing similar educational experiences for the pupils who fill them. Again, the controversial policy of bussing children to schools in different areas illustrates the perceived differences in the quality of education provided in different environments in different locations.

Third, the coarseness of the level of investigation in the quoted studies means that some significant but highly localised differences will not necessarily show up in analyses of complete local areas. Thus many cities have pockets of very affluent residents living immediately adjacent to such amenities as parks and communications, and dramatic declines in social composition only a street or two from the desirable amenity. The whole area may therefore appear as generally provided with a park whereas wealthy residents who live on the edge of that park enjoy extra benefits over those who are not within sight of it. In the same way, a sample of significant additions to property rights in a local area could just as easily miss the one or two buildings, like Euston Centre or Centre Point in London, which have contributed the most gains to wealthy individuals, as to include them in a study.

Fourth, the studies mentioned also tend to neglect the important fact that the whole level of public service provision in local areas is not necessarily determined by their residents or by local bureaucrats. Thus, the general level of provision is critically important in what is available for distribution. That level can be influenced by a number of factors including electoral revolts over the level of property taxes.

Fifth, even where the general levels of provision are set by central government, as in Britain, Davies (1968) has shown that there are significant variations in the relationships between 'need' and provision in different local authority areas. Again this is a function of complex factors, not the least being the relationships between local and national power groups.

Sixth, the American studies perforce do not examine the distribution of public goods, like housing, which are not supplied to the entire population. These, in Britain, are more significant examples of struggles over the number, quality, location and funding of public goods because some groups expect to benefit from them while others do not. In contrast, most groups expect to benefit in some way from facilities like parks.

The American studies quoted here do not, therefore, provide conclusive evidence that the distribution, particularly of impure public goods and services, by local governments does not reflect the distribution of power at some levels. What they do show is that, within given levels of provision, in specific local areas, administrative procedures for the allocation of quantities of goods and services are both important and relatively consistent as between constituencies. This consistency, however, may be less important than the differences, and the factors that cause them, between the rules and levels of provision in different areas.

Friedland (1976), for example, has tried to account for the levels of funding allocated to different areas in America. His hypothesis was that federal War on Poverty funds were not

> distributed among cities according to the local level of poverty, but according to the local power of national corporations and labour unions and the extent to which their political dominance was at stake. The War on Poverty provided a strategy for political control over poor and non-white communities who were growing in electoral and organisational strength and who were challenging the political power and policies of corporations and labour unions. (Friedland, 1976)

The picture he paints is a complex one. On the one hand, there are national struggles between corporations and trade unions to secure broad redistributive legislation at that level. On the other hand, there are local political disputes between these groups where each seeks to dominate, manipulate or influence local circumstances. Where these national organisations have powerful local representatives and their individual power is not too dissimilar, then, when they are challenged by other local organisations such as residents' groups, they use their national connections to divert central funds to their local areas. This has the effect of enhancing their own local power, preventing local political challenges from becoming too effective and incorporating them into the major political groupings. In this way, local political conflict is contained. It is not too dissimilar from the relationships between the British Urban Programme and the local distribution of its research and funds.

Friedland (1976) also argues that where the balance of local power is one-sided or the local constituency does not have any national significance, then the level of funding is depressed. He says that where, for example, local labour predominates, as in central cities, it has not been able to curtail central business district growth, urban renewal or highway construction. The reason for this is partly that other groups do not expect to gain political control in those areas and so they may behave with less regard to local interests because they do not believe they have much political potential to lose there. He concludes that

> It is necessary to go beyond 'mass' electoral studies in which acts of individual political participation are aggregated into party or programmatic victories, as well as 'elite' studies in which political and bureaucratic elites respond to potential demands latent in different social groups or objective technocratic needs of the system. The power of national class organisations – such as corporations and labour unions – intervenes between the city's potentially disruptive popular base and the city's public policy designed for that social base. (Friedland, 1976)

Conclusions

It has been argued above that the development of cities in industrial societies is best understood in terms of the objectives of different groups and organisations and their relative power as exemplified by their abilities to translate these objectives into actual land uses and buildings. The central concept in understanding urban development is therefore power. The main indicators of relative power, in this context, are the distributions of urban outcomes.

The application of contemporary power studies combined with an analysis of the output effects of political struggles has largely been confined to American cities. There is no valid theoretical reason why such analyses should be confined either to that country or only to local communities. Lack of research resources in Britain is a major reason why such a situation has existed for so long. Possibly the only notable exceptions to the lack of application of American power studies to British cities are those by Miller (1958) and Saunders (1979).

The first necessity in such studies is a definition of power and the distinction of this idea from related concepts such as authority and politics. Power has been defined above as a concept denoting the ability to produce effects by means of force, coercion, dominance, manipulation or influence. Authority has been defined as the rational and legal exercise of power. Politics has been conceived as the collection of processes by which power, and the different forms of exercising it, is translated into the results required by groups with particular and contending interests.

The empirical analysis of these concepts has changed over time. It has been argued above that the most significant contemporary strategy for their analysis is to examine the outcomes of the use of power. This, again, has been largely an American preoccupation. The different historical, economic, political and administrative conditions prevailing in that country means that the results of American studies will not necessarily be replicated in Britain. Davies (1968) has already shown the inequalities which exist in the provision of public goods and services as between local authorities. This study will seek to show some of the changes in urban inequalities which have taken place within one authority.

Part II

Social Structure, Cities and the State

Chapter 2

Social Class, Organisation and the City

Introduction

If the study of power is best conducted by examining the outcomes of its use and their distribution between different groups, then significant outcomes must be specified and relevant distributive groupings defined. Part IV describes the significant immediate outcomes of development planning. Chapter 2 examines some definitions of distributive groupings and outlines some previous analyses of their relationships in the context of urban development.

In Chapter 2 it is argued that significant distributive groupings must be defined by theorising the bases of their differences. These bases usually rest on different ways of holding power. Therefore the concept of power and the existence of different distributive groupings are closely related.

Second, it is argued that these groups must be relatively closed over time. Groups which individuals can join or leave at will cannot form the vehicles for the most significant distributive differences. If they did, then individuals could equalise their shares of scarce goods and services simply by changing from one group to another. Clearly most individuals are not able to do this and therefore there must be important barriers which prevent them from doing so and which also mark the boundaries between one distributive group and another.

Third, it is argued that, in the first instance, groups are distinguished from one another, in economic terms, as a result of the division of labour in society. This gives rise to distinctions between social classes. Contrary to Marxist belief, this is a particular and not a general way of holding power.

Fourth, as the division of labour develops together with increases in scientific and technological knowledge, so organisation becomes a prerequisite for the combination of different skills in the accomplishment of tasks. Organisation therefore becomes an indispensable vehicle for the exercise of power. It develops new bases for the possession of power and also becomes the main agency for securing distributions on behalf of parts of social classes. Organisations therefore contribute to the structure of the division of labour, provide bases for the uses of power and form the main agencies of social action and control in advanced industrial societies.

Fifth, it is argued that cities form the physical location of distributive groupings and the local geographic areas for the operations of organisations. Only a decreasing minority of economic and political organisations are confined within the administrative boundaries of cities. The latter therefore provide a physical locale marked by local, national and international uses of power by social classes, economic and political organisations. The outcomes of these uses of power depend upon the abilities of different groups to focus these uses on different economic, political and geographic levels.

Social structure

All societies contain structured and sometimes institutionalised forms of social relations which are largely beyond the control of individuals. Insofar as they are not susceptible to individual wishes, they are non-voluntary. Two such sets of relationships common to all societies are those of age and sex. As individuals cannot normally choose their age or sex, they are highly subject to the structured relationships between different age and sex groups prevalent in their particular society. Over time, however, these institutionalised positions may be changed by exercising the collective power of one group against others. The roles of old people or women may be changed in this way. These simple examples serve to illustrate that all societies contain structured social relationships which are maintained by a balance of power between different groups and can be changed by altering that balance.

The structured set of social relationships which has received most attention from analysts of industrial society is social class. The term has been used in so many different ways by different commentators that it no longer commands a clear and unambiguous meaning. A discussion of its content is therefore necessary before proceeding further.

In sociology, a social class is a stratum of society which is identified by theorising the conditions for its existence which differentiate it and close it off from other strata in a given society. While social strata are descriptive categories, social classes are analytical groups resting on some theorised conditions of their existence. The two main conditions determining the existence of social classes are an unequal distribution of power and different or unequal distributions of the bases of that power. These, combined with relative degrees of mobility closure between groups marked off in these ways, form the bases of structured, non-voluntary social relationships in industrial societies. Social classes are therefore institutionalised forms 'for acquiring, holding, and transferring differential power and its attendant privileges' (Bell, 1976, p. 361).

The main dispute or confusion over the notion of social class concerns whether it is a general or particular way of holding power in society. Marxists argue that it is a general combination of the different forms of power which differentiate vertically social strata from one another. Poulantzas, for example, says that

> social class is a concept which shows the effects of the ensemble of structures, of the matrix of a mode of production or of a social formation on the agents which constitute its supports; this concept reveals the effects of the global structure in the field of social relations. (Poulantzas, 1973b, p. 67)

Non-Marxists argue that there are other forms of vertical power differentiation in society which are not dependent on the property relationships defined by Marx as the bases of social class. For Weber, classes, status groups and parties are all different forms of the distribution of power. For Mosca and Pareto, power differentiations are essentially political between rulers and the ruled. The association of power, politics and social class has led Lipset and Bendix to assert that 'Discussions of different theories of class are often academic substitutes for a real conflict over political orientation' (Lipset and Bendix, 1951, p. 150). Thus what is said to constitute the bases of social class tends to differ according to the political persuasion of the author. These views can be diametrically opposed.

On one point, however, there is some agreement. This is that where social relations are structured according to the differential possession of power, these relations are maintained in a state of tension. Structures resting on such a condition are inherently unstable. Tension and instability are represented by conflicts over the distribution of power and the advantages which follow from its possession. Such societies are therefore subject to changes resulting from shifts in the balances of power following various levels of conflict.

Writers as different as Marx and Dahrendorf have then argued that social relations structured on the basis of conflict inevitably lead to societies composed of only two primary classes. Marx identified these as the bourgeoisie and the proletariat. Dahrendorf argued that 'from the point of view of a theory of conflict there can be no such thing as a middle class' (Dahrendorf, 1972, p. 52). This would be true if there were only one major base of power. If that base were, for example, property, then a group either owned or did not own it. There was no in-between condition forming the basis of a third class position. If, however, property is only a particular way of holding the more general phenomenon, power, then the other ways of holding power would form the bases of different class positions and of multidimensional conflicts. As both Marxists and non-Marxists describe the existence of more than two classes in industrial society there is at least an inference that there is more than one way of holding power in such a society.

Marx, for example, argued that the development of privately owned capital produced a set of social classes which were different from those of preceding feudal society. He enumerated them as capitalists or the big bourgeoisie, the middle class or petty bourgeoisie, intellectuals or manual workers, peasants and the lumpenproletariat or social scum, as he described them. Although he then devoted most attention to the relationships between capitalists and manual workers, it is important to note that he identified at least six different social classes.

While it has been argued above that class conflict is occasioned by power relationships and disputes over the distribution of scarce goods and services, Marx attributed it to the private ownership of the means of production. The cause of class antagonism was, for him, the expropriation by capitalists of the means of production from manual workers. The private ownership of these means of production both permitted and ensured this result.

The continuation of this process Marx believed would lead to the increasing misery of manual workers. 'Along with the constantly diminishing number of the magnates of capital, who usurp and monopolise all advantages of this process of transformation, grows the mass of misery, oppression, slavery, degradation, exploitation' (Marx, 1867, see 'undated', p. 97). In this way, capitalist production produced a social class, manual workers, who were supposed to bear all the burdens of society. These burdens and their accompanying misery would produce, according to Marx, a radical class with nothing to lose except its chains. This would inspire a social movement to overthrow the capitalists. Although this process was inevitable, it was also the duty of an active elite to hurry it along.

At other times, Marx does not seem so certain that growing misery among manual workers is inevitable. Engels pointed out that

> Certain kinds of work require a certain grade of civilisation, and to these belonged almost all forms of industrial occupation; hence the interest of the bourgeoisie requires in this case that wages should be high enough to enable the workman to keep himself upon the required plane. (Engels, 1845, see 1973, p. 116)

The plane he required, according to Marx himself, was relative to the standards prevailing in society at the time. Workers would obviously resist distributive reductions in this plane, particularly to the levels of misery described elsewhere.

Wages are therefore not necessarily reduced to subsistence levels of misery but are 'settled by the continuous struggle between capital and labour, the capitalist constantly tending to reduce wages to their physical minimum and to extend the working day to its physical maximum, while the working man constantly presses in the opposite direction' (Marx, 1898, see 1973, p. 223). The actual levels of wages and length of the working day are settled by 'the respective powers of the combatants' (Marx, 1898, see 1973, p. 223).

This is one of the most important conclusions to come from Marx. It admits the possibility of bargaining between social classes and that workers do not enter this process with no power. Private ownership of the means of production is therefore neither the only nor always the greatest source of power. If one class other than capitalists controls some power, then the possibility exists that other classes may do the same. The differential distribution of scarce goods and services between them will therefore be the result of the complex of their relative degrees of power.

If classes who do not own the means of production have some power, as Marx admits, then private ownership cannot be the only basis of social power. Although Marx fails to identify what these other bases may be, there is a suggestion that some of them must be related to politics or ideas. In various texts Marx argues that any class struggling for domination must acquire political power. In other places he maintains that the ideas of the ruling class are, in each epoch, the ruling ideas. The existence of these alternative bases of power partly led Marx to his totalitarian solution to the removal of social classes.

Marx's revolutionary elite, which was to hurry on the inevitable demise of capital, had to seize political before economic power and also control the ruling ideas. This dictatorship of the proletariat, although supposedly transitory, has proved remarkably elitist and persistent in all the countries which have experienced communist revolutions since Marx. This is more to do with the similarities between all totalitarian dictatorships than changes in who owns the means of production.

Indeed, a classless society, in Marx's terms, may be brought about in two opposite ways. Either private ownership can be abolished or it can be made universal. In practical terms, the effects of these changes are remarkably similar. In one case most investments and stocks are invested in the state. In the other, a large part of them are collectively 'owned' in the same way. Neither makes much difference to the forces of production and therefore to the social classes which exist as a result of the continuing division of labour. Power relations within and between social classes continue to exist.

In contrast to Marx, Weber gave four examples of social classes:

a. The 'working' class as whole. It approaches this type the more completely mechanised the productive process becomes.
b. The 'lower middle' classes.
c. The 'intelligentsia' without independent property and the persons whose social position is primarily dependent on technical training such as engineers, commercial and other officials, and civil servants. These groups may differ greatly among themselves, in particular according to costs of training.
d. The classes occupying a privileged position through property and education. (Weber, 1964, p. 427)

Although, in his later works, Marx recognised the likelihood that these middle two groups were more likely to expand than to polarise between the proletariat and the bourgeoisie, much of the subsequent dispute with his class model has focused on the empirical expansion of these classes as if this were a new and unpredicted phenomenon.

Some theorists of industrial society, following Weber, have argued that the expansion and rise of groups whose abilities rest on specialised training marks the development of a new ruling class. For Dahrendorf, 'the ruling political class of post-capitalist society consists of the administrative staff of the state, the governmental elites at its head and those interested parties which are represented by the governmental elite' (Dahrendorf, 1972, p. 303). This idea is expanded by Bell, who argues that

> The essential division in modern society today is not between those who own the means of production and an undifferentiated proletariat but the bureaucratic and authority relations between those who have powers of decision and those who have not, in all kinds of organisations, political and social. It becomes the task of the political system to

manage these relations in response to the various pressures for distributive shares and social justice. (Bell, 1976, p. 119)

Two points should be noticed in this exposition as they will be taken up below. The first is that differences between individuals are the result of the roles they fill in organisations. The second is that this type of analysis also leads to a view of state action which will be taken up in the next chapter. Galbraith identifies the collections of individuals who make decisions in organisations as technicians, scientists, advertisers, marketers and co-ordinators. Collectively they constitute the 'technostructure'.

The idea of a bureaucratic ruling class has also been applied to collective economies. Djilas, for example, says that 'the communist revolution, conducted in the name of doing away with classes, has resulted in the most complete authority of any single new class (the bureaucrats)' (Djilas, 1976, p. 36). Although some argue that the term class should not be applied to a group marked off in this way, Lane has argued that

> The state bureaucracy is ruling class because of the dominant role it plays in the production process. Control of the means of production is effectively in the hands of the bureaucrats as a collective. The relations between the workers and the bureaucrats is exploitive. (Lane, 1976, p. 31)

Finally, Marcuse describes this top ruling group as being composed of representatives from certain organisations such as economic, political, management, armed forces, and the party. It is only subject to the constraints of the Central Plan and the competitive terror.

In contrast to Marx, the theme running through the analyses of social class among these commentators on industrial society is that control and therefore power can be exercised on the basis of factors other than property. Ownership is therefore seen as a particular form of the more general concept - power. If the term social class is to be used in this analysis it either has to be confined to the particular economic usage associated with relationships to production and other terms used for different structured social relationships or it has to be redefined in a much more general way. The latter alternative would seem to produce a concept so vague and general as to be of little analytical value. Accordingly, the term social class will be reserved for those structured social relationships which arise as a result of economic divisions in society and which are relatively closed.

At the more general level of structured social relationships in industrial societies, the problem is therefore to identify the different types of power and control which cause involuntary social differentiation and social stratification. According to Giddens, 'There are three, related, sources of proximate structuration of class relationships: the division of labour within the productive enterprise; the authority relationships within the enterprise; and . . . distributive groupings' (Giddens, 1973, p. 108). These structure relationships between groups to the extent that there is lack of freedom of movement and mobility closure between the different groups.

The division of labour within enterprises tends to define groups who own or organise, who provide special technical abilities and who provide labour. Authority relations within the enterprise associate different degrees of power with these positions. The bases of this power tend to be different for different groups. For organisers, the basis of power is their control over the functions of the total organisation and its individual members. Specialised, scarce and expensive knowledge is the basis of the power of those who provide special skills. Collective numbers and control of labour inputs are the basis of power for those who provide labour. Taken together across the whole of society, individuals in these three main categories tend to form distributive groupings with respect to the acquisition of scarce and desirable goods and services from markets or queues. There is also a fourth, large and growing group in industrial societies which does not participate in economic enterprises. This group is dependent for its support on the rest of society or its own accumulated resources. It is composed of pensioners, the unemployed, the permanently sick and some large, or single-parent, families. It is both relatively heterogeneous and powerless.

Any industrial society is therefore composed of four main

groups which although they may be internally heterogeneous are marked off from one another by the possession of differential power emanating from different sources. These sources are hierarchically structured administrative systems, knowledge, numbers and moral considerations. The four groups are organisers, technocrats, labour and dependents. They represent a relatively closed system of vertical stratification.

The relationships between these main groups or parts of them are characterised by varying degrees of conflict. This is because they have different bases of power and hence different interests in the division of scarce goods and services. Arrow developed what he later recognised as the Condorcet paradox to show that a society stratified into at least three distinct groups with different interests and preferences had to be characterised by conflict.

Arrow argued that, in societies divided into three or more different distributive groupings with different interests, there was no way of generating majority choices and avoiding conflict without violating one or more of five democratic rules. These rules were:

1. Universal domain (that is to say resolution of all possible preference patterns).
2. Positive association of individual values.
3. Independence of irrelevant alternatives.
4. Citizen sovereignty.
5. Non-dictatorship.

Given these rules, Arrow showed that no majority choices could be reached by democratic means. His argument may be illustrated as in Table 2.1. In this X is preferred to Y by a majority; Y is preferred to Z by a majority. According to the transitivity principle, therefore, if X is preferred to Y and Y is preferred to Z, then X ought to be preferred to Z. In fact, this is not the case. Z is preferred to X by a majority; therefore no majority preference pattern of outputs can be formulated among the different interests of these three social classes. The result is that varying levels of conflict must take place between these groups before actual decisions or distributions take place. Normally, the most powerful group would be expected to acquire the most out of such activity.

TABLE 2.1 *An illustration of the Condorcet paradox*

Interests	Social class		
	Organisers	Technocrats	Labour
First	X	Z	Y
Second	Y	X	Z
Third	Z	Y	X

The division of labour and organisations

As a result of the complex division of labour in advanced industrial societies, power is normally exercised through organisations. The continuity, resources and range of abilities of organisations usually outweigh those of simple individuals or even unco-ordinated but well-endowed distributive groupings. Capitalists as individuals, for example, are a well-endowed distributive group, but individually and even, to some extent, collectively they do not have as much opportunity for the practical exercising of power as a large corporation. Only when capital itself is combined into financial institutions employing continuous organisational structures and bureaucratic control does it enter the same power level as, for example, a manufacturing corporation. Again, however, this means that high levels of power are associated with bureaucratic organisations rather than unco-ordinated individuals.

Manifest social-class relationships therefore take place within the organisational enterprises in which individuals make their living. It is the nature of these specific relationships which determines the latent class relationships in society as a whole. Within organisations, class relations can be relatively heterogeneous, varying from worker co-operatives through state-owned industry to old-style private capitalism. The latter is no longer and decreasingly the dominant mode of production in Britain. In tracing the effects of social-class relationships on distributive groupings one is thus concerned first with inter-organisational action and second with the effects of this action on individuals in similar class positions.

Few organisations or social classes are so powerful that they can control decisions which affect them by economic action alone. The ubiquitous production of a surplus in all industrial societies not experiencing economic decline is accomplished by economic organisations. Its distribution between different organisations and social classes is increasingly a matter of political action. From any given starting point, for example, a trade union organisation may engage in economic action within an enterprise to determine the share of profits accruing to workers or the corporation. Outside the enterprise it may pursue the same ends using political means such as a political party. Disputes between large organisations or over the production of goods and services in non-market conditions are also usually conducted at the political level and increasingly via state organisations.

The causes of the structuration of non-voluntary social relations are therefore complex and interdependent. They include the division of labour, the use of organisations to coordinate this divided labour, the hierarchical structuring of these organisations, the differential possession or use of goods, services and knowledge, economic and political action. While they may be relatively autonomous from one another, they may also overlay each other to produce a composite structure which might lead to radical change in a single direction. They are not all ultimately dependent on economic action. The number and complexity of these factors also reduces the practical probability that they will ever all combine to produce a unidirectional change.

The central problem of industrial societies geared to stability and growth is to ensure steady increases in investment and productivity. These become the main stated aims of economic and political units, and there are different ways of achieving them. In a society composed of unequal distributive groupings, different groups take different views of which method seems most desirable. As distributive groupings start from different positions with different bases of power, they also have different and mutually inconsistent interests in the distribution of goods and services together with the fruits of growth or the incidence of decline. It is therefore important to be involved in the decisions on economic strategy and investment. Those groups and organisations who are involved in these decisions and who carry power can expect to maximise beneficial distributions and minimise undesirable effects.

In the early forms of industrial society, decisions on economic strategy and their execution were largely in the hands of individual capitalists who owned and controlled their own enterprises. Non-unionised labour and a minimal state increasingly dedicated to the philosophy of *laissez-faire* had little influence on economic decisions and action. Both Marx and Weber recognised that this was a situation which labour would not submit to indefinitely. Unlike Marx, however, Weber saw the evolution of different forms of participation in deciding and executing economic strategies as a natural development of tendencies already present in original capitalism and not the emergence of an entirely new set of social relationships. The evolution of early nineteenth-century capitalism has not in practice led to the emergence of the kind of socialist society envisaged by Marx. Indeed, so far, no Marxist revolution has ever taken place in any society which had developed beyond early forms of capitalism.

The analysis offered by the Harvard School and other writers, like Dahrendorf, of the changes that have taken place in capitalism is summarised by Giddens. He says that their argument is

> that the essential component of 'capitalism' is the unfettered competition of a multiplicity of producers; that any movement towards a diminution in the number of competitive producers, in respect of capital, or towards the collective organisation of workers, in respect of labour, serves to threaten the hegemony of the capitalist system; and consequently that the decline of capitalism can be charted by the degree to which these latter two sets of processes are seen to take place. To these we may add the notion that the functioning of capitalism, as an economic and as a social order, is inhibited by the intervention of the state in economic life. (Giddens, 1973, p. 283)

Giddens then goes on to argue that in both these analyses and in political economy the roles actually played by working-class organisations and the state and the empirical variations found in these roles are not adequately explained. This is largely true and will require further elaboration in the following chapter.

It is also true that advanced industrial societies attempt to make more conscious decisions about economic actions rather than leaving things to the free play of market forces. Although Goldthorpe, a noted opponent of industrial society theses, has argued that such societies can have a variety of different regimes, it still remains true that all of them are seeking to rationalise their economic strategies. The main stimuli for this action are the need to co-ordinate large enterprises where that function is no longer performed by capitalists as such and to harness the processes of investment and innovation to productivity and growth.

The initiatives for economic strategy lie with the corporations and not with consumers. The only organisations which are of sufficient power, size and permanence to rival the corporations are the state and the trade unions. If the corporations were perfectly co-operative and generated large profits which were reinvested not only in their individual interests but also in the interests of total internal national growth and stability, and if the fruits of those strategies were distributed according to the needs of the total community, then most groups would be relatively satisfied and there would be little organised pressure for them to do otherwise. Economic units do not operate in that way, however, and so organised interests separate out and seek to change each other's actions.

Within organisations, the design of work tasks and the structure of the organisations themselves are not normally in the hands of workers. The decision-makers in these circumstances are normally the administrators and those with special technical expertise. This situation was predicted as long ago as the beginning of the nineteenth century by Saint Simon. He argued that, at the very minimum within organisations, workers would not be able to rule or make decisions on the design of their work because they did not have the necessary organising, scientific or technocratic skills. Important decisions about the internal organisation of economic units and their external roles are normally made, therefore, by the kind of people Galbraith has called the 'technostructure'.

To the extent that such decision-makers require organisations to grow both for their own ends of security, pay and promotion and to internalise some problems of planning, so markets are superseded by monopolies and/or monopsonies. Such developments are often seen as inimical to the interests of too many other groups in society and so organised pressure develops to alter such behaviour. Where this cannot be accomplished successfully within or between economic units, groups turn to political action. The decline of free market decisions is therefore marked by the increasing importance of political decision-making and hence the state. The role of the state is therefore central in who decides what in advanced industrial societies.

The greatly increased importance of the state is a major feature distinguishing original capitalism from modern industrial societies. It has a role of not only altering or co-ordinating the activities of profitable economic units but increasingly of directly controlling essential but non-profitable enterprises, indicating a changing balance between economic and political decision-making. Increasingly, large state-owned enterprises are geared to breaking even rather than making profits and are also used, rightly or wrongly, in the process of the political management of the economy.

Even in industrial societies where the state owns all the significant economic enterprises it is still not the workers who decide economic strategies or design their own work. Where a communist party is responsible for such decisions, party membership gives some indication of who the decision-makers are. In Russia, for example, the social composition of the party does not reflect the social groupings found in the wider society. Lane shows that while manual workers represented over half the population of the Union of Soviet Socialist Republics during the 1960s, they only formed just over a third of the members of the Communist Party of the Soviet Union. Conversely, while non-manual workers formed just under a quarter of the total population, they composed not far short of half the total party membership (Lane, 1976, p. 99). Djilas goes further and argues that a new ruling class emerges in countries like Yugoslavia. This class is 'made up of those who have special privileges and economic preference because of the administrative monopoly they hold' (Djilas, 1976, p. 39).

As with economic enterprises, representative control of managers by shareholders declines with size and time, so with the state. There, detailed electoral control over administrative organisations by voters also appears to be eroded by size and the passage of time. Djilas remarks that 'as the new class becomes stronger and attains a more perceptible physiognomy, the role of the party diminishes' (Djilas, 1976, p. 40). Galbraith, too, talks of the passage of significant decision-making into the hands of the planning system and the technostructure.

The important decisions on investment, productivity, growth and stability generally seem to be made within large organisations. Within those organisations the administrators and technocrats are the people who actually produce and process the information on which decisions are based and also implement those decisions once they have been taken. This provides them with a wide margin for action well beyond the detailed control of even large shareholders or voters' organisations like parties. Political action by organised groups can modify these conditions at some stages in the development of industrial societies. As they develop and as bureaucracy spreads and concentrates in even larger units, however, political action by organised labour unions is associated more with the power of veto than the power to produce positive strategies. This is reflected in the results of major investment decisions and conflicts over who pays, who gains and who loses among interested organisations and distributive groupings.

A generic characteristic of all industrial societies which are involuntarily structured into different organisations and distributive groups is a disparity between the returns from total production accruing to different organisations and social strata. This used to be thought of as peculiar to capitalism but it is now clearly evident in collective economies as well. Aron, for example, says that 'In the Soviet system during the early fifties the difference in earnings between a Soviet private and a Soviet general was said to be greater than in the United States' (Aron, 1967a, p. 89). Lane also notes the general finding that similar forms of social stratification occur in both the United

States and the Union of Soviet Socialist Republics (Lane, 1976, p. 54).

The main social effect of structuration in advanced industrial societies is therefore to counterpose organisations and individuals. Within administrative units, power hierarchies are established which serve the interests of the organisation as perceived by the top members of those hierarchies rather than the interests of all the members. In their external relations only similar, permanent organisations can compete on equal terms with other bureaucracies. Individuals are not generally able to alter the activities of organisations from outside those units. Conversely, public and private bureaucracies can follow courses of action which are in conflict with the interests of individuals. Only if the latter can group together and take organised economic or political action can they hope to modify organisational behaviour in ways different from those required by the organisation in question. In practice, therefore, the organisational structuring of industrial societies becomes more significant in terms of the actual distribution of power and social action than the economic divisions between relatively heterogeneous social classes containing internal competitions and not marked by uniform, organised social action or values.

Cities as the locations of distributional outcomes

Some Marxists believe that changes between the relative positions and conditions of capital and labour within advanced industrial societies constitute a significant divergence from the future predicted by Marx. On the other hand, they argue that something like this future is being realised on an international geographic scale. Imperialist theory therefore sees the exploitation of labour by capital as bound up with the relationships between advanced industrial societies and the so-called underdeveloped countries. In this analysis, international capital exports some of its problems in high wage economies by exploiting the resources, lack of union organisation and low wages found in the Third World. In this way the structure of development in one country maintains the condition of underdevelopment in another. The perceived way of breaking out of this condition is through revolutionary movements for independence. This is a thesis which merits further attention, for these have always been links between forms of structured social relationships and geographic development. The relevant horizons of these relationships have clearly expanded well beyond those examined by early theorists.

Saint Simon, for example, identified the development of industrial society with the establishment of free urban communes. This theme was developed by Weber, who extended it in his analysis of cities. Both of them believed that a necessary condition of the development of industrial society and social relationships was freedom from feudal control. The physical location of this freedom was the urban community in which the traditional rights of feudal landowners did not exist.

During the period of early capitalism, therefore, it was a minority condition confined within clearly defined geographic boundaries in cities and encompassed within predominantly feudal regulations. The city, for Weber, was therefore a particular kind of community with a special and different arrangement of constitutions normally limited to its physical confines. The complete urban community was composed of fortifications, a market, courts, trade associations and administration. According to Weber, such urban communities were total systems of life forces brought into some kind of equilibrium.

Once the process of industrialisation was set in motion this was not a situation which lasted for long. Bücher, a German economist, considered, for example, that economic history could be reduced to a series of three stages: closed domestic economy, urban economy and national economy (see Aron, 1967a, p. 79). To this he might have added international economy. Thus although cities were originally the product of the development of urban economies, the ramifications of those economies soon spread well beyond the physical limits of individual cities.

Another, relatively independent, cause of the development of the kind of urban communities analysed by Weber was politics. While urban communities grew physically as populations moved and concentrated there, with industrial development the established conditions permitting that development were essentially political. In the first instance, political action producing legislation freeing urban communities from feudal rule, permitting non-feudal administration and free land tenure, was an essential precondition of urban economic development. Although continued economic development subsequently became a more important reason for urban growth, political conditions remain an important determinant of that development. Consequently, from the very beginning of industrial urban communities the structuration of their populations into different groups and the political relationships between them had important effects expressed partly in the physical nature of urban development.

Early in the expansion of cities, groups would not only be separated socially, economically and politically but their interests would also be different according to the different physical attributes of different urban locations. The residential implications of these different interests formed the core of the urban sociology of the Chicago School as represented by Park, Burgess and McKenzie (1925). Without making any attempt to theorise the causes of social stratification, they argued that the division of society into different groups was reflected in terms of their urban locations and residential segregation. The processes affecting this result were said to be competition and selection.

Competition and selection between individual members of different social groups with respect to accommodation is, however, only one aspect of the relationships between structured classes and the physical characteristics of cities. Many of the most powerful organisations have interests in locations and buildings in which their members do not live. Indeed, some of the most significant buildings in cities are not used for residential purposes by anyone.

The development of urban and then national economies was accompanied by physical development for manufacturing, commerce, exchange, distribution and administration. These functions come to dominate urban structures in the same way that the organisations using them dominate economic, political and social action.

Part of the actions of organisations in pursuing their ends is concerned with arranging locations and buildings to facilitate those goals. Thus the development of industrial, urban settlements is a reflection of part of the activities of powerful organisations and their actions over time. At the level of early urban economies, organisations may seek to dominate certain locations in order to reduce competition by denying competing organisations the use of those spaces in order to carry out competing activities.

The development of urban economies during the nineteenth century was also accompanied by cultural modes of thought related to money, rational accounting and the intellect. Simmel (1903, 1936) made this the central feature of his analysis of cities. Although, like the Chicago School, a partial analysis, his examination of the mentality of urbanites served to cast some light on the results of the expansion of finance associated with the growth of urban economies. These latter were the seats of money exchanges, and the development of twenty-two regional stock exchanges in large cities serves to illustrate the point in Britain.

With the continued expansion of urban economies to become national and later international, the identification of economic action with specific cities declines. The competition between organisations which once contributed to city growth and structure becomes competition between organisations with horizons well beyond the city limits. Choices can be made which, instead of contributing to development in a given city, can locate that growth elsewhere and so depress conditions in original growth centres. This is again reflected in the decline and concentration of money exchanges. The history of British regional stock exchanges during the twentieth century has largely been one of closure and concentration on the largest one in London. All these developments lead Martindale to assert that 'the age of the city seems to be at an end' (Martindale, 1968, p. 62).

Certainly those social groups which competition has trapped in the ghettos and slums are entitled to agree. The rise of the international economy with many staple, heavy or even new industries more economically established not just in other cities but in other countries makes the future for certain organisations and groups in British cities in general, and the depressed parts of them in particular, extremely uncertain. This is already expressed in the characteristics which remain, unlike the international economy, confined within the limits of particular cities.

Individual cities are now essentially political and administrative units with a legal existence. They are corporations at law with artificial personalities which can act in more or less the same way as other organisations. This has long been the way that American political scientists have theorised about cities. Their work has been much neglected in this country.

A number of factors combine to alter the nature of cities from primary economic locations to primarily political units within which organisations and distributive groupings compete for scarce and desirable physical facilities. In the first place, the development of the international economy means that citizens of any given city have even less control over the economic activity taking place within their city's boundaries. National and international competition results in the decline or removal of many industrial organisations. The weakest groups feel the disadvantages of these changes first but more and more people find themselves unemployed in cities. Increasingly, political units or governments are the only agencies who can be persuaded to arrest the decline of manufacturing industries in cities. Alternatively, they are the ones responsible for financing the services on which unemployed dependent groups rely for their very existence. Short of ignoring such changes, political units are increasingly involved in cities either in trying to produce employment or in paying for those without it.

In the second place, projects for reorganising or redeveloping cities are usually beyond the interests or abilities of individual organisations or groups. They are not part of the interests of private organisations; they are beyond the abilities of those most in need and most likely to benefit from reorganisations. Insofar as political units are more susceptible to pressure from outside than economic enterprises, and insofar as urban projects require complex funding and organisation, political units appear to be the only adequate vehicle for urban improvement in the age of international economics.

Thirdly, once cities have developed it becomes clear that some groups can reduce their own costs by passing some of them on to other members of the community in the form of externalities. Noise, air pollution, proximity and accessibility would provide examples of this process at work. As individual organisations or groups do not usually extend to the same geographic boundaries as externality effects, the only body which may be called upon that does is usually the political unit. Political action therefore becomes the main way that organisations and groups in different social structural positions seek to avoid or share out the externality effects created in cities.

All these factors contribute to the expansion of political as opposed to economic or free market action in cities. A number of urban markets or parts of them are replaced by politically and administratively managed queues. Land, housing, education, retailing, industry, communications are all subject to this process in industrial societies. The direction of change is towards more rather than less of this type of intervention. In Britain, for example, central and local government are by far the largest landholders and are directly responsible for more than half of all building and construction work.

In countries like Czechoslovakia, where political units control most land and buildings in cities, the emerging socio-political nature of the relationships between people and cities is seen most clearly. As Musil has put it,

> Since there are practically no price mechanisms to regulate the use of land and since there is a great scarcity of it in towns, there a non-economic allocation of the resources must be effected. This means that the allocation becomes predominantly a socio-political process. The conflicts are solved by negotiations of political bodies with economic and interest organisations. (Musil, 1971, p. 19)

The decline of private ownership of land and buildings in British cities, especially in central areas, rented housing, declining industries, education, amenities and communications between them, hastens the emergence of similar conditions here.

Cities in industrial societies thus come to reflect past and present conflicts over the distribution and location of different types of land uses and buildings. These conflicts take place in different forms between different groups.

On the one hand there are social classes which are differentiated from one another in terms of the bases of their power or lack of it, and their interests. Social classes as such or as a whole do not usually engage in overt and direct conflicts. More often they are the relatively passive recipients of distributions meted out by organisations.

On the other hand there are organisations. These are brought into existence in industrial society as a prerequisite to the accomplishment of tasks using the division of labour. Organisations are both the active agents of distributions to external groups and a form of relatively closed stratification.

The overlapping and interaction of organisations and social classes produces a complex matrix of vertically and horizontally differentiated distributive groupings. Their actions and inactions at different levels and in different locations combine to produce the distributive outcomes found on the ground in particular cities.

The analysis of power and distributional outcomes in a particular city should therefore exhibit the following patterns. At the level of social action, different groups and interests will be divided by organisational boundaries. These boundaries may be confined within the local geographic area, such as local authorities or firms, or they may stretch to national or international levels such as the national state or international corporations. Where local organisations are parts of larger groups or can form alliances with such larger groups, then they may expect to gain a disproportionate share of local outputs. In this way, local political organisations can call on their national parties to assist them in obtaining satisfactory local outcomes. Large corporations can use the different conditions prevailing in the different geographic locations of their operations to cajole or manipulate particular outcomes in specific localities. These are essentially the political equivalent of the economic conditions of imperfect competition.

Smaller, essentially local organisations can mobilise local connections and knowledge in the service of their particular interests. Among these connections, organisations, like chambers of commerce, rotary and round-table clubs, masonic lodges and working men's clubs, can be employed to secure favourable urban outcomes.

In the first instance, urban outcomes will normally accrue to organisations and, secondly, be passed on to other distributive groupings such as social classes. For this reason the former provide what is this first visible manifestations of the distribution of urban outcomes. Their ability to acquire these distributions indicates their relative power in the urban context.

Urban conflicts cannot usually be identified directly with overt disputes between social classes. Few clashes and few distributions take place directly between social classes. On the contrary, where they take place they may be between urban residents drawn from a mixture of social classes and organisations such as the local state, or between organisations representing different social-class interests. In the main, social classes, as such, are the passive recipients of distributions which result from organised and institutionalised conflicts between representative organisations such as political parties, pressure groups, trade unions or corporations.

It could be that the long-term or general results of these institutionalised organisational clashes are to maintain a given pattern of distributions between social classes. This, however, can only take place at such a generalised and abstract level as to be of little value in understanding particular or local distributional outcomes. Indeed, at this level of resolution, contradictory evidence does not usually fit well with social-class explanations couched in Marxist theoretical terms. Many of the contemporary attempts to understand urban outcomes in these terms fail as a result of the credibility gap between theory and evidence.

To understand urban outcomes it is therefore necessary to define significant groups of formal and informal organisations and to trace the use of power between these groups and the immediate distributions to organisations which result from them. Second, it is necessary to examine the effects that these first-round distributions may have on different social classes. Normally, social classes will be the relatively passive recipients of such distributions. These are the tasks which are tackled in Chapters 5 and 6.

Conclusions

Many changes have taken place in industrial societies since the industrial revolution around the turn of the eighteenth and nineteenth centuries in Britain. Among the more significant has been the progressive replacement of free markets by planned queues. A number of crucial differences emerge in industrial societies as this change takes place.

While free markets predominate where numerous groups and individuals buy and sell their requirements in the processes of production and consumption, the most important form of social structure is social class. Individuals compete as individuals in similar competitive positions for goods, services and incomes. Some are more successful or powerful than others and consequently acquire a disproportionate share of scarce commodities.

The economic history of industrial societies is, however, marked by the decline of free markets and the rise of organisations, planning and queues. Economic units like the firm and social collectives like trade unions tend to grow and organise. Both seek to control the markets for their products and services by such devices as monopolies and closed shops. In these conditions the most important form of social structure is the organisation. The characteristics of large organisations come to dominate the causes and forms of social differentiation.

Social classes continue to exist but as distributive groupings. Even then their relative ability to compete in markets or queues often depends on the organisations to which they belong or their ability to generate alternative organisations with the relevant skills and resources.

A discrepancy develops, however, between local class organisations operating, for example, in a particular city, and the continued operation of markets at the level of the international economy. These large producing or political organisations cannot normally encompass and plan their activities in the same way that is possible at the national or city scale. This means that market relationships continue to exist at this level unless overtaken by such devices as trade agreements or combinations into economic communities.

Conflict is endemic in this system because different organisations and distributive groupings have different values and aspirations. Normally, the larger the organisation, the more power it possesses and the more successful it will be in conflict situations. The ubiquity of conflict means that industrial systems are subject to continuous change. Other factors like the growth of knowledge also contribute to change.

The ubiquity of conflict together with a complex division of labour in industrial societies make the disruption of necessary production a potentially frequent, effective and damaging occurrence. Insofar as all groups require a regular, reliable and continuous supply of material goods to sustain life, there is an incentive to institutionalise conflict in less damaging forms. Where this can be achieved at the level of a given productive unit no third organisation is required. Where conflicts spread beyond the confines of a given economic unit the state develops as a political forum for the institutionalised resolution of conflicts between other contending organisations.

While economic action is largely confined to particular urban or national locations, political action focused on the local or central state can reach enforceable compromises between different organisations. This is decreasingly the case with the development of the international economy. This provides opportunities for large organisations who do not get what they want in one location to direct future activities to other areas. In this way, if the state is to represent perceived local interests, it is drawn increasingly into the provision of goods, services and employment which the market will not provide.

Advanced industrial societies are generally characterised by massive and increasing state replacement of markets by queues. This has a number of effects. In the first place it reinforces the tendency towards and prevalence of bureaucratic forms of administration. This in turn increases the importance of those characteristics which follow from bureaucratisation, namely social stratification, the prevalence of planning and the importance of knowledge. In the second place, this trend also increases the importance of politics within national or urban boundaries as the main form of decision-making and allocation of scarce goods and services. In the third place, the sheer scale of state operations in a country like Britain introduces the possibility that the institution has interests of its own which are distinct and different from other contending organisations in society. The state in Britain, for example, is the largest single landowner, property-owner and wealth-holder.

Any understanding of contemporary industrial societies must therefore include an analysis of the role and functions of the state. For this reason, there follows a discussion of just these topics.

Chapter 3

Civil Society and the State

Introduction

It was argued in Chapter 2 that advanced industrial societies are divided into a complex overlapping matrix of social classes, groups and organisations. These divisions are not usually subject to alteration by individuals constrained within them. On the contrary, they are maintained in given forms by the relative power of collections of individuals with different interests in different locations within the matrix. This power may rest on a number of different bases, including organisational position, the possession of high technical knowledge and collective numbers. These bases of power have been added to the traditional ones of the ownership of land and capital. The net result of these changes taking place in advanced industrial societies is to generate an increasingly complex and multi-based system of power relationships and social divisions.

It was further argued in Chapter 2 that among the social divisions of advanced industrial societies, those marked off by organisational boundaries have become increasingly important. This was argued to result from the increasingly sophisticated and complex division of labour needed to accomplish tasks in production, which in turn leads to the use of complex organisations to co-ordinate and direct the necessary combinations of inputs and abilities. These developments result in important functional divisions within society.

Large and complex organisations tend to segregate production and society on the vertical axes of social divisions. This is because they mark off sectors and sections of production from one another and also create their own internal power hierarchies and distributions of rewards. Thus a worker, for example, in one producing organisation, in a

Civil Society and the State 61

given economic sector, will have more common interests with similar workers in that organisation than those in different organisations in different sectors, and will also share a common power position with his fellow workers as opposed to those in different sectors of the economy. Workers, for example in London's printing industry, do not share the same relative power, organisational situations, market position or interests as workers in what remains of Birmingham's motor-cycle industry. Consequently most of their collective actions are geared to maintaining or changing their particular organisational conditions. In terms of observable social action, therefore, vertical functional groupings such as production units, trade unions or political parties appear to form the most important divisional boundaries in advanced industrial societies as opposed to those of social class.

Social classes, of course, continue to exist as important horizontal but uneven divisions in modern societies. They are uneven in the sense that, as Weber and subsequent theorists have argued, a number of factors in addition to position in production contribute to the total situation of any given group in society. Essentially, however, with the rise of complex organisations in production goes the decline of similarity of common social-class situation and the increase of the importance of the consumption and distributive characteristics of different parts of social classes.

These summary remarks based on the discussion in Chapter 2 have important implications for the way in which the location and role of the state should be theorised in advanced industrial societies. In particular, any satisfactory theory must locate the state and its reciprocal relationship with production organisations and consuming social groups. In addition, the theory would have to comprehend the role of the state in both exchange and distribution.

The main reasons why it is important to theorise the location and role of the state in advanced industrial societies are, first, its sheer size in relation to those societies and, second, its role as a focus of political conflicts and the institutionalised adjustment of different interests. The state has become the central and most important institution in the political production, exchange, distribution and consumption of goods and services. It is the focus of power struggles at international, national and local levels. To understand these struggles it is therefore necessary to understand the state.

The dispute about the nature and structure of civil society conducted between Marxists and those often taking their lead from Weber is reflected in arguments concerning the position and role of the state in that society. In general, those regarding social-class divisions as the most important in society tend to adopt a Marxist view of the state. Theorists regarding functional or organisational divisions as predominant in society tend to support various corporatist analyses of the state. These two positions are therefore analysed in some detail. The conclusions follow those of Chapter 2 insofar as it was argued there that organisational divisions are the most significant in civil society so that corporatist analyses of the state should be the most appropriate in contemporary industrial societies.

Marxist theories commence with an analysis of society and proceed to make the activities of the state dependent on the nature of the society in which it is developed. Although Marxist theory represents a complex whole, it is treated here, for the purpose of analysis, as a relationship between economy, society and the state. Its relative failure to cope theoretically with the rise of bureaucracies and the growth of complex organisations is described.

At the level of economy, Marxist theories of the state are said to draw attention to the importance of divisions in production in determining the divisions into political antagonists. Too much importance is attached to juridical forms of ownership of the means of production in determining social-class struggles and therefore the forms of the state. In many cases these forms of ownership are incorrectly identified as monopolies within national states where they would be more accurately described as competitive oligopolies within the international economy. Concepts of monopoly or state-monopoly ownership therefore fail to locate the national state correctly with respect to the economy.

Some Marxist writers do locate national states with respect to the international economy. In doing so they have to discard a number of the traditional concepts employed by Marx

Civil Society and the State 63

himself. To this extent their analyses have as much in common with neo-Keynesian analysis as with the original Marx. It is therefore argued that traditional Marxist economic understandings of the location and role of the state should be consigned to the history of ideas.

In relation to society, Marxist analyses are particularly susceptible to empirical criticism. In the first place, Marx argued that the state develops as a result of class struggles but is used by the ruling class to dominate the ruled classes. The outcomes of this are supposed to be continuing favourable distributions as far as the ruling class is concerned. The problem with this is that during the latter half of the twentieth century there have been substantial distributions to groups other than the private owners of capital and this empirical fact requires some explanation.

The riposte of some Marxists to this problem has been to dissolve the uniformity of the ruling class and to allow the state a degree of autonomy from the bourgeoisie as a whole. Some fraction of capital is then said to be dominant at any particular time without much evidence being submitted to substantiate such claims. The interplay between different groups identified in this way can again be analysed without resort to Marx's original concepts, which often prove a hindrance rather than a help. In particular, some contemporary Marxist theorists suffer from an anxiety to 'explain' mutually inconsistent outcomes with the same theory. Thus, whether labourers acquire better welfare services or not, whether they become upwardly mobile or not, whether the state acts independently or not are all said to illustrate the validity of Marxist theory. This can only be a tenable position for the faithful.

As a result of these earlier confusions, the eventual analysis of the location and role of the state in Marxist theories also suffers from some inexactitudes. Most of these arise from the inability to demonstrate the daily existence of a ruling class at an empirical level and a consequent retreat to more abstract notions such as the existence of a set of core assumptions. These are never stated precisely nor are the ways in which they determine state action specified.

A final problem for Marxist theories of the state, which is

discussed below, is that of the rise of bureaucracy. This rise is a characteristic of both Western and Eastern bloc states. Insofar as these bureaucracies become permanent bearers of power, they and their organisations form a difficult empirical reality for Marxist theorists who regard social classes as the only possessors of power. Neither analyses of the social-class origins of bureaucrats nor defining them as a social category can do justice to their power and growth in modern states.

In contrast, corporatist theories concentrate on the functional and organisational relationships between producing organisations, consumers and the state. Although they are as much a disparate collection of slightly different theories as are their Marxist counterparts, they also have some features in common.

The first of these is a desire to explain the role of the state in conditions of industrial concentration, declining profitability, technological development and international competition. Following Weber, there is a willingness to allow a greater degree of separation between the economic and the political than is allowed by Marxists. This leads the analysis of the state to be conducted along a number of different dimensions.

In the economic dimension it is sometimes argued that a quantitative and qualitative change is taking place in the role of the state. Some analysts maintain that this is characterised by a significant shift from supportive to directive functions. In these conditions the state develops an important and relatively independent ability to control the activities of private producers.

In the political dimension, corporatists tend to concentrate on significant changes taking place in systems of representation. These generally involve an increase in continuous and extra-electoral negotiations between important functional groups and the state in the making and administering of public policies. They also involve the continued existence of a pluralist sector of interest group representation, mainly concerned with consumption and lacking the political power of major producing organisations.

Corporatists also consider an administrative dimension. This involves examining the degrees of autonomy held by state agents and also identifying the administrative principles and practices of the state. As far as the autonomy of the state is concerned, some analysis is made of the importance and role of a technocracy in mediating demands from the corporatist and pluralist sectors of the polity. The administrative principles of the corporatist state are variously identified as antinomianism, inquisitional justice, strategic control, delegated enforcement and extra-legal power. Following these principles the administrative practices of such a state are said to include a wide range of extra-democratic devices such as secret negotiations, background support for particular pressure groups, the establishment of extra-governmental enforcement agencies and a general willingness to exalt ends over means.

The conclusion is reached that elements of these theories represent a relatively accurate analysis of the current role and practices of the British state. The relevant theoretical elements are therefore combined under the general title of 'imperfect pluralism' with the object of allowing an empirical investigation to illustrate the relationships between power, society and the state.

Marxist theories

Marx commences with an analysis of civil society and proceeds to make the forms and activities of the state dependent on the nature of the society in which they are found. The relationships between government and individuals reflect a complex collection of dependent manifestations of the struggles between social classes. Marxist theories of the state represent a simultaneous analysis of economy, society and the state. These are combined within a framework of their discontinuous historical developments. They confront a changing historical reality and developing argument and counter-assertion. The differences between early and late analyses are as great, if not greater, than those between supposedly opposed positions. In order to unravel these developments it is necessary to look at parts of Marxist theory separately. During this analytical exercise it should be remembered that one of the special characteristics of Marxist theory is the consideration of society as a whole and that at the end of the exercise the parts should be thought of in their totality and not as individual areas of analysis.

An additional problem with Marxist theory is that, as time goes by, the number of Marxisms tends to increase. Often these differences are associated with the interpretation of particular national circumstances. For the purposes of the clarity of the analysis below, it has been judged more important to follow the chronological development of Marxist thought rather than to concentrate on separating the various schools of thought into sections. Most of their differences become evident during a chronological analysis anyway.

Economy

Marx's position on the state was summarised by Engels at his graveside in 1883. There he said that

> the production of the immediate material means of subsistence and consequently the degree of economic development attained by a given people or during a given epoch form the foundation upon which the state institution, the legal conceptions, art, and even the ideas on religion, of the people concerned have been evolved and in the light of which they must, therefore, be explained, instead of vice versa, as had hitherto been the case. *Marx and Engels Selected Works,* 1973, p. 429)

The development of the state, therefore, was to be seen in terms of the results of economic development. Elsewhere, Engels asserted that societies have existed without states, and only economic changes leading to the division of society into classes necessitated the development of political institutions like the state in order to prevent economic struggles interfering with continuous production. Aside from primitive tribal societies, it is difficult to see which societies Engels could have had in mind when setting up this historical starting point for the development of states.

Given the existence of industrial society Marx, however, sought to build up an analysis of the state from concepts like labour, the division of labour, demand and exchange value. In addition to these basic concepts, he also added the notions of international exchange and world markets. The initial problem with this line of reasoning is that while the characteristics of the state in industrial society are related to its economic and social development, no national state in history has ever newly risen only or primarily as a result of struggles between social classes. In the periods of history most relevant to the understanding of industrial states, military conquest, as Spencer argued, was the most common starting point for the imposition of various forms of national state and government. This is obliquely recognised by Engels. In examining the early functions of industrial states, he claims that they first divide their subjects according to territory and, second, substitute public power for the population acting as an armed force. This, he says, is necessary because once society is divided into classes the population can no longer be a self-acting armed organisation. Despite this, even contemporary theorists still regard class struggle as the appropriate starting point for an analysis of the state. According to one Marxist, therefore, 'the place of the state in the ensemble of structures provides us with a single scheme which cannot be established as a concept before we have examined this state's relation both to the economic class struggle and to the political class struggle' (Poulantzas, 1973b, p. 143).

The same author goes on to argue elsewhere that it is not possible to construct a general theory of the state on the basis of such an analysis because the nature of economic and political class struggle differs from one mode of production to another. In fact, only two main modes of capitalist production are identified by Marxists. One is associated with competitive and the other with monopoly capitalism. Much of Marx's analysis of capitalism rests 'on the assumption of a competitive economy' (Baran and Sweezy, 1966, p. 17). A preponderance of subsequent analyses of the state rests on imprecise and highly suspect analyses of monopoly capitalism. Nevertheless, it is reasonable to argue that if the state is related to economic and political struggles in the way Marx asserts, then differences in the latter should be reflected in the nature of the state.

Most of Marx's scarce and fragmented references to the relationships between the economy and the state refer to conditions of competitive markets in which the prevailing attitude of British governments was that of *laissez-faire*. This was a time when the contradictions between liberal philosophy and the condition of the masses was indeed stark. Under such conditions, Poulantzas argues, 'the economic instance almost constantly possesses I determination in the last instance, and II the dominant role. This, in turn, is expressed in the dominance of economic power over political power' (Poulantzas, 1973b, p. 172). This is not to say, as he points out elsewhere, that in the competitive stage of capitalism the state does not itself play an economic role, only that it is minimal and muted compared with the stage of monopoly capitalism.

No doubt most contemporary liberals would not wish to defend the social effects wrought by nineteenth-century industrial development in Britain or similar effects elsewhere at other times. Nor would those accepting the concept of positive freedom wish to defend the role of the British state during the same period. Thus, without necessarily accepting the analytical bases of Marx's critique of the period, it is not difficult to share his condemnation of the early effects of industrialisation.

The era of the dominance of competitive capital and free markets in Britain was relatively short-lived. Out of competitive capital and existing alongside it emerged what Marxists call monopoly capital. This reflected the process of accumulation and concentration of capital. According to writers like Mandel (1974), this process is central to the capitalist mode of production and gives rise to many of its so-called laws. Gamble and Walton (1976) accept this proposition and argue that it is therefore only possible to understand the role of the state in such economic circumstances by examining its relationships to accumulation and monopoly capital.

The basic Marxist position on the state and monopoly capital is found in works like those of Miliband (1969) and Mandel (1974). They both argue that concentrations of private economic power generate political power which, in turn, facilitates the use of the state in the interests of monopoly capital. According to Mandel, for example, 'The bourgeois state becomes the essential guarantor of monopoly profits' (Mandel, 1974, p. 502). Poulantzas sounds a word of warning on this analysis. He points out that monopoly capital represents a fraction of the capitalist class which is divided among itself more severely than other fractions of the same class' (Poulantzas, 1975, p. 137). It would therefore appear to be a difficult task for the state to satisfy all fractions of monopoly capital at the same time. If the kind of analyses put forward by writers exemplified by Miliband and Mandel is to be substantiated, a more detailed evaluation of why one fraction is favoured at one time rather than another is required. Poulantzas himself embarks on such an analysis from the position that the difference between monopoly

> and the state of competitive capitalism is not . . . a mere quantitative one. In the stage of monopoly capitalism, the role of the state in its decisive intervention into the economy is not restricted essentially to the reproduction of . . . the general conditions of the production of surplus-value; the state is also involved in the actual process of the extended reproduction of capital as a social relation. (Poulantzas, 1975, p. 100)

By the stage of monopoly capital the state is therefore seen as a separate entity. Although its general primary function may be the maintenance of monopoly profits it must, as Poulantzas recognised, have a degree of autonomy. This arises from the acknowledged fact that some fractions of monopoly capital are more successful than others in having their profits guaranteed by the state so that less successful fractions cannot dominate state action so effectively. Furthermore, although monopoly capital may be the dominant form, competitive capital remains a large and significant part of total capital. If it is being argued that the state is used to further the interests of some fractions of monopoly capital rather than others, then by the same token it must be even more independent of competitive capital than it is of the less successful fractions of monopoly capital.

Another difficulty with assertions about the role of monopoly capital is that by implication the concept refers mostly to manufacturing capital either because the analysis refers to stages of historical development before the development of a major service sector in economies or because most services do not lend themselves to monopoly anyway. The history of large manufacturing capital during the twentieth century in many industrial economies has not been one of unmitigated success. If it was so powerful in forcing national states to guarantee its profits it is reasonable to expect that at the very least existing profit quantities would have been maintained. Even Marx himself predicted that although the rate of profit would tend to fall as a result of the use of increasing proportions of capital, the actual mean or quantity of profit would rise. In many manufacturing enterprises this has not been the case. In a rather large number of instances, manufacturing concerns which were economically viable in the nineteenth century have seen their profitability collapse altogether in the twentieth. This does not support assertions that monopoly capital can usually use or force the state to guarantee or maintain its profitability.

Three different theories have been advanced to take account of these economic conditions and yet still maintain that the state is dominated by capital. One is that finance capital is now the dominant form, another is that the state has to make up for underconsumption in the private sector, and the most common argument is that the state itself becomes the monopoly capitalist.

The first theory is propounded by writers like Aaronovitch. He says that

> Whether we consider the Cabinet and its committees, or the so-called quasi-government bodies, or the government departments, all the evidence points to the conclusion that these policy-making and administrative organs of the State are not 'independent' bodies. They are manned and controlled by finance capital. Finance capital is not some 'lobby' outside the political system, but is built into its foundations. The finance capitalists are in truth the ruling class. (Aaronovitch, see Urry and Wakeford, 1973, p. 130)

While it is true that a great deal of current state activities require investment, stocks and money and therefore require capital in this sense, this is not the same as being ruled by it. Finance capital is by its very nature highly divisible and can be acquired in different ways, from different sources both inside and outside the state. For these reasons, it is not a homogeneous commodity but a highly differentiated and competitive resource required by any industrial society. If there are contradictions within monopoly industrial capital, there are certainly more within the realm of finance capital. Fragmentation, competition and contradictions make it difficult to accept the idea that finance capitalists are a unified ruling class.

Baran and Sweezy put forward an alternative view of the relationships between the economy and the state in the era of monopoly capital. In 1966 they argued that industrial capital was so good at producing goods that the population at large was not capable of absorbing all the surplus. Capital, therefore, got into difficulties exemplified by declining profits because of underconsumption of the goods it produced. The role of the state in these conditions was to absorb the surplus for which industry could find no profitable outlets. This process should preferably not have reintroduced more goods into the economy and thus contributed to the size of the surplus which already could not be consumed. Space expenditure and arms expenditure were ideal for this purpose. The problems with this theory were, first, that it was peculiarly related to American experience and, second, that, apart from some of the terminology, it was too close to liberal Keynesian analyses to be acceptable to most European Marxists.

The most generally accepted theory concerning the position of the state in modern industrial economies is that in both East and West varying degrees of state monopoly capital exist. This concept is designed to convey Marx's idea that the more the state takes over productive forces the more it becomes the national capitalist. According to Trotsky,

> State capitalism means the substitution of state property for private property, and for that very reason remains partial in character. State-ism [as he calls it, adopting a

translation of the French 'étatism'] no matter where ... means state intervention on the basis of private property, and with the goal of preserving it. (Trotsky, 1936, see 1973, p. 246)

In addition to the activities which the state itself acquires, the era of state monopoly capitalism also sees the increasing dependence of private capital on the awards and support of the state. If demand and employment are to be maintained in such conditions, many economists would agree that government expenditures to this end are necessary. All this led Baran and Sweezy to the conclusion that

In State and Revolution (1917) Lenin spoke of the epoch of the development of monopoly capitalism into state monopoly capitalism, and it is now the accepted view in the communist world that the advanced capitalist countries have long since passed through this transitional stage and entered that of state monopoly capitalism. (Baran and Sweezy, 1966, p. 25)

If this is indeed the case, then much of the early Marxist analysis of the relationships between economy and state must be abandoned as irrelevant because it refers to conditions of competitive market capitalism. Even some Marxist critics of Poulantzas have raised this argument saying, as he summarises them, that 'The analyses of Marx, Engels, Lenin and Gramsci on which I based myself were certainly correct in terms of the specific situation that the latter confronted, but they are no longer applicable to the state of state monopoly capitalism' (Poulantzas, 1975, p. 157). Although Poulantzas himself disputes this, it remains an important criticism of the contemporary relevance of the authors mentioned.

Another problem with the idea of state monopoly capital is that many of the activities pursued by modern states have been acquired because they were not profitable as private enterprises or because they were not generally available at a price most people could afford. This means that many of them are essentially loss-making. Such losses must be made up from surpluses made elsewhere and, in the short run at least, must be deductions from the total surplus available to capital in the form of profit. Again this does not really confirm the picture of a state either itself committed to or dominated by capital pursuing profit.

The most serious deficiency in the ideas of monopoly and state monopoly capital, however, is that in practice there is virtually no such thing. In the context of a world economy which also includes the socialist countries, even the most giant of enterprises seldom have an absolute monopoly. More often the industrial world economy is composed of oligopolies in fierce competition with each other. Many national states have economies which are in fact smaller than some of the giant oligopolies. Often the national state is in the position of supporting enterprises within its territorial boundaries in the face of international competition both from other similar enterprises and other national states. Even the relatively closed economies of socialist states are subject to these kinds of pressures as oil crises, unemployment and inflation tend to demonstrate. Lenin was therefore both confused and contradictory when he identified the age of imperialism and the international economy with 'the era of bank capital, the era of gigantic capitalist monopolies, of the development of monopoly capitalism into state-monopoly capitalism' (Lenin, 1919, see 1972, p. 31).

Within the territorial boundaries of a given national state it is also seldom the case that the state as such has an absolute monopoly. Either a small private sector maintains a privileged market alternative such as in health and education or the state itself provides substitutes for its own services such as in energy and transport. In the case of production, the state often appears as the defender of weak national enterprises in the face of strong international competition rather than as dominated by its own internal oligopolies or as a monopoly itself in the world economy. Some of these problems are recognised by Poulantzas when he admits that 'by considering the capitalist state as a regional instance of the (capitalist mode of production), and so in its complex relations with the relations of production, we can establish its specific autonomy relative to the economic' (Poulantzas, 1973b, p. 127).

The specific autonomy of the national state with respect

to its own internal economy will tend to increase in proportion to the weakness of its own oligopolies within the context of the international economy, the existence of organised countervailing oligopolies such as the trade unions and the size of the role played by the state in its own economy. The general direction of these trends, at least in Britain, has been a weakening of manufacturing oligopolies, an increase in the countervailing powers of organised trade unions and a massive increase in the proportion of total capital and income directly controlled by the various state agencies. This has led to a considerable degree of autonomy for the state within its boundaries combined with a general decline in the context of the world economy.

Despite these problems associated with the real nature of state monopoly capitalism and the degrees of its autonomy, Marx argues that even national states with large public sectors of production or welfare functions are really directed by private capital. He says that

> the modern state ... purchased gradually by the owners of property by means of taxation, has fallen entirely into (the hands of private property) through the national debt, and its existence has become wholly dependent on the commercial credit which the owners of property, the bourgeois, extend to it, as reflected in the rise and fall of state funds on the stock exchange. (Marx, 1846, see 1974, p. 79)

Thus state ownership does not, according to Marx, do away with capitalist control or the underlying capitalistic nature of productive forces.

Somewhat surprisingly, therefore, in view of this position, as late as 1892 Engels was still developing the thesis that 'The proletariat [seize] political power and [turn] the means of production into state property' (Engels, 1892, see Marx and Engels, 1973, p. 423). This action was supposed to do away with the underlying nature of capitalistic productive forces by a trick of definition, for 'in doing this, it abolishes itself as proletariat, abolishes all class distinctions and class antagonisms, abolishes also the state as state' (Engels, 1892, see

Marx and Engels, 1973, p. 424). This view was repeated with approval by Lenin in *The State and Revolution* in 1919 (see 1972, p. 16). He went on to argue that this action was necessary to centralise and organise a socialist economy with the main objective of increasing production, that is to say, economic growth and accumulation.

The practical results of this semantic trickery and utopian philosophy were outlined by Trotsky. During the 1930s, after the revolution in Russia, he argued that

> The Soviet Union is a contradictory society halfway between capitalism and socialism, in which:
> (a) The productive forces are still far from adequate to give the state a socialist character;
> (b) the tendency toward primitive accumulation created by want breaks out through innumerable pores of the planned economy;
> (c) norms of distribution preserving a bourgeois character lie at the basis of a new differentiation of society;
> (d) the economic growth, while slowly bettering the situation of the toilers, promotes a swift formation of privileged strata;
> (e) exploiting the social antagonisms, a bureaucrarcy has converted itself into an uncontrolled caste alien to socialism;
> (f) the social revolution, betrayed by the ruling party, still exists in property relations and in the consciousness of the toiling masses;
> (g) a further development of the accumulating contradictions can as well lead to socialism as back to capitalism;
> (h) on the road to capitalism the counterrevolution would have to break the resistance of the workers;
> (i) on the road to socialism the workers would have to overthrow the bureaucracy.
> In the last analysis, the question will be decided by a struggle of living social forces, both on the national and the world arena. (Trotsky, 1936, see 1973, p. 255)

Some of these views are again echoed much later still by

Westergaard and Resler, who argue that 'state ownership has not been translated into effective public ownership: access to control remains privileged. But the economy is not, as in Western countries, governed by a pursuit of market profit on the part of separate private corporations' (Westergaard and Resler, 1976, p. 15).

It is clear that a simple change in the ownership of economic resources does not result in the utopian train of events outlined by Marx and Engels and advocated by Lenin. Changes in ownership do not necessarily lead to actual control by workers or the abolition of social differences and the state. In practice, the reverse has been the case in most countries subject to elite communist revolutions. Workers do not control the use and application of economic resources. The state has grown larger and extended its functions rather than wither away. A new party bureaucratic elite has emerged. Social classes are not abolished, they reappear in different guises. The question of the distribution of resources between them arises. The nature and labels of distributive groupings may be different but they exist just as much as in the work of Ricardo, from which Marx took his starting point.

Until the utopian and unlikely conditions of complete communism arise in industrial societies, distributive groupings will continue to exist. In these conditions, 'there still remains the need for a state which, while safeguarding the common ownership of the means of production, would safeguard equality of labour and in the distribution of products' (Lenin, 1919, see 1972, p. 86). This is easier said than done for, if the revolution is to be judged by the fact that it brings a higher economy of time than capitalism, as Trotsky argued, then it must increase productivity. This must entail increasing the total amounts of investment, plant, machinery and therefore the organic composition of capital. In order to do this a surplus must be generated from existing production.

> Superficial 'theoreticians' can comfort themselves, of course, that the distribution of wealth is a factor secondary to its production. The dialectic of interaction, however, retains here all its force. The destiny of the state-appropriated means of production will be decided in the long run

according as these differences in personal existence, evolve in one direction or the other. If a ship is declared collective property but the passengers continue to be divided into first, second and third class, it is clear that, for the third class passengers, differences in the conditions of life will have infinitely more importance than that juridical change in proprietorship. The first class passengers, on the other hand, will propound, together with their coffee and cigars, the thought that collective ownership is everything and a comfortable cabin nothing at all. (Trotsky, 1936, see 1973, p. 239)

As long as such distributive groupings exist there will be conflict between them over the shares of production going to each group and retained for further investment. As long as such conflicts exist they will be reflected at the political level in the state.

At the level of economy, Marxist theories of the state draw attention to the importance of production in determining the political combatants in industrial society. With a few notable exceptions, like Trotsky and to a lesser extent Poulantzas, they tend to focus on the juridical forms of ownership of the means of production as the bases of class struggles and therefore of the state. These forms of ownership are often incorrectly identified as monopolies within national states whereas in fact they are more often competitive oligopolies within the world economy. Concepts of monopoly or state-monopoly ownership therefore often fail to locate the national state correctly in its relationships with economic forces.

Trotsky and Poulantzas, on the other hand, do consider the national state as a regional instance of a capitalist mode of production and the questions of its relative autonomy and distributive groupings in relation to its own internal economy. Both the autonomy of the state and the differences between distributive groupings are matters of degree. Their degrees may be considerable. To this extent it may be questioned whether returning to traditional Marxist analysis and the intangible determination in the last instance of the social and political by the economic contributes much to current analyses. The valuable works of Baran and Sweezy (1966) and Glyn and Sutcliffe (1972) in the analysis of political economy would, in this context, seem to have as much in common with modern Keynesian analysis as with the original Marx.

Society

For Marx, 'civil society' was the context of the national state. This phrase, often translated as bourgeois society, was intended to convey both the idea of a civilised society with settled laws and institutions. Both he and Engels consistently argued that civil society was the real basis of the state. Thus, in Marx's view, 'it is not the state which conditions and regulates civil society, but civil society which conditions and regulates the state' (Engels, 1885, see Marx and Engels, 1973, p. 436).

The actual relationships between civil society and the state, and the processes engendering the dependent relationship, are not made clear in Marx and indeed sometimes vary. In his earlier works, civil society evolved out of the empirical life processes of real individuals, which by no means depends merely on their "will", their mode of production and form of intercourse, which mutually determine each other ... is the real basis of the state' (Marx and Engels, 1846, see 1974, p. 106). In this formulation the character of the state is determined by the antagonisms of individuals who find themselves in opposed structured positions in civil society. The struggles between them both necessitate and maintain the institution of the state as the routine political reflection of their economic struggles.

In another formulation, 'social organisation evolving directly out of production and commerce ... forms the basis of the state' (Marx and Engels, 1846, see 1974, p. 57). In other words, it is not so much the empirical experiences of separate individuals as individuals which necessitate the development of the state but the activities of combinations of them in social or political groups and organisations.

In yet another view, Marx argues that the division of labour establishes a difference of interest between individuals and the community. 'Out of this very contradiction between the interest of the individual and that of the community the latter takes an independent form as the state' (Marx and Engels, 1846, see 1974, p. 53). In this sense the satisfaction of individual interests may run counter to the supposed interests of the hypothetical community as a whole and therefore necessitate the development of the state to represent the community rather than partial private interests. This is a view wholly consistent with the tenets of modern non-Marxist welfare economics.

For the moment, it is enough to see that Marx encompasses at least three different notions of the relationships between civil society and the state. One view stresses the relationships between individuals, another between groups and organisations and a third the differences in interests between individuals and the community. What Marx is clear upon, however, is that struggles in society determine the nature of the state but that the state is governed for the benefit of the bourgeoisie. Bearing in mind that Marx himself acknowledges three possible types of antagonism, and that any of them are argued to be sufficiently important to warrant the development of state institutions, it might have been expected that Marx would have analysed more closely possible different results from these complex origins. It was Lenin, however, who first paid much attention to the possible differences in civil society and the state arising from what he called the process of uneven development.

Somewhat surprisingly, however, Lenin was satisfied with the entirely circular argument that

> The state is a product and a manifestation of the irreconcilability of class antagonisms. The state arises where, when and insofar as class antagonisms objectively cannot be reconciled. And, conversely, the existence of the state proves that the class antagonisms are irreconcilable. (Lenin, 1919, see 1972, p. 9)

To dispense with both, Marx and Lenin argued that class antagonisms would have to be abolished and that this could only be accomplished, by definition, by the introduction of a classless society. For them this meant the abolition of private property and therefore of the bourgeois social class. In theory, even a totally bourgeois society would also satisfy their requirements for a society free from class antagonisms.

In order that the proletariat should introduce a classless society composed solely of proletarians, however, Marx and Lenin argued that a political party should be formed in order to educate and act as the vanguard for workers. This view was echoed by Gramsci, who thought that the necessary revolutionary action could only be instigated and led by a revolutionary vanguard. This had to be a prepared and conscious elite. In practice, this elite has tended to remain in power long after communist revolutions have taken place. In 1936, for example, Trotsky complained that 'The Soviet proletariat still exists as a class deeply distinct from the peasantry, the technical intelligentsia and the bureaucracy' (see Trotsky, 1973, p. 261).

Despite the obvious contradictions between the idea of a classless and stateless society and the practices of revolutionary elites, Gramsci devoted some considerable attention to justifying the continued existence of the latter as the Modern Prince. For him, as for Lenin, the activities of this minority were justified, as the Prince had been for Machiavelli, by the need to acquire and hold power for specific ends. For Lenin and Gramsci, the end was the creation of a workers' state which was defined as a bourgeois state without the bourgeoisie. In this context it would have similar internal and external problems and use similar methods to the bourgeois state. To achieve this end, discipline and sacrifice were required. As Lenin recognised, discipline presupposes a hierarchy of authority and minority rule. The justification for minority rule in the case of the workers' state was the consciousness of its historical task by the party. Again the argument is internally consistent if both the premises of a science of history are correct and the moral evaluation of its analysis can be substantiated. Both are doubtful.

Poulantzas takes up the analysis by arguing that

> Marx distinguishes the economic struggle . . . from the political class struggle, and seems to acknowledge the existence of fully constituted classes only at the level of the

political struggle; with regard to the economic struggle of the agents of production ... he says that it is a case of class struggle, and with regard to the economic trade union struggle he speaks of 'class-in-itself', i.e. he seems to reserve the status of class-for-itself, of class 'as such', for the political struggle alone. (Poulantzas, 1973b, p. 23)

Having, to some extent, separated the political from the economic in this way, he goes on to analyse the relationships between social class, power and the state.

He says that bourgeois social science and politics based on Weber and ultimately on Hegel are characterised by the idea that 'it is the structures/institutions which hold/wield power, with the relations of power between "social groups" flowing from this institutional power' (Poulantzas, 1976). In contrast, he argues that power relations and hence the state should be understood in terms of the relationships between social classes. For Poulantzas, social classes are not, however, empirical things but concepts of social relations and 'social ensembles'. He defines social class as

a concept which shows the effects of the ensemble of structures, of the matrix of a mode of production or of a social formation, on the agents which constitute its supports: this concept reveals the effects of the global structure in the field of social relations. (Poulantzas, 1973b, p. 67)

Within the concept of social class he designates three further distinctions between social categories, social strata and fractions. Social categories are groups with significant effects in society in fields other than economic ones. He cites as examples of these the bureaucracy in its relations with the state and intellectuals in relation to ideology. Fractions, on the other hand, are parts of social classes which can have significant individual effects on society and in doing so constitute autonomous social forces with respect to their class position. In contrast, social strata are defined as secondary effects of modes of production insofar as they designate differences within social classes, categories or fractions.

Examples of social strata are the working-class aristocracy and top bureaucrats.

The problem with this analysis is that, if the political and the national state are to be understood in terms of the power relationships between social classes, but they are only concepts, then the 'real action' generating these concepts, at the political level, must take place between categories, fractions and strata. These groups are not, however, mutually exclusive, as the original Marxist definitions of social classes were, nor are they clearly defined *per se*. The bureaucracy and intellectuals do have important relationships to the economy such as in the nationalised industries or economists. The existence and bases of fractions are not theorised. No explanation is offered of the bases of the differences, say, between industrial and finance capital. They could equally well be social strata defined according to their 'possession' of special characteristics such as knowledge or skill. Thus working-class aristocracies could just as well be labelled fractions as strata in Poulantzas' formulation.

What Poulantzas is trying to accomplish, with these semantic distinctions, is the maintenance of a Marxist class analysis of the political and the national state, when it is evident to many critics that social classes as a whole do not struggle in the way Marx envisaged, and that it is therefore not possible to see the development and maintenance of the national state wholly in these terms. In practice, it is necessary to account for the roles different and often elite groups and organisations play in the determination of state action and characteristics. Frequently these groups do not exist or act in the kind of ways suggested by Marx. Unionised working-class elite groups, for example, often support conservative governments or action against the interests of their less well-organised brothers. Competition among capitalists can be as fierce as the struggles between capital and labour. Hence the need for the definition of groups other than social classes and the idea of autonomy to explain the political and national state.

Nevertheless, in order for Poulantzas' analysis to be Marxist rather than 'imperfect pluralism' he has to link the activities of various groups to the concept of class structure. In doing so he has to argue that sometimes social class is more than just a concept. For example, he says that 'the proletariat exists as a class only through its organisation in a distinct party' (Poulantzas, 1973b, p. 59). Indeed, the only effective way to exercise class power would seem to be by the establishment of concrete organisations such as trade unions and political parties. Once the analysis moves from class as a concept to class as specific organisations, however, a number of awkward empirical questions come to light.

Class relations, for example, are seen as power relations. Therefore, according to a Marxist analysis, bourgeois organisations ought to be seen to be at least hegemonic if not dominant. The apparent weakness of some manufacturing organisations and the undoubted strength of some trade unions does not always fit this picture. So Poulantzas seeks to argue that 'class relations are at every level relations of power: power, however, is only a concept indicating the effect of the ensemble of the structures on the relations of the practices of various classes in conflict' (Poulantzas, 1973b, p. 101). In effect, what this means is that according to Poulantzas the general relationships between the concept of social class and the concept of power are characterised by the superiority of capital and the inferiority of labour. This is despite the fact that, at the level of organisations which can be examined empirically, examples to the contrary can be found, or organisations do not act according to a Marxist definition of their class interests as a whole. In this way the connection between Poulantzas' detailed analysis of the interactions between different social groups within particular structures with classic Marxist formulations seems more of an encumbrance than an insightful starting point.

This difficulty is particularly evident when Poulantzas and his followers come to explain the development of the 'welfare state' in 'capitalist economies'. While some analysts might be content to see such developments in terms of lengthy conflicts between organisations representing different interests, Poulantzas prefers to conceptualise welfare provisions as the 'extended reproduction' of social classes and their determination. Accordingly he argues that 'the state apparatuses, and the ideological state apparatuses in particular, have a decisive role in the reproduction of social classes'

(Poulantzas, 1975, p. 27). In this way, the establishment of a free educational service, which one would expect to find in any communist society, is seen not so much as a victory in the continuous struggle between different interest groups, but as a way that some fractions of capital can acquire the kind of labour they require while not having to finance its training directly out of their own surplus and shifting that cost either to other fractions of capital or preferably to labour itself. The content of education is also supposed to be geared to the interests of capital. In this way, following a Marxist analysis leads to the conclusion that either the provision or the non-provision of facilities like free education in capitalist countries, by the state, are in the interests of capital and, conversely, that the same education is in the interests of the workers if provided by a communist national state.

In addition to these contradictory conclusions, the relative autonomy of Poulantzas' national state must be considerable if, as he argues, it plays 'a decisive role in the reproduction of social classes'. Yet he is scornful of the view that in some circumstances the state can be sufficiently autonomous to play a non-determined role between the proletariat and the bourgeoisie. This view he associates with the interests of the petite bourgeoisie rather than the general or public interest. For the petite bourgeoisie, he says,

> The role of the state as an apparatus of class domination is seen as a pervasion of a state whose authority is to be restored by 'democratising' it, i.e. by opening it up to the petty bourgeoisie, making it respect the 'general interest', it being understood that this general interest corresponds to that of the intermediate class, the mediator between the bourgeoisie and the proletariat. This is the origin of the conception of the 'corporate state', a debased form of state socialism. (Poulantzas, 1975, p. 293)

In these circumstances it is difficult to locate the relative autonomy of Poulantzas' national state. It may be relatively autonomous with respect to capital although the argument cannot proceed too far down that path before the Marxist framework must be abandoned. It can be independent from labour although this has never been in question. It is unlikely that the state could have a different interest from capital, labour and the petite bourgeoisie if only because its agents are largely members of the petite bourgeoisie themselves and this is becoming the most numerous class in advanced industrial societies.

If Poulantzas' reformulations of a Marxist analysis of the relationships between society and the state are pressed to their logical conclusions, many questions are left unsolved. Not the least of these are the relationships between the theory and empirical evidence.

Miliband (1969), in contrast, sets out to show empirical relationships between capital and the state. He argues that because members of the business and state elites are drawn from the same social background and they have greater rapport with each other than do labour representatives and ministers, the state agents act largely in the interests of business. This partiality is disguised and propagandised by virtue of the fact that the ruling class controls the means of mental production such as the mass media. In addition, power is exerted over state agents by business interests and the state has to support these interests because of its own dependence on continued accumulation.

In this analysis the state is described as a separate set of political institutions. They may be dominated by business interests. The main problems with Miliband's analysis are, however, that the mechanisms and limits of this dominance are not specified and the ways in which working-class organisations have made gains by using state institutions are not given sufficient consideration.

State

Marx was among the first theorists to define what constituted the empirical reality of the state. This he did by listing what he considered to be the ubiquitous organs or agents of the state. These included a standing army, police, bureaucracy, clergy and the judicature. For Lenin, these embodied the power of the state, together with prisons and the ability toraise taxes and loans. Gramsci is less clear about what constitutes the state. Sometimes it is contained within economic forces, sometimes it is the boundary within economic forces and sometimes it is the boundary within which national industrialists operate. Elsewhere he defines the state as political society and civil society, elsewhere as a balance between political and civil society and finally that they are all identical. Poulantzas extends the concept of state apparatus to embrace, in addition to those of Marx and Lenin, radio, television, the press, cinema, theatre, publishing, trade unions, political parties and, in some circumstances, the family. Miliband lists the elements of the state as government, administration, military, police, judiciary and local government. It is clear, therefore, that there is no standard Marxist definition of the state and different theorists have different combinations of specific elements in mind when discussing the concept.

As a result of their economic and social analyses, however, Marxists are clear that the function of these various manifestations may be summarised in the sentence that 'the state is nothing but a machine for the oppression of one class by another' (Engels, 1891, see Marx and Engels, 1973, p. 258). The state is said to create an order which 'legalises and perpetuates this oppression by moderating the conflict between classes' (Lenin, 1919, see 1972, p. 9). The social class whose interests are best served by this machinery, according to Marx, Lenin and Gramsci, is the bourgeoisie.

This basic and simplistic position, although the starting point for many Marxist analyses of the state, is substantially modified in particular instances. Thus Marx talks of Bonapartism as a condition where the powers of social protagonists are not so dissimilar as to permit political domination by one of them. Gramsci develops the concept of Caesarism which, while not identical to Bonapartism, is related to it. Caesarism represents a compromise between two fundamental social forces and is perhaps illustrated in action by the British National Government of 1931. Poulantzas also remarks that the bourgeoisie are not necessarily dominant in capitalist states but rather hegemonic. The function of the state in such cases is to interfere with the political organisation of the proletariat and to help to organise the bourgeoisie at the political level. He says that its function is to disorganise the dominated classes politically, and at the same time to organise the dominant classes politically; to prevent the dominated classes from being present in its centre as classes, whilst introducing the dominant classes there as classes; by relating itself to the dominated classes as representative of the unity of the people-nation, whilst at the same time relating itself to the dominant classes qua politically organised classes. Poulantzas, 1973b, p. 189)

All this leads him to the conclusion that the modern national state cannot be seen as a mere instrument of force in the hands of a dominant class.

Much of this sounds familiar to non-Marxist political scientists accustomed to analysing the cut and thrust of political pressure in the determination of state action. It again raises the question of how far one could proceed down such a path of analysis without at least implicity abandoning its Marxist origins. So, for example, 'if the notion of relative autonomy is taken to its logical extreme, [the base/superstructure distinction] . . . should really disappear or be drastically changed in a topological sense, in that the superstructures do not have a necessary base in class' (Glucksmann, 1974, p. 134).

Marx, however, following his assertion that the state was a machine for the oppression of one class by another, went on to recommend what action the dominated class should take. His revolutionary solution involved seizure of state machinery by the proletariat and changing ownership relations by centralising all the means of production in the hands of the state. Freedom for the proletariat thus consisted in subordinating the state to society. The political vehicle for accomplishing this end was to be revolutionary dictatorship of the proletariat. Somewhat contradictorily this was said to produce a free state which was 'free in relation to its citizens hence a state with a despotic government' (Engels, 1875, see Marx and Engels, 1973, p. 355). Lenin supported the use of violent revolution to liberate oppressed classes. If, as he argued, the bourgeois state was an organisation of violence for the suppression of the proletariat, then the same machinery could be used in reverse. History, he said,

> compels us to regard the state as the organ of class rule and leads us to the inevitable conclusion that the proletariat cannot overthrow the bourgeoisie without first winning political power, without transforming the state into the proletariat organised as the ruling class. (Lenin, 1919, see 1972, p. 28)

It was not consistent with Marx's notions of oppression and the class base of the state that, following the victory of the proletariat and the establishment of a utopian classless society, there would be any *raison d'être* for the continued existence of the state. As, for him, such human emancipation would destroy the basis of the state, the continuation of its institutions after the revolution would be transitional. State interference in social relations would become superfluous and so the state would wither away. So, as Lenin argued, 'as soon as it becomes possible to speak of freedom the state as such ceases to exist' (Lenin, 1919, see 1972, p. 60). Trotsky went even further and argued that in a communist society both the state and money would disappear.

History, far from confirming the revolutionary outcome of class struggles and the subsequent withering away of the state, has tended to confound both the prediction that the proletariat in advanced industrial socieities would rise up against their exploiters and the expectation that where communist regimes were established, the state would wither away. In the first place, no Marxist revolution has ever taken place in an advanced industrial country. In the second place, the countries that have experienced such revolutions have seen the state flourish rather than wither. If, as some Marxists argue, it is the fact that Marxism has been applied which illustrates the validity of its analysis, then presumably the reverse should be true. At any rate, both the lack of revolutions in advanced capitalist countries and the enormous growth in state agencies in communist ones calls for a more complex analysis of the state than those offered by Marx and Lenin.

Subsequent analyses in coping with these requirements have tended to focus on what, for Marx, might have been considered a somewhat illegitimate separation of power and politics from economy. Indeed, as Poulantzas points out, Marx, Engels, Lenin and Gramsci never produced a theoretical conceptualisation of the idea - power.

Poulantzas, however, takes up Marx and Lenin's idea of the 'conjuncture' as a framework for considering the particular outcomes of political struggles in any given time or place. The elements of a conjuncture or present moment are social classes or parts of them which have a significant effect on a particular political issue and thus constitute social forces at that time. Contradictorily, Poulantzas goes on to argue that although a particular conjuncture may exhibit the effects of the activities of a number of different types of groups, power can only be conceptualised in terms of class practices. He defines power as 'the capacity of a social class to realise its specific objective interests' (Poulantzas, 1973b, p. 104).

A necessary condition of the existence of class power, according to Poulantzas, is organisation. Without a specific organisation he thinks that social classes do not have a sufficient concrete existence to participate in political struggles. Even with organisations the degree of effective power of a given class within a particular social structure is said to depend on the relative power of other social classes. It is therefore an interactive concept. Power may therefore be mobilised in a number of different ways and so he argues that

> Insofar as we can distinguish between several forms of power, we can by use of concrete situations proceed to a concrete examination of the existing plurality of power centres (institutions at a given moment) and of their relations: for example companies, the state, cultural institutions, etc. (Poulantzas, 1973b, p. 115)

These remarks represent a considerable modification of the Marxist position outlined above. With an actual class analysis based on economic divisions so far in the background, this approach would be perfectly consistent with that of 'imperfect pluralism'. In other words, examining the interaction between various organisations which might represent parts of social classes in the struggles for scarce goods and services and expecting the outcomes at any given moment to reflect their relative degrees of power represents a perfectly acceptable conceptual and methodological framework for non-Marxist political scientists.

Poulantzas goes further and acknowledges that the results of such struggles can satisfy the objective interests of some groups, forming parts of the so-called dominated social classes, at a more general level. While admittedly such a political situation is founded on an unstable equilibrium based on continually renegotiated compromises, this is to be expected in any society composed of conflicting interest groups.

Having moved this far, Poulantzas then creates confusion by criticising social-democratic misconceptions for seeking to conduct a somewhat similar analysis. He maintains that they underestimate the specific importance of the political, parcel out institutionalised political power among a plurality of groups, do not consider the autonomous importance of political power or overestimate the neutrality of the state and finally lack a conception of the class struggle. Apart from the last point, these are criticisms which could be levelled by traditional Marxists at Poulantzas himself.

In a subsequent work, Poulantzas (1975) has returned to the theme of how the state serves the interests of monopoly capital. In this work the analysis is thoroughly confused and it is not at all clear whether the state organises the political hegemony of monopoly capital or only takes responsibility for a hegemonic fraction or monopoly capital as a whole. Eventually he also acknowledges 'that the contemporary state is not a simple tool or instrument that can be freely manipulated by a simple coherent "will", any more than it has been in the past' (Poulantzas, 1975, p. 158). In the study of the national state it is therefore to be expected that a limited number of groups or organisations will exercise effective power through its institutions, but that this does not mean that the same group is always the most successful, partly because all issues do not affect it equally and partly because its power is checked by the relative power of other groups. In essence, this is a situation of 'imperfect pluralism'.

Contemporary Marxist analyses of the state tend to adopt

this stance while at the same time maintaining tenuous links with Marx's analysis of the class struggle and caricaturing the works of so-called pluralists. Miliband, for example, argues correctly that 'A theory of the state is also a theory of society and of the distribution of power in that society. (Miliband, 1969, p. 4). Certainly any adequate theory of the national state would have to embrace an understanding of the nature of the society in which that institution was located. Equally it would have to provide some conceptualisation of the location and distribution of power. Miliband then, however, criticises Western political scientists who have embarked on those tasks for assuming 'that power in Western societies, is competitive, fragmented and diffused; everybody, directly or though organised groups, has some power and nobody has or can have too much of it' (Miliband, 1969, p. 4). No major study of power by Western political scientists has ever shown that power is distributed equally among all members of the community. The argument is not about whether everybody or only one group has power in such societies but whether a limited number of groups and organisations hold power as opposed to a single, albeit fractured, ruling class.

Miliband devotes most of his work to argue that an authentic ruling class exists in Britain. His 'evidence' for this line of reasoning is that the command positions of the state are filled either directly from the world of business and property or by individuals from similar social backgrounds. This is said to create a set of presumptions concerning the outlook and political bias of the top agents of the state. They are said to be generally conservative and active allies of existing economic and social elites. Despite the undoubted truth of this analysis up to a point, it is not an adequate or sufficient analysis of the actual net outcomes of state action. Miliband himself is forced to admit that

> governments, acting in the name of the state, have in fact been compelled over the years to act against some property rights, to erode some managerial prerogative, to help redress somewhat the balance between capital and labour, between property and those who are subject to it. (Miliband, 1969, p. 71)

One of the main reasons for this apparent contradiction is the assumption on the part of Marxist writers that the main problem exercising liberal theorists is of no significance. Thus, for Marxists, sovereignty, the rule of the law and the legislature are of no significance for all are ultimately based on the domination of a ruling class resting on its economic position in society. In fact, despite the class background and predispositions of British civil servants, the legislature, reflecting the clash of organised interests, has often set them to implement laws which are in the interests of classes other than their own. Neither Miliband nor most other Marxist writers can or will interpret events in these terms. There is a tendency for their theories, particularly of the state, to be phrased in irrefutable and abstract terms. Quite opposite outcomes are said to be 'explained' by the same theory. On the one hand, workers are seen as dominated and powerless. On the other hand, gains made for them by their apparently powerful organisations are only ransoms paid to keep them docile. Upward mobility, by definition, turns workers into bourgeoisie. Schools, health services, housing and all the panoply of the welfare state in social democracies are explained away as part of the strategy of some parts of capital. This is despite the fact that similar types of service appear in collective economies. Few but the faithful could accept such contradictory evidence as supporting similar theoretical positions.

A further argument is that these compromises are restricted to actions which are congruent with a set of core assumptions. Thus, for Westergard and Resler,

> There are . . . two levels to the study of power. At one level the questions concern 'core assumptions'. What are the implicit terms of reference within which conflict about policy is confined for all practical purposes; which exclude alternatives outside that range from consideration? Whose and what interests do these core assumptions favour? At the other, and lower, level the questions concern the conflict and outcome of pressures within the boundaries set by the core assumptions. (Westergaard and Resler, 1976, p. 248).

In some ways this analysis is similar to Poulantzas' in arguing that the detailed empirical evidence of power struggles within capitalist societies is complex and can run counter to Marxist assertions, but that, nevertheless, at a general and more important level, Marxist relationships hold good despite some examples to the contrary.

Undoubtedly there is a framework of core assumptions influencing state action at any given time but equally these core assumptions change over time. The acceptable framework for legislative action in Britain in the last quarter of the twentieth century is not the same as it was at the time of the industrial revolution. What is more, core assumptions can be challenged by group action. The development of trade unions and the Labour Party has done precisely that.

The final test of power, however, is 'not who decides, but what is decided - and what not' (Westergaard and Resler, 1976, p. 246). The degree to which various interests are satisfied or not by state action is exemplified by the actual outcomes of that action. It is these which illustrate the real power of different groups and organisations rather than their social characteristics or backgrounds. In this way the distributional effects of state action are the most telling illustration of the power of different groups and their relationships to the role of the state.

Bureaucracy

Two of the main quantitative and qualitative changes in all industrial societies since the time that Marx was writing are the general rise in large formal organisations for the accomplishment of economic and political tasks and the huge increase in the size of the state employing similar forms of hierarchically structured organisations. Large organisations, complex divisions of labour, high levels of technological knowledge, relative bureaucratic autonomy and new bases of power are all, therefore, important characteristics of contemporary industrial societies. They combine to make both the power structures and the nature of these societies qualitatively different from their nineteenth-century predecessors.

The existence of growing numbers of bureaucrats maintaining a public allegiance to independent codes of conduct and knowledge is a problem for a Marxist class analysis of the state as much as it is in the economic sphere. Marx himself was unequivocal on this point. He said that 'The executive of the modern state is but a committee for managing the common affairs of the whole bourgeoisie' (Marx and Engels, 1848, see 1975, p. 82). Engels, however, was not quite so sure and towards the end of the century was remarking that the drift from jointstock companies to trusts and then to the state of various productive and service functions showed the bourgeoisie to be superfluous and also that their functions were being performed by salaried employees. In addition, he thought that having public power and the right to levy taxes placed state officials above society.

Lenin noted this problem but failed to produce a satisfactory solution. He argued that the two most characteristic institutions of the state were a bureacracy and a standing army. He agreed with Marx that the destruction of the bureaucratic military machine was a precondition for every real people's revolution. Paradoxically, however, he recognised that no state could be without one. He merely asserted that after the revolution 'We shall reduce the role of state officials to that of simply carrying out our instructions as responsible, revocable, modestly paid "foremen and accountants" ' (Lenin, 1919, sec 1972, p. 46).

Internal critics of some communist revolutions have noticed a different result. Trotsky, for example, designated the bureaucrary as the new ruling stratum in post-revolutionary Russia. According to him

> The soviet bureaucracy has expropriated the proletariat politically in order by methods of its own to defend the social conquests. But the very fact of its appropriation of political power in a country where the principal means of production are in the hands of the state, creates a new and hitherto unknown relation between the bureaucracy and the riches of the nation. The means of production belong to the state. But the state, so to speak, 'belongs' to the bureaucracy. (Trotsky, 1936, see 1973, p. 249)

The so-called dictatorship of the proletariat, therefore, neither meant the abolition of the state bureaucratic military machine nor that the proletariat as such participated in the management of that machine.

Gramsci also noted that in industrial countries not experiencing communist revolutions a new kind of career functionary was developing and multiplying to do technical and bureaucratic work. Such arguments have led some theorists to talk of convergence between different types of industrial systems. There is no reason to suppose, however, that unless the societies and social forces surrounding bureaucracies are similar, their characteristics and actions should have more than varying combinations of similarity and dissimilarity.

The real problem of bureaucracy for Marxists is identified by Trotsky (1936), Burnham (1941) Schumpeter (1976), Dahrendorf (1957) and Djilas (1957). In different ways they point to the possibility that power is not only or even necessarily the preserve of social classes but may reside within and between institutions, and that hierarchies of control correspond to hierarchies of power. Power and the state could therefore ultimately reside in factors other than social class.

Poulantzas confronts this problem by arguing that such an analysis involves a confusion between structures and class practices and unduly restricts a Marxist reply within an alien ideological framework. His obscure and unconvincing attempt to remedy this dilemma relies again on establishing an abstract level of structures and ensembles within which actual class or power relations take place but which cannot be equated with actual structures such as real institutions or organisations. Like the lonely hour of the Althusserian 'last instance', these abstract structures may be considered so remote as to be irrelevant.

When Poulantzas comes to detail the characteristics of bureaucracies his description, as the listing of his sources implies, is remarkably similar to those he seeks to criticise. As he says,

> bureaucratism represents an hierarchical organisation of the state apparatus, by means of delegation of power, having

particular effects on the functioning of that apparatus. As a general rule it is correlative with:

1. The axiomatisation of the juridical system into rules/laws, which are abstract, general, formal and strictly regulated and which distribute the domains of activities and competence . . .
2. The concentration of functions and the administrative centralisation of the apparatus . . .
3. The impersonal character of the functions of the state apparatus . . .
4. The mode of payment of these functions by fixed salaries . . .
5. The mode of recruitment of civil servants by co-option or nomination by the 'heights' or again by a particular system of competition . . .
6. The separation between the civil servants' private life and public function, separation between 'home' and 'office' . . .
7. A systematic masking of knowledge of the apparatus, i.e. bureaucratic secrecy, vis-à-vis the classes . . .
8. A masking of knowledge within the apparatus itself, with the 'top civil servants' holding the keys of science . . .
9. A characteristic disparity between the scientific education of the 'height' and the subordinate strata's lack of culture . . . (Poulantzas, 1973b, p. 349)

Despite the size of modern state bureaucracies organised in this way and the unquestioned hierarchy of power within them, Poulantzas goes on to assert that the bureaucracy has no power of its own. Power, he says, is only held by classes and the state is only a power centre. As a matter of definition, he argues that as the bureaucracy is neither a social class nor a fraction of a class it cannot be a social force in a particular conjuncture and therefore it cannot play a principal role in determining the actions of the state. All the state can do anyway is to materialise class relations.

This is a purely semantic argument. There is no evidence that social classes as such are the only bearers of power.

Indeed, even Poulantzas himself has argued that they only bear economic or political power when they organise themselves as trade unions or political parties. In this sense, collective organisations are bearers of power in a way that their individual members would not be if they were not organised. Conversely, the fact of organisation develops the holding of power so that a view of large state bureaucracies as powerless agents of class domination is to stretch credibility beyond its limits.

Nevertheless, Poulantzas maintains that criticisms such as these are based on the false epistemological assumptions that there is a separation between relations of production and powers of decision; also that classes are based on agents. Both assumptions would seem to have more justification than he allows them. In the first place, a variety of decisions are possible by different groups within a particular set of social relationships. In the second place, classes as concepts cannot engage in struggles and when they form themselves into trade unions and parties or classes for themselves they are clearly composed of agents.

Poulantzas does allow, however, that state functionaries constitute a social category. In opposition to Miliband, however, he says that the functioning of this category cannot be reduced to the class origin of its members. Instead the function of the bureaucracy, for Poulantzas, is seen as operationalising the relations of political domination. In this way he refuses to account for any autonomy of the state in terms of the activities of a group making up the agents of the state. Instead, the possible relative autonomy of the state is seen in terms of the relationships between forces external to its own institutions. He argues that the agents of the state are themselves divided among these forces, they belong to different social classes and do not constitute homogeneous groups with origins necessarily similar to those of top business and property owners.

Poulantzas' attitude to bureaucracy illustrates his general ambivalence in maintaining a Marxist class analysis on the one hand and doing justice to the complexity of modern power structures on the other. There is a gap between his conceptual framework and his detailed analysis. The former is obscure and contradictory; the latter bears interpretation from non-Marxist viewpoints.

With the notable exceptions of Marx's concept of 'Bonapartism', Gramsci's analysis of 'Caesarism' and Troksky's evaluation of the soviet bureaucracy, most Marxist theorists have failed to give sufficient importance to the role of organisations in structuring power relationships and in developing degrees of autonomy from outside pressures such as those of social classes. Even Poulantzas' analysis of the relative autonomy of the state does not go far enough in recognising the power of organisations and relinquishing the importance of social class struggles as determinants of state forms and actions.

The only theories of the state which attempt to produce an extended analysis of these issues, apart from those mentioned above, are those of corporatists. It is argued, therefore, that, in combination, these should provide the most fruitful approach to conceptualising the location and role of the state in advanced industrial societies. Accordingly these theories are reviewed next.

Corporatist theories

Corporatist theories are the most appropriate for analysing the role of the state in contemporary industrial societies, first because the main causal factors leading to corporatism can be demonstrated empirically and constitute fundamental characteristics of such societies. Secondly, corporatist theories also offer an analysis of functional interest representation in conditions where functional divisions in society can be argued to be more significant than those of social class.

According to Winkler, for example, the four main structural conditions leading to the development of a corporatist state in Britain are 'industrial commercialisation, declining profitability, technological development and international competition' (Winkler, 1976). There can be little doubt that these are in fact crucial changing characteristics of the British economy. They generate corporate forms of economic activity in the following ways.

The process of industrial commercialisation leads to sectoral dominance in the economy by a small number of relatively large companies. In turn, this increases the abilities of the few companies to determine the conditions of production in their particular sectors. This results in declining competition within the domestic economy. Large firms can therefore plan their production without much regard to the 'normal' controls of market competition. In order to safeguard the 'national interest', the state therefore becomes involved in planning the production of these large firms either for the purposes of co-ordinating production so that a product mix arises which approximates to the requirements of the nation as a whole, or for the purposes of generating necessary goods and services, which are not profitable enough to be produced by the private sector if left entirely to its own devices.

The state also becomes involved in the economy when the rate of profit in critical sectors falls below that at which private corporations are prepared to produce goods or services. If these goods and services are regarded as an essential part of national production, then the state may support, direct or even undertake their production itself. In this way the state comes to develop a corporate or national role in the economy.

This role may also be expanded as the scale, costs and complexities of technological innovations increase beyond the willingness or ability of the private sector to undertake them. Here again the state may step in to support private production or to research and produce the technology itself.

International competition in, for example, the production of manufactured goods also leads to changes and developments in the role of the state. Its corporatist functions are manifested in attempts to protect and foster its own national industries in the face of competition from those of other countries. This is particularly the case where domestic industries find increasing difficulty in competing with those abroad.

These economic changes, together with the state responses to them, are of sufficient magnitude to warrant the argument that a new form of the state is in the process of emerging.

One of the main reasons why this form is more accurately described by corporatist than by Marxist theories is the decline of the importance of profit maximisation and therefore capital accumulation as a major objective of production. This trend is identified, for example, by Cawson. He says that

> industrial commercialisation produces private firms which, individually or in collusion, seek to regulate competition to secure stability and growth, even at the expense of profit maximisation. An increasing degree of control over market conditions takes the form of forward planning, vertical integrations or horizontal conglomeration. In order for the planning function to be successful in the private sector, corporate business increasingly seeks government intervention to help stabilise the business cycle and make the future less uncertain. (Cawson, 1977, p. 6)

The decline in the importance of profit maximisation as the major objective of production, together with the increasing demand for a private and public planning function to reduce risk and uncertainty, also leads to the second major defining characteristic of corporatist states, namely that of functional interest representation.

Where societies are divided into functional interest groups as a result of the increasing significance and complexity of the division of labour, and where oligopolistic competition dominates most sectors of production as in contemporary Britain, then corporatist forms of interest representation tend to develop in the polity. Such forms of representation tend to be most crucial in the making of important economic decisions because oligopolies are among the most powerful functional interest groups.

A corporatist evaluation of the relationships between polity and state therefore seems more apposite than a Marxist analysis of those relationships in contemporary Britain. Cawson (1978) has also noted two of the main reasons why this should be so. In the first place, there is an emphasis in British public policy-making on the national or public interest which reflects an underlying holistic social theory in which the interests of society as a whole are argued to tran-

Civil Society and the State 101

scend narrow sectional interests, and thus dictate specific policy approaches. Society is held to comprise interdependent parts with the health of the whole contingent upon the 'correct' functioning of the parts (see also Simmie, 1974, pp. 17-43). In the second place, as was argued above in Chapter 2, 'the emergence of functional groups with real socio-economic and political power has emphasised the reality of interdependence in modern industrial society. Whether these groups be trade unions or business corporations, governments have had to adjust to the existence of centres of power outside the state.' The combination of these political doctrines and functional power groupings are particularly characteristic of some forms of corporatist political economies. This is not to argue, however, that corporatism is a coherent body of theory any more than is Marxism. This lack of coherence is evident in definitions of the concept.

A major cause of the differences and ambiguities in definitions of corporatism derives from one of Weber's key principles of political sociology. He argued that there was no necessary or complete connection between economics and politics. This meant first that political power could accrue to groups or organisations on a number of different bases. Social class divisions were only one among a number of such bases. Second, it led to a sometimes unfortunate division of politics and economics for the purposes of study. Corporate theory has suffered from this division. Sometimes it has been defined solely in terms of economic administration and at other times it has been regarded solely as a form of political representation. Among the former definitions, Pahl and Winkler have written that 'corporatism is a comprehensive economic system under which the state intensively channels predominantly privately-owned business towards four goals ... order, unity, nationalism and success' (Pahl and Winkler, 1974). In contrast, Schmitter has defined corporatism as

> a system of interest representation in which the constituent units are organised into a limited number of singular, compulsory, non-competitive, hierarchically ordered and functionally differentiated categories, recognised or

licensed (if not created) by the state and granted a deliberate representational monopoly within their respective categories in exhange for observing certain controls on their selection of leaders and articulation of demands and supports. (Schmitter, 1974)

Such differences in the definition of corporatism, and divergences among analysts emphasising either economic or political power, have given rise to a variety of conceptualisations of the essence of corporatism. This variety is usually based on differences of opinion concerning the main loci of power and how it is exercised.

Differences of opinion on how and where major power centres are located according to corporatist theory are exemplified by Winkler (1976), and Marsh and Grant (1977). Winkler notes that the essence of corporatism has been seen as the process of incorporation, the commercial corporation or the corporate state. Marsh and Grant identify the existence of five subtypes of corporatism. These subtypes are labelled state, societal, liberal and authoritarian corporatism and tripartism.

Winkler notes that the process of incorporation has been seen as the co-option of interest groups into governmental decision-making and the formalisation of their role, because they have become too important to ignore. Alternatively, it has been interpreted as a suborning of dissident elements and their conversion into agents of control of a powerful state (Winkler, 1976). This definition therefore emphasises the political representational aspect of corporatism and the absorption of powerful oligopolies and monopsonies into political decision-making or the blunting of fragmented pressure groups by the embrace of a powerful state. As Winkler summarises these processes, they all assume the existence of a powerful and somewhat independent state.

In contrast, the rise of large, powerful, industrial and commercial corporations has been seen as leading to

a system of rule by business corporations, either in the malign sense of domination by monopoly capital or benignly as socially responsible managerialism leadership by corporate managers. An alternative conception sees the corporatist society as the modern business corporation expanded to a national scale and hence as a comprehensive pyramid of authority controlled from the top. (Winkler, 1976)

In this version of corporatism, power resides primarily with large private corporations and lies in the hands of whoever is thought to control these organisations. Opinions on this again differ and vary from finance capitalists, to managers to the conjunction of economic, political and military elites.

Winkler also summarises a third version of corporatism. This again is divided into two categories. The first is

a limited conception of the corporate state as a system of political representation in which geographical parliamentary constituencies are replaced by industrial/occupational/ functional groups organised in national syndicates. It is the formalisation of economic interest groups into a political institution. An expanded conception sees the corporate state as a 'megabureaucracy', the all encompassing polity that attempts to control everything. (Winkler, 1976)

In this version powerful, functionally differentiated groups or organisations stand aloof from the state but further their economic interests by political negotiations with it. Alternatively, the major functional grouping is thought to be an all-embracing state managerial and bureaucratic system of power.

The disputes concerning definitions of corporatism which are evident in these alternative views centre primarily on the roles and power of oligopolistic and monopsonistic functional groups with respect to those of the state. They are essentially arguments about the changes taking place in the exercise of political power as a result of the development of new forms of economic administration associated with the extended division of labour and the deployment of highly specialised science and technology. They focus almost exclusively on the relationships between large private organisations and public bureaucracies.

The exclusive concentration on the economic and political relationships between large groups is exemplified by Marsh and Grant (1977). They note a major distinction between state or authoritarian corporatism and societal or liberal corporatism. In the former, 'the state plays a directive role in the establishment of class harmony and the organisations representing different economic interests within society are subordinate to and dependent on the state'. In the latter type, 'the representative organisations are autonomous but cooperate with the state and each other because they recognise that they are mutually interdependent' (Marsh and Grant, 1977). The authors go on to argue that, in contrast to Pahl and Winkler (1974), most students of corporatism regard liberal corporatism as best exemplifying contemporary political representation in Britain. They restrict this reference, however, to tripartite relationships between the peak organisations exemplified by the Confederation of British Industry, the Trades Union Congress and the Government. Clearly these are important organisations in political and economic decision-making, but they are by no means the only functional groups influencing such decisions in Britain. They are also not always able to make their decisions binding on the members of their own firms, trade unions or parties.

Winkler also takes a relatively one-dimensional view of corporatism. He makes its definition depend on the degree to which the state facilitates, supports or directs privately owned productive organisations. He argues that 'stripped to its essentials, corporatism is principally defined by one particularly important qualitative change, the shift from a supportive to a directive role for the state in the economy' (Winkler, 1977). The shift, according to Winkler, involves the state telling private business organisations what they may and may not do, establishing goals that they must work towards, allocating the resources with which they must achieve them and generally structuring the economic life of the country. Labour government failures at national planning and planning agreements, and Conservative withdrawals from state involvement in the economy, together with the unwillingness of trade unions and private firms to comply with government directives, make Winkler's analysis of the corporate state in

Britain unconvincing. Such evidence as is available does not support his contention that the state is achieving such a powerful directive role in the British economy.

A satisfactory definition of corporatism must include the possibility of theorising not only the power relationships between functionally differentiated large economic and political units but also the relationships between such organisations and small producers or consumers. The British political economy includes not only oligopolistic producers, monopsonistic consumers and large political groups or institutions, but also small producing organisations, individual consumers and a multitude of small political pressure groups. A comprehensive definition of corporatism must therefore embrace the power relationships between an economy composed of a few large organisations and many small producers in most of its sectors, a polity also composed of a few large organisations and many small ones and a state engaged in power relationships with both types of producers and consumers.

For the purposes of this study, therefore, corporatism is defined as a politico-economic system characterised by the exercise of power through functionally differentiated organisations seeking to achieve compromises in economically and politically approved actions which are as favourable to their particular interests as possible and which are often legitimated by their incorporation in the objectives of the state. The main negotiating groups in this system are oligopolies and smaller producers in economic sectors; monopsonies, parties, pressure groups and individual consumers; the government and bureaucratic agencies of the state. In general, the larger and more powerful of these elements are incorporated in various ways into state policy-making and its implementation. In contrast, the smaller and less powerful elements are not usually incorporated and constitute a market system of economic activity and a pluralistic system of interest representation. Corporatism therefore represents an important development in the location and use of power. It represents a shift away from market and electoral power towards oligopolistic, functionally differentiated and hierarchically structured organisations. It also involves a lessening of the electoral accountability of the decisions reached as a result of negotiations between members of the higher echelons of such organisations.

Corporatism, defined in this way, represents an extension of the study of the conditions pertaining to imperfect competition in the economy to embrace their political ramifications. As such it could be described as 'imperfect pluralism'. It requires an analysis of the three-way interrelationships between producers, consumers and the state. For this reason the next three sections of this chapter are devoted to analyses of the relationships between corporatism and the economy, the polity and the state.

Corporate economy

Economic systems are composed of relatively stable patterns of production, exchange, distribution and consumption. These patterns are established and maintained by the acquisition and use of different degrees of power by the different organisations, groups and individuals engaged in economic activities. Corporatists have usually regarded the ownership and control of production as the key source of power in the economy. Consequently they have either been interested in changing the distribution of ownership and control in order to effect a change in the nature of the economy or they have argued that such distributions are defining characteristics of economies.

French syndicalists have argued, for example, that it was necessary to nationalise the means of production. This was to be achieved not by the state but by corporations based on the trade unions and professional associations. This was somewhat similar to the pattern of ownership and control advocated by English guild socialists, a partnership between the state and the workers. This was to take place after the state had been captured by the workers, and industry had been brought under public ownership. After that they wanted the management to be delegated to chartered guilds which would be obliged to conduct firms in accordance with the wishes and interests of the local community. In these conditions the guilds were argued to be on a par with the state in the economic sphere.

Winkler regards economic systems as characterisable by their structures of ownership and control. Thus, for him, 'Corporatism is an economic system in which the state directs and controls predominantly privately owned business according to four principles - unity, order, nationalism and success' (Winkler, 1976). He repeats on several occasions (1974, 1976 and 1977) that the essence of corporatism is therefore distinguished by a particular state role in privately owned economies. This role is described as the public control of privately owned business. It makes a qualitative shift in state action from facilitating through supporting to directing what private business may or may not do.

According to this version of corporatism,

> the state directs the internal decision-making process of private business using such devices as the National Economic Development Organisation, consensus planning, planning agreements, controls over prices, profit margins, dividends, wages, rents and capital movements ... [and attempts] to regulate industrial relations, state stimulation of industrial re-organisation, a proliferation of devices for export subsidisation and import substitution, increasing state provision of investment funds and plans for the direction of private capital sources. (Winkler, 1977)

As has been mentioned above, these devices are said to be used to direct private business towards the goals of unity, order, nationalism and success.

It is argued that the goal of unity should be sought because economic objectives can best be achieved by co-operation rather than conflict. This leads the corporate state to see no merit in price competition nor in competing sources of supply. These are regarded as creating waste rather than efficient production.

The same attitude is evident in the search for order. Here again, market economies are seen as anarchic and therefore in need of more stability. This characteristic is said to assist in the elimination both of company collapses and of windfall profits. Corporatist governments seek to achieve this goal by eliminating market forms of economic activity.

Such policies are said to be pursued in the name of nationalism. This principle elevates the general welfare over that of self-interest and also establishes national performance *vis-à-vis* the rest of the world as an important objective.

Finally, according to Winkler, the corporate state directs private business to the goal of success. Success, however, is defined in terms of the achievement of national rather than sectoral objectives. It involves the elevation of ends above means and control of the allocation of resources in order to achieve efficiently the attainment of collective goals.

Winkler correctly argues that 'at the level of theory, corporatism is antithetical to some of the central institutions of a capitalist economy - the market, profit and private property' (Winkler, 1976). It is surprising, therefore, that in his analysis outlined above, he devotes little or no attention to how the state comes to direct privately owned business or indeed to what the reactions of such businesses are to state direction of them and to attacks on some of the institutions dear to their hearts. In this way he neglects both the role of private producers in shaping government economic policies and their reactions to such policies whether shaped by them or not.

It would be expected, for example, that at least major oligopolies would have some negotiations and exert some power over government decisions concerning the conditions prevailing in their economic sectors. It could even be that collections of small producers might also engage in such bargaining. It might even be expected that major producers would seek to circumvent government directives that they did not wish to comply with, as exemplified by British Petroleum's sales of oil to Rhodesia during a government embargo. Small producers might also evade government directives by trading, at least in part, in the 'hidden economy'.

Winkler's emphasis on the importance of a change from state support to state direction of the economy, as a defining characteristic of corporatism, is therefore a unidirectional view of the pattern of relationships between the state and private economic activity. It is deficient insofar as it neglects the two-way nature of such relationships. It is also deficient insofar as it neglects the continued exercise of power by private corporations with respect to state policies and their continuing ability to evade directives they do not wish to comply with.

An analysis of the economic aspects of corporatism must therefore deal with the two-way interrelationships between oligopolistic and competitive producers and the state. If, as Winkler argues, corporatist controls seek to constrain the rights of private owners to use, direct and dispose of their property as they think fit, then it should be expected that the establishment of such controls will generate both conflict and evasion. Attention should thus be devoted to analysing these relationships between producing organisations and the state and not just to the rhetoric of published government policies and directives.

Corporate polity

The defining characteristic of a corporate polity is functional representation of interests. In such a polity the most important divisions for the purposes of political representation are those between vertically segregated functional groups rather than those between horizontally defined social classes. Vertical segregation and functional interest representation are usually the result of the development of horizontally structured formal organisations for the accomplishment of economic and political objectives where the division of labour and the deployment of science and technology are highly developed. Some theorists allocate the state a small role in such conditions while others regard it as a central focus of political struggles.

French syndicalists, for example, advocated small, free, self-governing communities. They repudiated all attempts to use the state for social betterment and maintained that parliamentarism led inevitably to bureaucracy and autocratic government. Following these premises they were strongly hostile to communism because of its disciplined and authoritarian character. They had no place for a national state, whether capitalist or a dictatorship of the proletariat.

In contrast, guild socialists allowed a legitimate role for the state but only in conditions of functional democracy. For this reason they opposed collectivism and state management of industry on the grounds that it would lead to bureaucracy and therefore not release workers from wage slavery but simply substitute one set of masters for another. They argued that communities or organisations could not be really democratic unless principles of democratic government were applied not only to the state but also in every form of social organisation.

Given these conditions, some guild socialists regarded the state as the appropriate guardian of community interest while others moved closer to political pluralism, arguing that the state should be based on, and subject to, functional representation. The former advocated the chartering of guilds by the state. The latter regarded the democratised state as the representative organ of the community for political purposes but not superior to it or its guilds. It would be subject to requirements emanating from a guild congress representing men as producers, and a co-operative congress representing men as consumers. Other bodies were to be developed to represent other functional interests. These democratic characteristics are conspicuously absent from contemporary analyses of the corporate polity.

In Britain, interest representation has changed with the development of oligopolies, monopsonies and pressure groups. In most sectors of the economy a majority of total output is produced by a small number of relatively large companies. In some instances a majority of total output is also bought and 'consumed' by a limited number of large organisations. Among the largest of these is the state itself. Recent years have also seen the development and proliferation of numerous pressure groups representing the interests of both small producers and consumers.

The crucial change in interest representation indicating the development of a corporate state within such a polity is the development of access to and negotiations with the state by the kinds of functional interest groups outlined above. This access, negotiation and bargaining tends to be both informal and beyond the control of electoral processes. As a result,

> The liberal-democratic emphasis on individual interest representation mediated through political parties and

independent pressure groups increasingly gives way to a stress on the representation of functional groups corresponding to the social organisation of economic production and distribution. With or without encouragement and support from governments, associational groups seek to monopolise the representation of functional interests. Such groups aim to use their power to gain access to governmental decision-making on a permanent and stable basis, as well as to protect the interests of their members against interference by central authority. (Cawson, 1977).

The development of this type of functional interest representation has important consequences for political power structures. In such conditions, power will tend to shift away from parliamentary processes and genuine electoral participation in government decision-making. Elected representatives play a decreasing role in the evolution of major decisions. Political parties can also become less important as representatives of collected political interests. They may become the legitimators of policies generated as a result of informal negotiations between corporations and governments. The gap between state policies and popular control widens. Genuine participation by individuals is not assisted by the tendency to centralise and concentrate power in the hands of major functional groups and governments.

Conversely, major functional interest groups seek to move into regular access and negotiations with central authorities. For its part, the state often encourages or generates such access and negotiations.

A major transformation in interest representation takes place when private organisations establish ready and sometimes regular access to government decision-making. This transformation is reinforced when interaction between them becomes mutually supportive and some responsibility for the enforcement of the resulting decisions is even delegated to private organisations from governments. In this instance the flows of power and influence are both from private organisations to governments and vice versa. An important characteristic of corporatism is therefore two-way interaction between interest groups and governments.

The state itself also sometimes contributes to the development of corporatism. It does this either because it is administratively easier to deal with organised interests or because it requires certain interest inputs to justify policies it wishes to pursue. In the first case, state agencies have difficulty in combining unreconciled conflicts of interest into policies. The more such unreconciled conflicts there are the more difficult it is for the state to combine them into apparently representative policies. There is therefore a tendency for the state to acquire co-ordinated pressures by conferring representative status on a limited number of private organisations rather than negotiating with large numbers of pressure groups or individuals.

In the second case, the state may help to create functional interest groups in order to generate co-ordinated pressures from a particular quarter. This was the case, for example, with the development of the Confederation of British Industry. It can also follow from the wishes of interventionist ministers to generate support for policies they wish to follow. An example of this process was the pressure group support generated by the Swedish government for its public housing programmes.

A critical indicator of where power resides in such a system of interest representation is the outcomes of decisions. Who gains and who loses as a result of the effects of corporate decision-making is a touch-stone against which political rhetoric may be assessed. Unlike syndicalism or guild socialism, there is no prescription in modern corporatism in favour of equalitarian distributional outcomes as a result of state policies. There is only a predilection for orderly, efficient and co-operative decision-making. The output effects of corporate public policies are, therefore, likely to reflect the interests and power of the organisations engaged in generating them. They are not so likely to incorporate the interests of unorganised individuals, small organisations and pressure groups who do not have informal access to the internal decision-making centres of government.

The main characteristics of the corporate polity may be summarised. First, there is the development of functional interest representation. Among producers, this is based primarily on the incorporation of major oligopolies into interrelationships with state decision-making. These interrelationships involve both the exercise of power by the major organisations over government and the delegation of some responsibilities from public to private organisations for the execution of public policies. The mass of small producers are not usually incorporated in this way and constitute the market sector of production.

Among consumers, functional interest representation also involves the incorporation of monopsonists into public decision-making. Often, however, the largest consuming organisation is the state itself. This places it in a relatively autonomous and powerful position *vis-à-vis* its supplies of such things as defence equipment, health, educational and housing facilities. The necessity to form organisations in order to enter negotiation with state agencies also develops many pressure groups among consumers. These constitute a pluralistic sector of political representation.

The second main characteristic of the corporate polity is the different degrees of access that different groups have to public decision-making. On the whole, larger organisations have greater degrees of informal and internal access to government decision-making processes. In contrast, smaller organisations tend to have more formal and external relationships with the state.

This leads to the third main characteristic of the corporate policy. In general, power resides with those organisations who are incorporated into government decision-making rather than with those who are not. Most power is therefore associated with large, hierarchically structured formal organisations, including agencies of the state, and is exercised by the extra-parliamentary and electoral negotiations and bargains which take place between them.

A fourth feature of the corporate polity is the relatively high level of interdependence and inter-organisational relationships between the larger and more powerful public and private organisations. These relationships are characteristic of the corporate and incorporated producers and consumers. They are usually not so important in the market sectors of the economy, nor the pluralistic sectors of the polity. Where such relationships exist, however, they usually involve the exercise of power, flows of information or the exchange of goods and services in multi-directional ways. In Britain, it would not be accurate to regard the most important of these exchanges as only, or even mainly, emanating and flowing from governments to producing and consuming organisations. In practice, exchanges take place between all three major categories and in all possible combinations of directions.

The corporate state

The institutional boundaries of the corporate state do not define the limits of its action. This ranges from that undertaken by its visible and permanent legislative and executive branches, through those corporations set up by the state with nominal independence to produce particular goods and services, to action undertaken by private organisations on behalf of the state as a result of private negotiations. It is evident, therefore, that

> the difficulty of distinguishing the state in institutional terms becomes greater the more one is committed to an idea of close inter-relation between private interests and the state. This mitigates the idea of the state as something objectively identifiable. The issue is an important one for corporatism, where the state would attempt ... control through nominally autonomous, 'self-regulating' private bodies, that is, shift the institutional form of its activity toward a more indirect or disguised end of the continuum. (Winkler, 1976)

It is therefore necessary to think of the corporatist state no so much as a clearly defined set of visible agencies but more in terms of what it does, how it executes these functions, how independent it may be and what the outcomes of its actions are.

Again, Winkler gives some examples of what the corporate state does in order to achieve the objectives he identifies of unity, order, nationalism and success. He argues that the operating principle for the achievement of unity is co-operation. Following this principle, the corporate state introduces price control, industrial reorganisation and state-organised cartels. To achieve order, the state uses discipline and introduces such policies as wage control, anti-strike legislation, compulsory arbitration and inquisitorial tribunals. Nationalism is followed by the principles of collectivism and neo-mercantilism. These involve such policies as import control, export subsidisation, control on foreign enterprises, buying British and autarchic provisioning. Finally, success is sought by mobilisation and antinomianism. These involve investment direction, national planning, enabling acts and quasi-governmental organisations (see Winkler, 1977).

These actions are the result of negotiations and bargaining between major organised groups and the state. As some of these groups represent organised labour, some state actions represent compromises with their interests. Contrary to some Marxist hypotheses, therefore, state action does not always favour the interests of capital or some part of it. Such policies as price control, compulsory arbitration, control on foreign enterprises, investment direction and national planning can all be antithetical to the immediate and long-term interests of capital. Some nationalistic policies such as state-organised cartels, import control, export subsidisation, home-purchasing preferences and autarchic provisioning can also be antithetical to the interests of capital as a whole. Taken together, therefore, policies like the examples given above indicate more and different forces and processes at work in the devising of state policies than are allowed by most Marxist theories.

The combination of public and private organisations in negotiating what the state seeks to do has important implications for the origins of major state policy objectives. There has been a dispute not only between Marxists and managerialists as to the relative importance of capitalists and managers in the organisation of state policies but also between corporatists as to whether the corporate state favours or is antithetical towards bureaucracy.

The managerialist school of corporatist thought is therefore divided among those following the tradition illustrated by Burnham (1941) and an alternative exemplified by Marcuse (1964). The former develops the argument that power has shifted from the owners of private capital towards its non-proprietory executive controllers. For the state, this entails some origination and mediation of its policies by bureaucrats. The latter regard the corporate state as generating a mega-bureaucracy from which emanates most policies and control.

The first tradition has been related to the government of cities by such writers as Rex and Moore (1967), Pahl (1968), Dennis (1970), Davies (1972a) and Ford (1975). These writers have tended to focus on the internal workings of organisations. With the exception of Ford (1975), who studied building-society managers, the main thrust of their arguments has been that state policies originate from within the bureaucracy. Bureaucrats are said to define the national, public or community interest and to derive relevant policies for its pursuit. Little attention is paid in this formulation to the part played by external political forces in originating state policies.

Early versions of the managerialist thesis argued, for example, that inequalities in urban systems were the product of a 'naturally occurring' socio-ecological system in which spatial inequalities were generated, reinforced or mediated by strategic urban gatekeepers. This version lacked a theory of the general power structure within which the gatekeepers were located and therefore could not assess either the relative importance of their actions or the constraints limiting their extent.

Later versions of the same theses have reiterated the importance of studying the ideologies and motives of those who control the allocation of resources in urban systems. In addition, however, it has also been argued that such an analysis should be conducted within a specific theory of the state in which urban managers are defined as local bureaucrats. Furthermore, in this analysis, specific account is to be taken of both the internal structure of the state and its external relationships with private organisations.

Pahl, however, conducts this analysis based on assumptions about the corporate state outlined by himself and Winkler (1974). These, as has been noted above, concentrate on the relationships between the state and the economy to the relative exclusion of political considerations. The critical qualitative change said to be taking place between the state and the economy is that from support to direction. This argument establishes the autonomous state origination of policies but does not consider either the multi-dimensional nature of negotiations between private economic organisations and the state or the importance of similar political bargaining.

The alternative thesis, which sees bureaucrats as a primary source of state policies, follows a Weberian tradition. This is the argument that the mode of political (possibly as opposed to economic) domination in modern societies is increasingly bureaucratic and centralised. The results of these tendencies are said to be that the state is not primarily class-biased, neutral nor equalitarian. Instead, it is argued that the state is both independent of external influences and also dominates them. These arguments apply primarily to the central state. In this way they contradict some of the assertions made in the alternative managerialist analyses about the importance of local state bureaucrats. In this version, local state bureaucrats actually lose power and independence to the central agencies of the state.

While it may be argued that the mandarins of Whitehall do have extensive and, to some extent, unaccountable powers, they still appear to be politically limited in some important internal and external respects. Internally, inter-departmental and ministerial rivalries, conflicting objectives, less than perfect communication and financial constraints, all limit the possibilities for a single, coherent megabureaucratic dominance. Externally the interplay of public and private economic and political organisations, a healthy scepticism about mandarin competence and the efficiency of public bureaucracies and national parameters set by international conditions, levels of economic and political development, all limit the independence and dominance of central state bureaucracies. Pahl and Winkler are, therefore, probably right to conclude that 'Unlike the "technocracy" of Galbraith's New Industrial State, where experts rule in the name of science and efficiency, corporatism openly acknowledges political control directed towards ends determined by the state itself' (Pahl and Winkler, 1974).

Although the development of corporatism in Britain has coincided with a substantial growth in state activity, exemplified by the size of its revenue, expenditures and increases in the number of bureaucrats, corporatist methods of government are not particularly favourable to the latter. The guild socialist movement in Britain, for example, was responsible for some discrediting of the bureaucratic conception of nationalisation and the emergence of an alternative public management of industries through public corporations. They also campaigned for the idea of workers' control of industry. This helped to set an appropriate tenor for the development of corporatism in Britain by contributing to the general acceptance of a political theory which readily accepts interest groups as a normal part of politics. This acceptance means that state interventions in the internal decisions of external organisations do not necessarily lead to increased bureaucracy. This is because the larger of these external organisations may be vertically integrated into state decision-making and may therefore be parties to the making of those state decisions in the first instance. The ways that the state may administer those policies do not therefore inevitably necessitate the etablishment or expansion of public bureaucracies.

The principles of corporatist adminstration have been illustrated by Winkler. Most of them do not require the expansion of bureaucracy. They are 'antinomianism, inquisitorial justice, strategic control, delegated enforcement, mediated enforcement and extra-legal power' (Winkler, 1977).

Antinomianism is the principle which leads the corporate state to avoid, as far as possible, formalising its operating procedures. Its concern with efficiency and effectiveness elevates prompt and flexible responses to changing conditions above formal, inflexible and long-term planning. Bureaucratic forms of administration are thought to interfere with corporatist requirements for flexibility in policy responses and so the state uses devices for loosening the restrictions of formal rules and hence the control of bureaucrats. Examples of such devices are discretionary elements in statutes and regulations, enabling acts and quasi-contracts. It should be noted, however, that while such devices offer a range of opportunities to the state for altering policies, they also offer discretion to bureaucrats in implementing them. Antinomianism can therefore both increase the freedom of manoeuvre of the state in major policy decisions and increase the discretion of bureaucrats when it comes to operationalising those decisions.

Winkler's second major principle of corporatist administration is inquisitorial justice. The role of judicial institutions in this instance is to assert the general principle of order by discovering the causes of disputes and restoring co-operation.

> The format for settling issues is not an advocacy proceeding in which each side presents the strongest possible version of its case but an investigation in which all parties have an obligation to co-operate and divulge information, in pursuit of a single, 'true' understanding of the situation. (Winkler, 1977)

This is not unlike the procedures adopted in town-planning enquiries. There, an inspector, sometimes supported by others forming a tribunal, appointed by the Department of the Environment, listens to different arguments but eventually seeks to produce a report identifying the one best use of land. Neither the inspector nor his expert assistants are independent judges or lawyers: they are all appointed representatives of the state.

The corporatist state also seeks to achieve its aims by stategic control. With development of small numbers of large oligopolies in economic sectors and the large production and consumption functions of the state itself, the corporatist state can exert a strategic influence on the entire political economy by controlling only the oligopolies. This it does by using the processes of informal and internal negotiations. The strategic control of the state is, however, limited by the degree of reciprocal influence exercised by the oligopolies over the state itself.

Once bargains have been struck between these organisations and the state, the latter can delegate some of the responsibility for enforcing policies to the former. Thus, 'once the state reaches "voluntary" agreements with a few large or representative private bodies, it then obliges them to enforce these bargains themselves, to control their own members, associates, clients and suppliers' (Winkler, 1977). This takes an element of responsibility for the potential daily maintenance of state policies out of the hands of public bureaucrats and places it into the care of private managers. This would tend to decrease the powers of bureaucracy.

A further principle of corporatist administration is mediated enforcement. Again, according to Winkler, 'A corporatist regime would conduct some of its public administration through intermediary institutions ... state control does not [therefore] necessarily mean civil service control' (Winkler, 1977). Among the best known categories of such institutions are quasi-governmental organisations and quasi-non-governmental organisations. In Britain, these are numbered in hundreds. They are used to minimise the permanent costs of public administration by avoiding formal expansions in the civil service. They are also used to minimise apparent government responsibility for contentious activities. In passing, they also provide a way of maintaining political debts by providing a lucrative range of jobs for mostly unelected and unaccountable members of the establishment.

Finally, the corporatist state employs extra-legal powers. This involves the use of private decision in support of public policies. It arises as incremental extensions are made of 'normal' pressure group politics. 'The militancy of private groups may easily escalate from peaceful campaigns, through energetic protests, civil disobedience, violent demonstrations, rioting, attacks on opposed groups to planned acts of intimidation - all in support of a proposed government policy' (Winkler, 1977). Recent events at the Grunwick factory may not be too far removed from this process at work.

It may be seen, therefore, that a number of the important methods of administration of the corporate state do not encourage either bureaucratic control or growth. While some elements of state policy are mediated and executed by its own bureaucrats, others are subject to development as a result of negotiations among the higher echelons of public and private organisations. Some of the policies devised in this way are also executed by private rather than public managers. This raises the question of the autonomy of the corporatist state.

The burden of the arguments so far is that the corporatist state is not autonomous or independent by virtue of the neutrality or internal control of its bureaucrats. They do have some relatively independent effects on the daily working of state policies but the state employs administrative devices which mitigate their importance and is also subject to external pressures by virtue of its incorporation of external organisations. Any comprehensive theory of the corporatist state must therefore consider the level of independent effects that internal bureaucrats have on the working of its policies, together with the effects produced by external organisations and the resulting degrees of freedom that these allow the main governmental decision-makers.

Under corporatist conditions, the autonomy of the state is limited by the actions of its own bureaucrats and the power of external, functional interest groups. Despite these main limitations, there are still sources of autonomy for the state in such conditions.

In the nineteenth century, for example, German jurists developed the theory that a corporation is not just a collection of individuals but a being in its own right and having a will of its own. For some of them, the highest corporation was the state. A corporatist state could therefore have a degree of autonomy by virtue of its organisational will which could be greater than the sum of its parts. In this sense the state as a whole has a degree of autonomy both from the individual wills of its own members and from those of organisational outsiders.

A more convincing and frequently deployed argument is that some state autonomy arises as a result of its ability to play off different sections of the community against each other. This view is surprisingly developed both by some liberals and by some Marxists. Liberal pluralists have argued that the state can play one interest group against another in order to leave itself in a position to make the final decision. Marx's concept of 'Bonapartism' and Gramsci's analysis of 'Caesarism' are somewhat similar. In both conceptions, conditions arose in society which produced a relatively even balance of power between major classes, which left the state relatively free to follow its preferred course of action. More recently, some neo-Marxists have also noted the balance of interest between factions of the dominant class which also lead to a degree of autonomy for the state.

The corporatist state is therefore a complex of actions resulting from both internal and external pressures, some of which are executed from within its institutional boundaries and some of which are adminstered externally. The main organisations engaged in the setting of state objectives are those oligopolies and monopsonies which are incorporated into its higher levels of decision-making, the upper echelons of state institutions and, to a lesser extent, state bureaucracies. The main groups which are excluded from regular access to major decision-making are small producers in conditions of market competition, pluralistic pressure groups and most individuals as individuals. These groups may exert some external pressure on the state from time to time. It is easier, however, for the state to remain autonomous of these groups by playing some off against others than it is for it to establish a similar degree of autonomy from incorporated oligopolies and monopsonies or, to a lesser extent, its own bureaucracies. Nevertheless, there are times when the interests of such groups are in conflict, leaving the state relatively free to pursue its own objectives. State autonomy is therefore a continually changing phenomenon. It changes with the moving balance of forces among different sectors of the economy and the polity.

Conclusions

It was argued in Chapter 2 that vertical, functional divisions in modern industrial societies are more significant than horizontal divisions between social classes. This has important implications for theorising about the bases and characteristics of power in such societies. This chapter has examined the two major categories of theories of the state and power. Marxist theories follow a class analysis while corporatist theories are based on functional and organisational divisions in society.

Marx set out to produce a theory of political economy

which embraced both society and the state. Civil society was, for him, the basis of the national state. It was irrevocably based on economic divisions which formed the basis of different social classes. The more powerful of these were said to be able to use the state for their own ends. Originally, Marx's analysis applied to an essentially competitive economy. Later theorists have tried to accommodate both the ideas of monopoly capital and divisions within the class of capital. After the projected dénouement of capitalist society, an interregnum of proletarian dictatorship was forecast, followed by an unlikely utopian vision of the withering away of the state. Subsequent communist critics of Marx and Lenin, like Trotsky and Djilas, have pointed to the fact that the dictatorship of the proletariat tends to become the permanent rule of a bureaucratic, party and military elite. Despite this, other writers like Miliband and Poulantzas have continued to apply Marxist propositions to the analysis of the national state in capitalist societies. Poulantzas, in particular, has tried to wrestle with the problems that skilled working-class conditions have undoubtedly improved in social democracies and that the state in such countries does not always seem to favour capital as a whole.

The main problems with early Marxist formulations of theories of the national state were that they attributed causal primacy to effects they disapproved of to the institution of private ownership and they did not foresee either the extent of the changes that took place in that particular institution, social democracies as a whole or in societies in which it was diminished or abolished. The two reasons for this were first that works of Marx, Engels, Lenin and Gramsci contain no satisfactory theory of power, partly because it was thought to be axiomatic, and second that they did not have an accurate analysis of the changing nature of private property. The first was thought to follow from their class analysis and the second was thought to remain essentially constant despite the changes associated with the transition from competitive to monopoly capital.

The most telling deficiencies in Marxist analysis were exposed by contemporary French writers. Faced with the enormous differences between living conditions in early and modern capitalist societies, and still wanting to maintain the original Marxist base and superstructure analysis of the state, they argue that apparent social advances are still to the advantage of capital. To do this they have to maintain that the national state has more autonomy than Marx allowed, that it is used by some fractions of capital rather than others and that the same advances in capitalist and communist societies either have different causes and significance or that those communist countries are still in a transitional state of state-monopoly capitalism. Thus, common 'evidence' is used in mutually inconsistent ways depending on the normative beliefs of the writers concerned. In addition, the location and significance of the national state, with respect to capital, is often incorrectly or only partially recognised.

Trotsky and, to some extent, some members of the Frankfurt School, have located the role and nature of the national state more accurately. In the first place, they see it as a regional location for international capital within the context of the world economy. International capital is both competitive and fragmented. National states are usually concerned with their own local interests both at home and abroad within this context. No national state is large enough to have a monopoly of capital at this scale and few organisations employing capital do not have one or more competitors within the boundaries of national states. The monopoly capital of other Marxists is therefore mostly a myth.

In the second place, the role of state agencies is more accurately identified by these writers. The abolition of private ownership is seen not to be so significant as the rise of large, welfare-oriented bureaucracies which can become both the agents of a stereotyped form of comfortable welfare and a new kind of ruling group. These analyses lead in somewhat different directions from those of Marxist/Leninists, both old and new.

The Marxist class analysis of the state is also unclear when it comes to the question of how a particular social class establishes a relationship with the concrete reality of the state. The idea that the national state operates in the interests of a class as a whole which is defined purely on the basis of its ownership characteristics is quite unsatisfactory. It contains an unacceptable mixture of theory and practice. On the one hand, there is a theoretical group without any specified vehicles for the concerted exercise of power and, on the other, are real governments composed of specific institutions and bureaux making or refraining from taking real decisions. In order for a social class to have any real effects on these institutions it must become a class 'for itself' at which point it has specific organisations and/or political parties. At this point the relationships between social class and the state become an empirical question exemplified by the exercise of power in the processes of politics.

Class-based organisations such as trade unions and parties are formal and hierarchically structured, represent important vertical divisions in society and are not the only such organisations to exercise power *vis-à-vis* the state. Corporatist theories have started to develop a more comprehensive analysis of the role of functional interest groups and the state.

The factors leading to the development of corporatism are somewhat similar to those identified by Marx as leading to the dénouement of capitalist political economies. They are industrial concentration, declining profitability, technological development and international competition. They are argued here, however, to lead to politico-economic systems characterised by the exercise of power through functionally differentiated organisations seeking to achieve compromises in economically and politically approved actions which are as favourable to their particular interests as possible, and which are often legitimated by their incorporation in the objectives of the state. The main negotiating groups in this system are oligopolies and smaller producers in economic sectors; monopolies, parties, pressure groups and individual consumers; the government and bureaucratic agencies of the state. An important characteristic of corporatism is that the larger and/or more powerful organisations tend to be incorporated in various ways into state policy decisions and are sometimes used as agencies for implementing these policies. Smaller and/or less powerful organisations are not usually incorporated in this way. The producing groups among them constitute a market system of economic activity. The primarily consuming groups form a pluralistic system of interest representation in the polity.

The corporate economy is characterised by the division of producers into functional sectors. Within these sectors a few large oligopolies are usually responsible for the majority of total output. These are the organisations which are often incorporated in state decision-making in a multilateral, informal and sometimes secret collection of negotiations. Most sectors of the British economy also have a large number of small firms producing a substantial proportion of total output. These firms usually operate in market conditions. They can, however, join together to form trade associations which may either allow them to negotiate on more even terms with governments or form a secondary level of incorporation into state policy-making. Both sets of producers may conduct multilateral negotiations between themselves and the state. The corporate economy is not state-directed: it is a negotiated and bargained system of production.

The corporate polity is marked by the establishment of functional interest representation. This is based on the development of interest and pressure groups mainly among collections of individual consumers. Some of these groups can be quite large. Among the largest of them is the state itself in its role as the purchaser of goods and services, particularly from the private sector. In this instance, political pressure on the state by organised interest groups such as trade unions or political parties can produce distributions to consumers in much the same ways as pressures by oligopolies generate distributions to producers. These large political groups are also incorporated into state decision-making and have access to some of its internal decision-making systems.

Like the corporate economy, the polity also has a large number of non-incorporated pressure groups. These constitute a pluralist sector of politics and usually seek to exert pressure on political institutions from outside.

In both the incorporated and the pluralistic sectors of the polity, the acceptance of pressure groups as a central feature of political life also involves a decline in the importance of genuine electoral participation and democratic accountability. The internal access enjoyed by larger organisations and the representative monopolies conferred on formal pressure groups by the state contribute to a decline in the abilities of individuals to influence policies or hold administrations to account.

These changes have important consequences for power structures. They are exemplified by who gains and who loses as a result of corporate decisions. In general, it is to be expected that larger pressure groups like trade unions and political parties who are incorporated in varying degrees into government decision-making will gain most for those they represent. External pressure groups may make gains, particularly if the state grants them representational monopolies. In such a polity it is not to be expected that individuals who are not organised into formal pressure groups will gain much from state decisions.

The corporate state itself cannot be defined by its institutional boundaries. It is better conceptualised as a collection of public policies and adminstration. A significant characteristic of the corporate state is that these policies and the responsibilities for implementing them tend to move along a continuum from open government towards secret informal policy-making and from purely public authority implementation towards extra-governmental executive responsibility.

These tendencies are partly responsible for the neutral or antithetical attitude of the corporate state towards bureaucracy. On the whole, policies followed by such a state, and the administrative principles employed to implement them, do not necessarily lead to increases in the number of bureaucrats.

Nevertheless, the role of bureaucrats in administering those elements of corporate state policies which are kept within the wholly public sector is important. They do have opportunities to mediate public sector policies, particularly between the state agencies and the unincorporated elements of the economy and the polity. This is because they are a main point of access to the state for market producers and pluralistic consumers. They do not have such extensive opportunities to mediate state policies between themselves and incorporated sectors of the economy and polity because the organisations in these sectors are often partly responsible both for the establishment of those policies and, in some cases, their implementation.

This limited freedom of manoeuvre by state bureaucrats contributes a correspondingly limited degree of autonomy to the state. Another element in this relative autonomy arises as a result of the balance of power between the major incorporated organisations. Where this balance of power over a particular issue is relatively even, then the state may play one evenly balanced organisation off against another, leaving it relatively free to follow either the views of its bureaucrats or those of other central decision-makers. Another element in the relative autonomy of the corporate state is its sheer size. In many ways it is *primus inter pares* even when negotiating with large oligopolies. Its own production functions, its purchasing power and its administrative size and capabilities all contribute to making it a powerful organisation in its own right.

Some aspects of the power of such a state and its roles in the economy and polity can be illustrated empirically. How this may be done is outlined in *Chapter 4*. The results of one such illustrative analysis are shown in *Part IV*.

Part III

Aims and Methods of the Study

Chapter 4
The Empirical Analysis of Power

Introduction

In order to illustrate the use of power in conditions of corporatism it is necessary to choose a field of government activity which is both of central importance to production and consumption and susceptible to empirical investigation. Among the items most critical to the public and private sectors alike are capital, labour and land. Most scholars are agreed that these form the main factors of production. As such, they are crucial resources in terms of private and public production, their combination forms the basis of consumption and governments are particularly concerned with their exchange and distribution.

The criteria for choosing between capital, labour and land as subjects for this study were first the length and level of public planning of them, second the degree of visibility of the exercise of power over them, and third the degree of ability to measure the immediate distributional outcomes of the use of its power. As a result of these criteria, land was chosen to illustrate the development of corporatism.

Land was chosen because it has been the subject of formal attempts to plan its use, at least since the Housing, Town Planning Etc., Act of 1909. Where free markets and pluralistic interests are being superseded by planning, there the growth of corporatism is likely to be greatest. By the time of this study, statutory land-use planning had been in existence in Britain for nearly two generations. It was therefore expected to provide a strong example of the development of corporatist conditions of power. In particular, the period since 1947, when major local authorities were allocated a mandatory land-use planning function by central government, was expected to provide evidence of the development of corporatism, at least at the level of the local state.

Land-use planning was also chosen for study because, although many corporate negotiations are secret, their results become visible at three important points. The first of these, during the period of this study, was development plans. At the end of negotiating and bargaining, a detailed statutory plan showing the planned outcomes of these processes was produced. The second was the process of development control. This provides a point at which the property rights and land uses which different organisations, groups and individuals are seeking to acquire become visible in terms of formal planning applications, permissions and refusals. Finally, the immediate outcomes and their distributional patterns become visible as land is developed and physical properties are constructed. Land-use planning therefore provides some important points at which the uses of power over this major factor of production become visible and are, therefore, susceptible to empirical investigation.

A further reason for choosing to study land-use planning was because, although it deals with a major factor of production, it is a function delegated by central to local government. Its characteristics may therefore be studied at the local level. Insofar as differences in local circumstances may be specified or controlled, then local planning studies may be said to illustrate more general processes at work and their significance need not be confined within the administrative boundaries of the areas analysed. Analysing land-use planning, therefore, has the double merit of providing a subject for study which may be legitimately confined within meagre research resources and at the same time producing results which may be argued to have some general significance.

Aims

The main aim of the study was to examine whether there was any evidence to support the hypothesis that power in cities has been characterised by the kind of corporatist structures and processes outlined in Chapter 3. To investigate this proposition, an analysis was made of which organisations, groups and individuals exerted most power over the production of a development plan for land uses and which of these acquired the greatest value of property rights and properties over the statutory period of this plan.

In doing this, the aim was to discover whether major producing and consuming organisations exerted the most power over land-use decisions and, conversely, whether unorganised individuals, particularly the poorest among them, were not able to exercise much power over the content of a development plan. This was done by analysing the detailed political history of such a plan over the period from its inception to the end of its statutory jurisdiction.

Following this analysis, it was also aimed to find out whether the relative power of organisations, groups and individuals could also be illustrated by the distributional outcomes of the process of development control. This was attempted by examining the main applications for developments in three wards of a city over the statutory life of the development plan. The immediate outcomes of these applications in terms of the acquisition of property rights, buildings and their relative costs and values were used to illustrate the incidence of distributions resulting from development control.

Methods of study

For the purposes of post-war, historical and longitudinal studies of British cities, different types of communities have been usefully classified by Moser and Scott (1961). They analysed the characteristics of all the 157 towns in England and Wales which had populations in 1951 of 50,000 or more people. These accounted for slightly more than half of the population of England and Wales at that time. Moser and Scott analysed sixty variables for all these towns, grouped into eight different categories as follows:

1. Population size and structure
2. Population change
3. Households and housing
4. Economic character
5. Social class

134 *Aims and Methods of the Study*

6. Voting
7. Health
8. Education. (Moser and Scott, 1961, p. 7)

From these they extracted four major components which accounted for 60.4 per cent of the variation in the sixty variables. These major components were as shown in Table 4.1. Using

TABLE 4.1 *Principal component analysis of British towns*

Component			Per cent of total variance accounted for by the component
I	Social class		30.1
II	Population change between 1931 and 1951	town's stage of development	13.2
III	Population change between 1951 and 1958		9.8
IV	Overcrowding		7.3
Total percentage accounted for by components I–IV			60.4

SOURCE C. A. Moser and W. Scott, *British Towns* (Edinburgh: Oliver and Boyd, 1961) p. 14.

these components in a principal component analysis, the authors were able to classify the towns they studied into fifteen groups and to plot the relative differentiation of these groups. These groups could then be combined into six or three larger categories as follows:

Mainly resorts, administrative and commercial towns

A. 1. Seaside resorts.
B. 2. Spas, professional and administrative centres.
   3. Commercial centres with some industry, London.

Mainly industrial towns

C. 4. Most of the traditional railway centres.
   5. Many of the large ports as well as two Black Country towns.
   6. Mainly textile centres in Yorkshire and Lancashire.

D. 7. Industrial towns of the north-east seaboard and mining towns of Wales.
   8. More recent metal-manufacturing towns.

Suburbs and suburban type towns

E. 9. Mainly 'exclusive' residential suburbs.
   10. Mainly older mixed residential suburbs.
   11. Mainly newer mixed residential suburbs.
F. 12. Light industry suburbs, national defence centres and towns within the sphere of influence of large conurbations.
   13. Mainly older working-class and industrial suburbs.
   14. Mainly newer industrial suburbs.
   15. Huyton and Roby. (Moser and Scott, 1961, pp. 17 and 18)

Although no comparative studies of the power structures of communities grouped in this way have been conducted in Britain, it might be expected that some variations in findings would correlate at least with the major groupings if not some of the more refined categories as well. Conversely, studies of towns in any particular group should only be assumed to be characteristic of similar towns rather than those categories in a different group.

The town chosen for detailed study in this analysis is Oxford. This falls into group 2, which also includes Bath, Cheltenham, Poole, Cambridge, Exeter, Maidstone, Bedford, Colchester and Southend-on-Sea. Oxford might also, for the purposes of this analysis, be considered not altogether untypical of the towns also included in groups 1 and 3 under the general category of resorts, administrative and commercial towns. The advantages of choosing Oxford were that small-area census data were available for the city from 1951; that some knowledge of the formal and informal political processes were available as a result of thirty-six years residence in the area by the author; and that the main political groups in the city were relatively visible.

For the moment, it is interesting to note the detailed characteristics of Oxford in 1951, the year in which the

136 *Aims and Methods of the Study*

TABLE 4.2 *England and Wales, urban characteristics compared with those of Oxford*

Population size and structure	England and Wales (157 towns population 50 000)	Oxford
Population ('000)	84	99
% of population aged 0-14	21.8	20.5
% of population aged 15-64	67.3	68.3
% of population aged 64 or over	10.4	11.2
Females per 1000 males	1 108	1 125
Females per 1000 males aged 25-44	1 042	1 007
% of females 20-4	48.1	43.1
Population change		
1931-51 total %	11.0	22.5
1931-51 births and deaths %	9.0	12.0
1931-41 balance of change %	2.5	10.5
1951-8 %	-0.2	5.5
Birth rate ratio 1950-2	96	91
Birth rate ratio 1955-7	94	84
% illegitimate births 1950-2	4.9	7.0
% illegitimate births 1955-7	4.7	7.0
Households and housing		
% persons in private households	92.5*	92.8
% one-person households	9.9	11.3
% six or more person households	7.2	8.1
% 1-3 room dwellings	10.6	8.0
Persons per room	0.74	0.71
% overcrowded households (1-3 person households, 4ppr, 4+ person households, 5ppr)	5.9	5.7
% households at over 1% persons per room	4.3	4.0
% households in shared dwellings	12.2	18.7
% households with piped water	94	94
% households with WC	97	98
% households with 5 amenities	65	72
% households with 5, or only bath missing	91	93
New housing rate 1945-8 total	48	46
New housing rate 1945-8 LAs	32	38
% LA of total houses 1945-8	72.8	82.6
Economic character		
Occupied as % of total population	59.7	59.2
% of women in labour force	32.6	33.4
% in manufacture etc.	41.6	39.4
% in all service industries	37.4	47.1
% in retail	10.3	10.1
% in finance etc.	1.4	1.5
% in professional services	6.8	17.4
Job ratio	99	132
Community ratio	51	42
Per capita retail sales 1950 (£)	125	202

TABLE 4.2 *(continued)*

Population size and structure	England and Wales (157 towns population 50 000)		Oxford	
Social class				
% in social classes 1 + 11		15.8		19.3
% in social classes IV + V		26.0		27.2
Social class index		99		100
Social survey J - index 1954		5.5		4.04
Voting				
General elections 1951 poll	83.7		82.0	
1951 % voting left	49.6		44.0	
1955 % voting left	48.8		37.6	
Local % voting in contested elections 1956-8	42.8		40.0	
Health				
Infant mortality rate 1950-2		28		21
Infant mortality rate 1955-7		23		20
TB notification rate 1957		88		129
Mortality rate 1957 lung cancer		116		109
Mortality rate 1957 other cancer		106		84
Mortality rate 1957 bronchitis		106		81
Education				
% with terminal edn. age under 15	67.8		58.8	
% aged 15-24 in full-time edn.	8.1		15.6	

* Probably printed in error as 2.5

SOURCE C.A. Moser and W. Scott, *British Towns* (Edinburgh: Oliver and Boyd, 1961) pp. 54, 55, 136 and 137.

following study commences, compared with those for England and Wales as a whole. These are set out in Table 4.2. If the four principal components are examined, it will be seen that Oxford had rather more than the national average of its population in both social classes 1 and 2, and 4 and 5. The rate of population growth between 1931 and 1951 was twice the national average. On the other hand, slightly less than the national average were living in overcrowded households. As these components were said to account for 60 per cent of the total variance in urban characteristics, it can be seen that the group of towns to which Oxford belonged were less than typical of British towns in general. The main differentiating characteristic accounting for this would seem to be economic growth. Thus Oxford and other towns in the group were all

138 *Aims and Methods of the Study*

subject to the growth of industrial, commercial and service industries like vehicles, administration, education and tourism. This would clearly differentiate them from areas suffering from economic decline during the same period.

Clark points out that

> A crucial variable generally intertwined with the extent of economic diversification, the percentage of absentee ownership, the non-local character of inputs and outputs, the development of labour organisations and the nationalisation of many economic decisions is the degree of industrialisation. Indeed, some writers have focused on industrialisation and the accompanying bureaucratisation and rationalisation of economic life as the central independent economic variable underlying these other changes. (Clark, 1967)

The city should therefore provide a strong example of the development of corporatism.

Table 4.2 shows that in 1950/1 the economic character of Oxford was somewhat different from that of England and Wales as a whole. It had nearly three times the national proportion of professional service jobs and 10 per cent more in service industries. Incomes, as reflected by per capita retail sales, were substantially higher than average. The level of industrialisation, its sophistication, the proportion of the workforce engaged in tertiary occupations and income levels all combine to illustrate Oxford's relatively advanced economy at the beginning of the study period.

The universes covered in this analysis were the political, legislative and administrative processes and outputs of national and local urban planning in Oxford. The primary focus in these areas was on the history of the political and legislative framework within which Oxford's development planning was conducted and the detailed development control decisions taken in three wards of the city. The time period for the whole analysis covers the introduction of the 1947 Town and Country Planning Act up to 1977 when the fieldwork was completed. The analysis of development control records covers the period from 1953, when Oxford's development plan was submitted, up to 1973, when both the planning system

The Empirical Analysis of Power 139

and local government were reorganised. The results of these development control decisions up to 1977 were analysed.

In the case of the political analyses of urban development, the samples used covered the entire visible universe of action focused on the development plan. All available sources of information on this topic were investigated for the period 1947 to 1977. These included newspaper reports, council and committee minutes, historical studies and personal informants. In the particular examples of important development control decisions selected for detailed study, the sample was drawn from the development control records of the local planning authority.

In the general analysis of the distributional outcomes of development control decisions taken between 1953 and 1973, a two-stage stratified sample was drawn from the local planning authority's development control records. First the wards of Oxford, as they existed in 1951, were stratified according to their social class composition in that year. Three wards were then chosen for detailed study on that basis. North ward was chosen because it contained the highest proportions of social classes 1 and 2; Cowley and Iffley was chosen because its resident population had the highest proportion of social class 3; and South ward had the highest proportion of social classes 4 and 5 of any ward in the city at that time. The location of these wards in 1951 is shown in Figure 4.1.

The boundaries of the City of Oxford and its component wards changed considerably over the period from 1947. The city was enlarged on 1 April 1957 to include the area known as Blackbird Leys, which became a ward in its own right in 1967. In 1969 a large-scale reorganisation of ward boundaries took place, in which all three of the chosen wards experienced boundary changes. In North and South wards these were only small alterations. Cowley and Iffley, however, was subdivided to form, in whole or in part, five new wards: Temple, Cowley, Iffley, Donnington, Wood Farm and East.

So that the original (1951) ward boundaries could be adhered to, it was necessary to draw up a list of the roads forming each ward in 1951. As new roads were added to the wards so these too were included in the directory drawn up. This directory was used as a check-list in the subsequent collection

140 *Aims and Methods of the Study*

FIGURE 4.1 *Oxford wards, 1951*

of data. The list of roads came from information kept in the Register of Electors and the City Engineer's Department of the City of Oxford.

The selection of areas for study in this way allowed two types of analysis to be conducted. First, the organisations and individuals who approached the local planning authority for planning permission could be identified empirically. Second, because of the levels of residential segregation which existed in Oxford, as illustrated by Table 4.3, reasonably strong relationships could be established between distributions to local areas and consequent distributions to residents with particular social class characteristics.

The organisations and groups involved in formal and, to a much lesser extent, informal negotiations with the local planning authority over land uses could be identified from the lists of objectors and participants at public inquiries and from the records of development control. They were composed of five main categories. One group were long-term and large landowners in the city. Land, for them, was a major resource, much as it had been in the days of feudalism before the industrial revolution. Another group were the commercial and industrial concerns of the city who used land as a necessary incidental to their main form of business. The state was another organisation with large and distinguishable interests in land use. Voluntary associations could also be distinguished as usually non-profit-making users of land. Finally, private and separate individuals formed a group seeking to influence planning decisions, acquire benefits and avoid costs.

Distributions to social classes are less precisely identified by this method. The well-known ecological fallacy which assumes unwarranted degrees of social homogeneity in residential areas has to be borne in mind when interpreting the level of significance of results gathered in this way. Nevertheless, Collison and Mogey (1959) computed a segregation index for Oxford using small-area data taken from the census of 1951. Such an index shows the degree to which particular social classes are residentially segregated from each other in terms of the difference between their levels of residential segregation compared with the average for the city as a whole. Collison and Mogey's index is shown in Table 4.3. The higher the index number, the higher the level of residential segregation of the particular class from others in the city.

Table 4.3 shows that professional and intermediate classes were substantially segregated in residential terms from others in the town. Thus, distributions to North ward, chosen because it had the highest proportion of residents in these social classes in 1951, would have had a higher than average probability of affecting those social classes than they would have had in other wards. Similarly, skilled manual workers were relatively segregated from both the professional and inter-

TABLE 4.3 *Index of residential segregation in Oxford, 1951*

Social class	Segregation
1. Professional	35
2. Intermediate	25
3. Skilled manual	13
4. Partly-skilled manual	8
5. Unskilled manual	18

SOURCE P. Collison and J. Mogey, 'Residence and Social Class in Oxford' *American Journal of Sociology*, 54 (1959) pp. 339-605.

mediate groups. Consequently, Cowley and Iffley ward, which had the highest proportion of skilled manual residents of any ward in 1951, serves as a spatial proxy for distributions having a higher than average probability of affecting that social class.

Residential segregation between professional and intermediate social classes and the remainder are reinforced by municipal housing programmes. Collison and Mogey comment on their data for Oxford 'that the effect of the municipal housing programme is to segregate classes 1 and 2 from the remainder while reducing the degree of segregation among classes 3, 4 and 5' (Collison and Mogey, 1959). Initially, however, the index figure for segregation of partly-skilled manual workers was low in Oxford. This illustrates their residence in some of the privately rented flats in the areas of larger, privately owned housing also inhabited by social classes 1 and 2. The index of segregation for unskilled manual workers was higher, indicating their residence in the cheaper privately rented accommodation of the city. Changes in the amount of this accommodation available, together with movement into public authority housing and movement into private ownership by some skilled manual workers, will require careful interpretation in Chapter 7 when distributions to areas are related to distributions to social classes.

Because of the lower levels of residential segregation among partly-skilled manual workers in Oxford in 1951, South ward, which contained the highest proportion of social classes 4 and 5, in that year, was not as distinctively segregated as either North or Cowley and Iffley wards. In the case of the latter,

55 and 48 per cent of households were respectively in the upper two social classes and social class 3. In South ward, 39 per cent were headed by partly and unskilled manual, and a further 40 per cent were headed by skilled manual workers. These figures should be borne in mind when interpreting the significance of the distributional analysis in Chapter 6.

Finally, as far as the ward figures on social class were concerned, some adjustments had to be made in order to compare the small-area, social-class data found in the censuses of 1951, 1961 and 1971. Here the technique used was, as far as possible, to reconstruct the socioeconomic composition of social classes as defined in the 1951 census by adding or subtracting the same socioeconomic groups found in 1961 and 1971.

Having stratified the wards of Oxford according to their social-class composition and chosen three to represent roughly upper, skilled manual and lower social classes respectively, the development control records in those areas were also stratified. Following Dobry (see Department of the Environment, 1975), they were divided into two main types. 'A' type applications were individually insignificant requests for development permissions such as advertisements, extensions, additions, conversions, garages, shop fronts and the like. None of them involved site developments covering more than 1000 square feet, roughly the size of one small dwelling. Most of them involved very much less than this in terms of physical works. 'B' type applications were all those requiring developments or changes of use involving more than 1000 square feet. A 10 per cent random sample of 'A' type applications was taken. All 'B' type applications were examined. This yielded a total sample of 2266 development control records for the period 1953 to 1973 from the three wards chosen for study. The total universe of records in those areas was reconstructed by multiplying the 'A' type sample by 10 and adding it to the 'B' type applications. Because of the relative triviality of 'A' type applications, the results obtained by this method were not thought to be politically or distributionally as significant as the 'B' type applications above. Some information was obtained on virtually the entire sample. Where cases were deficient in some way, their numbers have been listed on the relevant tables.

144 *Aims and Methods of the Study*

The applications were examined via the individual application files held in the City Architect and Planning Officer's Department. Missing files were cross-checked with the Decision Notice files of the same department and the files kept in the Building Control Section of the City Engineer's Department.

Checking on the completion of a physical development – an extension as well as a new building on a virgin site – was done in one of two ways. The first involved the completion notices kept in the building control filing system. Although these must be submitted by law, this has not always happened, and visiting sites or interviewing the relevant officers of the council often became necessary. This, in fact, proved one of the largest gaps in the supply of information encountered during the project.

Site areas and floorspace figures were often difficult to obtain. This was because they were not required by the Planning Department and therefore not given on the application forms, or because the figures given were not accurate. Although glaringly inaccurate examples of the latter were easily dealt with, it was necessary to take on trust most of the figures given in the applications. The figures calculated from the site plans and floor plans were, because of time limitations, close approximations rather than exact figures. Some cross-checking was possible for new developments by using the 1965 and 1971 land-use surveys carried out by the City Planning Department.

Most of the information required concerning housing data was taken from the filing system of the various sections of the Director of Housing and Estates Department. In particular, this information came from Section 5 (Housing Management) and Section 7 (Administration). Much of this information is also available to the general public in either the Abstracts of the Treasurer's Accounts for each year ending 31 March, or in the Reports and Minutes of the Housing Committee. Less detailed information may also be found in the quarterly reports the Housing Department submits to full council, found in the Council Minutes and Reports of Committees.

The annual Abstract of the Treasurer's Accounts provides data on the capital costs of all major projects such as Cowley

The Empirical Analysis of Power 145

Centre, Westgate and Horspath Industrial Estate. Some projects, particuarly road - Donnington Bridge Road and Marston Ferry Road - were not recorded in this source and had to be checked via the City Treasury direct.

The above-mentioned abstracts also provide information on the committee expenditures and revenues. This applies to both the Housing Revenue Account and the General Rate Fund.

All the information concerning the rateable values of properties within the city came from the ledgers and direction sheets kept in the Rating Section of the City Treasury, Exchequer Division.

In order to calculate the rate income to the city from any property or development, assessed rateable value was multiplied by the appropriate rate poundage for the type of property, which changes annually.

The information used in the case studies was taken from the application files, street files (more correspondence is kept in these than in the majority of application files), articles and reports in the *Oxford Mail* and *Times,* interviews with council officials, and the files kept in the City Secretary and Solicitor's Department. The latter are not readily available to the general public and may not be removed from the department. It should also be noted that correspondence relating to any application is not available to anyone outside the department dealing with the application, and that this restriction applies across departments as well as to the public.

The council structure for any particular year was taken from information kept in the Council Minutes and Reports of Committees for that year. The political composition of the council was taken from articles and reports in the *Oxford Mail* and *Times.* Committee memberships were culled from the Council Minutes. The internal structures of the council departments servicing the committees were taken from the establishment records of the Personnel Department and the Administrative Section of the City Architect and Planning Officer's Department.

The data were extracted from local authority files as a result of the kind permission granted by the City of Oxford to locate a research assistant in the City Architect's and Planning Department for the period 1975 to 1977.

146 *Aims and Methods of the Study*

Information on the political history of development planning in Oxford was culled from the *Oxford Mail* and *Times*, the numerous books, articles and reports on the subject cited in the bibliography and from the personal recollections of some of those who were closely involved. These form the basis of Chapter 5.

Conclusion

In the social sciences, no methodology is perfect. The study of power has been beset with less perfect methodologies than most. The methods employed in this study are, hopefully, a careful step in a more fruitful direction. As far as possible they have been devised so as not to predetermine the results. Even so the results which do emerge need to be understood and interpreted in the light of the theory outlined above and the various caveats on accuracy, change and relevance interspersed in the text.

The methods are employed to analyse the nature and processes involved in the City District of Oxford's concern with production in the form of development planning and with consumption in the form of who gained and who lost as a result of the activity. Chapter 5 examines the local planning authority's concern with production. Chapter 6 analyses the immediate distributions of land and buildings for both production and consumption. Part IV therefore offers some empirical evidence to substantiate the theoretical arguments propounded above.

Part IV

Planning, Production and Consumption in Oxford, 1947–77

Chapter 5

The Political History of the Planning of Development and Production

Introduction

Central government established a mandatory planning function for designated local planning authorities with the Town and Country Planning Act of 1947. In Oxford, some substantial landowners were also in a position to produce small development plans. Land, in combination with capital and labour, is one of three essential prerequisites of production. Development planning therefore illustrates an important aspect of, particularly, the local state's role in private and public production.

Chapter 5 outlines the relationships between the planning of land uses, private producing organisations, state production and the autonomy of planning bureaucrats. It shows that the relationships are not always uniform, but that often they demonstrate the ability of large private organisations to influence state actions in their own interests; the corporate nature of state involvement in production; the minor levels of bureaucratic autonomy; and the difficulties of unorganised individuals in influencing these relationships.

Central to the planning of land uses is the local council. The County Borough of the City of Oxford was designated as the local planning authority. The central state therefore made the authority responsible for the production of a development plan and the implementation of its various provisions either by direct works or by the control of development.

The council was generally composed of sixty-eight elected members and growing numbers of appointed staff. The avowed political allegiances of the elected members between 1953 and 1973 are shown in Table 5.1.

With the exception of 1964, 1965, 1972 and 1973, the

TABLE 5.1 Oxford City Council political composition, 1953-73

Year	Conservative	Labour	University	Liberal	Independent
1953	36	20	12	–	–
1954	34	22	12	–	–
1955	39	17	12	–	–
1956	35	21	12	–	–
1957	31	24	12	–	–
1958	28	28	12	–	–
1959	30	25	12	–	–
1960	31	24	12	–	–
1961	34	21	12	–	1
1962	31	21	12	4	–
1963	26	25	12	5	–
1964	24	27	11	5	–
1965	27	28	11	1	–
1966	29	27	12	–	–
1967	37	22	9	–	–
1968	46	14	8	–	–
1969	51	9	8	–	–
1970	46	13	8	–	–
1971	36	22	8	2	–
1972	25	33	8	1	–
1973	12	30	–	3	–

SOURCE *Oxford Mail/Oxford Times* (1953-73).

Conservatives had a majority over Labour in the council chamber over the study period. But Table 5.1 shows that the Conservatives only had an absolute majority in 1953, 1955, 1956 and 1967. The university members held the balance of power most of the time from 1957 to 1961. They then shared it with the Liberals from 1962 to 1965. They held the numeric balance in the council only twice more, in 1966 and 1972, before they were removed altogether in the elections of 1973. Representation of the university extended beyond their specific members of the council. A number of representatives of both the Conservative and Labour Parties had direct or indirect university connections throughout the period. Thus, until about 1966, the university could usually count on holding the balance of power in the council on matters affecting its interests.

In contrast, the composition of the council was not particularly sensitive to electoral sentiment. Seventeen of the seats were normally occupied by aldermen. These were elected by council members and not by the electorate. Until 1966, three of them were drawn from the twelve members who were selected by the university and not by the local electorate. In this way, twenty-three out of a total of sixty-eight seats were usually held by members not directly elected by the voters of Oxford. In addition, the practice of electing only one-third of the councillors at each annual election also meant that the composition of the council was slow to respond to electoral wishes.

In 1963 a proposal to reduce the number of university members from twelve to four and to abolish the office of alderman was voted out, partly by the aldermen themselves and partly because the council did not want to reduce its own size. Eventually, in 1967, the university representation was cut from twelve to eight, with three council seats being transferred to the new ward of Blackbird Leys. Not until local government reform in 1974 were aldermen and university representatives finally removed from the council.

Councillors are, of course, elected on a ward basis. The definition and numbers of these local constituencies are determined by the council's Parliamentary Committee. As the residential location of the supporters of different parties varies in the city, so the parties, via the Parliamentary Committee, seek to draw ward boundaries most likely to ensure their electoral success. In doing this they recognise the importance of residential segregation and ecological factors with respect to the composition of the elected section of the council.

To some extent, ward boundary changes reflect the shifting concentrations of residential populations over the years as the number of electors is supposed to be roughly equal between the different wards. Nevertheless, they do little to disguise the fact that much of the support for each of the major parties comes, inappropriately enough, from the right or left of Magdalen Bridge (looking north). To the left is North Oxford, a Tory stronghold, and to the right is Cowley, the centre of Labour support.

The results of these electoral conditions and ward boundaries are that strategic planning in Oxford was only in the hands of an overall Labour majority once, in 1973. The reorganisation of local government has ensured that this brief encounter is not likely to reoccur in the near future. The lack of electoral interest in local government can therefore be explained, in part, as a recognition that, subject only to dictates from central government and bounded by vaguely defined consensus on the necessity for the kind of goods and services it provides, the local state is not particularly sensitive to the needs of the consumers for its goods and services. This indicates a degree of autonomy at least from specific electoral control.

Powerful interests like the university, business and commerce have always known this and operated accordingly. This recognition appears to be spreading and, throughout the study period, a steady growth took place in local associations to further specific aims via different forms of political pressure. The legitimacy of these claims was recognised by the Skeffington Report (Ministry of Housing and Local Government, 1969) and enshrined in planning legislation from 1968 onwards, albeit in an even more restrained form than the report itself.

Political control of the local authority is, however, only partially reflected in the composition of the council. While this provides a focus for formal political action, a great deal of power is exercised over local government machinery, either by central government and the pressures it is subjected to, or by local groups acting outside the formal democratic processes. Once the latter was the preserve of the more powerful of these groups, but grass-roots community action may be altering this balance a little. Insofar as such action is growing, then the local council as a focus of political power is declining. It is decreasingly possible, for example, for powerful groups on the council to arrange comprehensive redevelopment areas.

History of Planning of Development and Production 153

COUNCIL
| Lord Mayor's Advisory

Selection

Finance   *Town Clerk*

Finance   *City Treasurer*
Parliamentary
Old-Age Pensions   *Town Clerk*
Emergency

Establishment   *Town Clerk, City Treasurer*

Valuation
Assessment   *City Treasurer*

Baths
Highways etc.
Parks and Cemeteries   *City Engineer*
Sewage Disposal
Town Planning

Plans
Aerodrome   *City Engineer, City Architect*

Housing
Estates
Allotments
Port Meadow   *City Architect*
Markets and Fairs
South Oxford Smallholdings

Public Health
Mental Health   *Public Health*
Blind Welfare

FIGURE 5.1 (*contin. overleaf*)

Public Assistance	*Public Assistance*
Education	*Education*
Watch	*Police, Other Services*
Electricity	*Electricity*
Library	*Library*
Waterworks	*City Water Engineer*
Catering	*Catering*

Roman type indicates committes, *italic* type indicates departments.

FIGURE 5.1 *Oxford County Borough council structure, 1946-7*

Residents' associations like those in Jericho and East Oxford are conscious of the fate of St Ebbe's, and have some determination to develop the kind of living conditions they themselves require, rather than those that the council might once have thought appropriate for them.

Thus, although the increasing role of the state at central and local levels makes political action more appropriate than economic action in the acquisition of its goods and services, formal democratic procedures are not necessarily the most effective. Indeed, they are decreasingly the channels by which groups achieve their aims. In Oxford, this has always been the case with the university, business and commercial interests. An increasingly knowledgeable society is also finding, in the shape of local action groups, that informal methods of exercising power and refusing to accept disadvantageous rules or results are the way to achieve favourable distributions in political society.

Within the council, formal control over its activities is exercised via committees. Figure 5.1 shows that in 1946/7 the council had no less than thirty-two committees controlling thirteen departments.

In view of the central role of committees in policy, financial and detailed control of the council's departments, any outsider wanting to know what the council was doing on a day-to-day basis would have to have access to these committees. To the degree that their activities were secret, not subject to public scrutiny, and determined by chief officers and council members, so the local departments could pursue interests as they saw fit, and only those outside interests with representation or power could directly seek to influence their activities.

In 1962, Councillor Davies (Liberal) proposed that certain committees should open to the public and press. The motion was heavily defeated (*Oxford Times*, 16 November 1962, p. 28). The next year, Councillor Butler (Liberal) complained that even the council did not know much about the activities of the Planning Committee. He said that there was no possibility of debate in the council about disputed planning decisions taken under delegated powers. Furthermore, as the Planning Committee quorum consisted of only four people (including the chief officer), planning decisions could be in the hands of only three elected members (*Oxford Times*, 10 May 1963, p. 15).

In 1965, the council eventually adopted a motion by Councillor Brooks (Labour) that the Planning Committee should consider proposals to give planning applications wider publicity before they were considered. After a year's deliberation, the committee said that it would not be worthwhile. In 1971, a member of the public complained to the council, 'It is unacceptable that, apart from the enterprise of local journalists, the only way for members of the public to safeguard their interests is to make visits twice a month to their local library [to see the Planning Committee Minutes], (*Oxford Times*, 15 January 1971, p. 5). Not until 1972 were lists of planning applications published in the local press.

Secrecy is beneficial to some interests rather than others. Only two main groups can gain much from it. They are, first, the bureaucrats who can further their interests in 'a quiet and secure existence', since as long as their activities can proceed peacefully behind closed doors, a measure of autonomy is accorded to the way they conduct their affairs, process information and reach judgements. The chief officer is then in a strong position to further these interests in closed committees, partly because he has a staff to back him up which councillors do not have, and partly because the committee quorum is so small. A dominant chief officer in these circumstances can achieve considerable autonomy for the activities of his department.

The second group of interests to benefit from secrecy are those acquiring direct influence in the committee. These are usually the more powerful groups in the locality. In these circumstances, a strong chairman has been known to achieve his objectives in committee almost without check.

Either way, secrecy in government tends to foster rule by unpredictable factors such as individual characteristics, the power of unelected groups and covert influences of all kinds. Insofar as these are often in the possession of already privileged groups, secrecy becomes the handmaiden of the powerful and the enemy of the underprivileged.

To the extent that committee membership gives some indication of the interests served by the decisions of that committee, membership of the Planning, Central Area Redevelopment and Cowley Centre Committees between 1953 and 1973 exhibited some interesting characteristics (see Appendix 1). A total of seventy-two members served on these committees during the period. Of these, at least twenty-two had direct or indirect connections with the university. Eight were university, five Labour and nine Conservative members. Most of the remaining members came from the local professions, although three representatives from local building firms were also among them. Otherwise, very few members had local industrial backgrounds at either management or worker level. Part of the explanation of this lies in the fact that a major role of the university was, and is, that of a major landowner in the city, with holdings dating back to feudal times. As an owner of large amounts of land, the university is particularly sensitive to the effects of land-use planning on its interests. Large landowners can be crucially affected by the operation of planning legislation. Industrialists, on the other hand, while they require some large sites, do not have much interest in land outside those sites. Furthermore, once acquired, and in Oxford this usually meant before the 1947 Act, industrialists were free to do much as they liked despite the strictures and agreements of the planning authority.

A final characteristic of the committee structures of local government is their search for rational and efficient administrative machinery. Figure 5.2 shows that in Oxford this search took the form of reducing the number of committees to four-

COUNCIL
|
| Lord Mayor's Advisory
|
Co-ordinating

Finance and Resources	*Town Clerk, City Treasurer*
Highways } Traffic }	*City Engineer*
Estates and Amenities	*City Engineer, Catering, City Estates and Surveyor*
Central Area Redevelopment	*City Engineer, City Estates and Surveyor, City Architect and Planning Officer*
Planning	*City Engineer, City Architect and Planning Officer*
Housing	*City Estates and Surveyor, City Architect and Planning Officer, Health, Social Services*
Health	*Health, Social Services*
Social Services	*Social Services*
Education	*Social Services, Education, Polytechnic*
Library	*Library*
General Services	*Fire, Weights and Measures*

Roman type indicates committees, *italic* type indicates departments.

FIGURE 5.2 *City of Oxford Council structure, 1970-1*

teen by 1970/1 and maintaining the number of departments, usually with increased staffs, at thirteen. The latter is a reflection of the growth of state involvement in the direction of the national product and the tendency of institutions to grow regardless of function. The former marks some attempt to increase formal political control over the activities of the authority's departments.

The establishment of a co-ordinating committee is one example of the attempt to overcome fragmentation of effort due to the growth and maintenance of departmental empires. It also marks a recognition that the combination of total state outputs is as important as the individual activities of separate departments. Whether a committee to co-ordinate other committees and hierarchically structured departments is an effective way of achieving this end is debatable. It does little to alter the balance of power to which the local authority is subjected. In this sense, the search for rational and efficient administration may have the effect of implementing more efficiently the desires of those who already possess power and influence over the local authority. The problem for those not wielding such power is not so much how the local authority does things, but more what it does.

Turning to the appointed sector of the council's planning function, in 1948 the council rejected a recommendation to set up a separate planning department. Instead, they decided to transfer planning from the City Engineer to the City Architect's Department (Figure 5.3). Successive reorganisations over the years meant that the department had a staff of seventy-five out of the 1970/1 total for the authority of 1418, divided between thirteen departments. The City Architect and Planning Officer's Department itself was divided between architects, administrators and planners as shown in Figure 5.4. The hierarchical and fragmented structure should be noted.

City Architect and Planning Officer

Deputy City Architect and Planning Officer

Chief Architectural Assistants — Assistant Architects (1) — Architectural Assistants (4)

Chief Planning Assistant — Senior Planning Assistants (1) — Planning Assistants — Junior Planning Assistants (1) — Trainee

Assistant Surveyors — Assistants (Estates) (4)

Assistant Housing Manager — Senior Housing Assistant — Housing Assistants

Mayor's Sergeant etc. — Assistant Town Hall Keeper — Telephonist

Markets Superintendent

Assistant Surveyors — Accounts and/or Stores Clerks (1)

Chief Clerk of Works — Clerks of Work (2) — Works Superintendent — Assistant Works Superintendent (1)

Figures in brackets show the number of vacant posts. Nineteen posts were in Administration: five of these were vacant

FIGURE 5.3 *City Architect and Planning Officer's Department, April 1949*

Three factors should be observed in these figures and numbers. The first is the growth in sheer size of the total bureauc-

City Architect and Planning Officer

    Secretary to City Architect and Planning Officer

Deputy City Architect and Planning Officer

Architecture
Chief Assistant Architects — Principal Assistant Architects — Senior Assistant
   Architects — Assistant Architects
      — Chief Clerk of Works — Clerks of Works
      — Model Maker — Technical Assistants (Trainees)

Central Area Redevelopment
Chief Assistant Architect — Principal Assistant Architects
      — Senior Assistant Architects — Assistant Architects) — Librarian/
      — Senior Assistant Planners   ) Research Assistant

Chief Clerk — Administrative Assistant
      — Senior Shorthand Typist — Shorthand Typists
      — Clerks

Planning
Deputy City Planning Officer — Principal Assistant Planner — Senior
   Assistant Planner
      — Assistant Planners — Planning Trainees) Draughtsmen
      — Development Control Assistant   ) Technical Assistant (Records)

FIGURE 5.4 *City Architect and Planning Officer's Department, 1970-1*

racy. In 1946/7, council departments employed 627 people. In 1960/1 this had risen to 882, and by 1970/1 to 1418, representing a 126 per cent increase over the immediate post-war figure. While these figures disguise some structural changes, such as responsibility for the police being lost, the trend towards larger numbers of local officers and staff is clear. Insofar as this was associated with a continuation or growth in acceptance or commitment to various professional codes, so the actual or technical rationality of these activities would be set against complete domination by external groups.

In other words, the growth of bureaucracy, the increasingly specialised knowledge required to execute its functions, the scarcity of this knowledge and a commitment to a set of external professional values places some autonomous power in the hands of local state officials, both from the central state and local interest groups. This autonomy is of course limited, but nevertheless is important.

A second factor giving some autonomy to bureaucrats is the fact observed by many students of hierarchically structured organisations that such a structure does not always follow the objectives of those who seek to control it. Following the virtues extolled by Weber, Western bureaucracies have long exhibited many if not all of the following characteristics:

1. Hierarchy of office, each with its own area of competence and ordered by official rules.
2. A hierarchy of status among members corresponding to the hierarchy of office.
3. Calculability of the behaviour of members which is important in the efficient running of the organisation and in its relationships with clients.
4. An allocation of roles, filled from above, the top posts sometimes being filled by election.
5. A high security of tenure and remuneration associated with posts.
6. Assistance in a career to be followed without reference to pressure from outside and ensuring the loyalty of the official to the bureaucracy.
7. Maintenance of impersonality in the social relationships between the members of the organisation and their clients.

Many of those who have adopted such structures would presumably agree with Weber's comment that

> experience tends universally to show that the purely bureaucratic type of administrative organisation . . . is, from a purely technical point of view, capable of attaining the highest degree of efficiency and is in this sense formally the most rational means of carrying out imperative control over human beings. (Weber, in Bell, 1967, p. 86)

Unfortunately, experience tends decreasingly to support Weber's contentions. Many students of bureaucracy, most notably Merton, Selznick and Gouldner (see Bell, 1967), have pointed to the unintended consequences following from attempts to achieve given objectives using hierarchically structured control organisations. In general, they point to the differences between control intentions and actual outputs which arise. Emphasis on defensibility and reliability often results in rigid and conservative administration. Delegation and specialisation seem to increase the amount of departmentalisation and internal empire building. The use of general and impersonal rules can lead to performance at the minimum level defined by these rules and a low level of acceptance of the goals of the institutions.

Taken together, these features show the difficulty that both the elected controllers of local government bureaucracies and external influences can have in seeking to achieve specific objectives. Bureaucrats are quite capable of constructing a red-tape autonomy with considerable imperviousness to attempts at control. There are a number of reasons for supposing therefore that state bureaucracies do have a degree of autonomy both from their immediate political masters and from powerful social classes. At some point in its development this autonomy must reach a level at which some aspects of bureaucratic action take on an interest in their own right. It may be a misplaced technical interest or self-interest, or something which favours inadvertently one social class rather than another. Nevertheless, its existence gives it a role in the parallelogram of forces which determine the eventual exchange results of goods and services in society.

Finally, the growth of bureaucracies illustrates the growth logic which tends to be followed by large institutions, especially among those responsible for their organisation. It is difficult for outsiders to assess and control the demands for more organisers made by the organisers themselves. The 126 per cent increase in local government officers in Oxford between 1946/7 and 1970/1 could have been the result of genuine requirements to meet increased workloads or of organisers acquiring more officers to pass workloads down the hierarchy and to build departmental empires. Table 5.2 shows

162 *Planning, Production and Consumption in Oxford*

TABLE 5.2 *Total planning applications for Cowley and Iffley, North and South wards, 1953-73*

Year	Number	Per cent
1953	301	3
1954	349	4
1955	294	3
1956	232	3
1957	318	3
1958	389	4
1959	409	4
1960	601	6
1961	515	6
1962	508	5
1963	539	6
1964	541	6
1965	434	5
1966	407	4
1967	477	5
1968	469	5
1969	455	5
1970	412	4
1971	469	5
1972	549	6
1973	753	8
Total	9 421	100

that for the three wards of Cowley and Iffley, North and South, the workload in development control as measured by the total number of planning applications did increase over the period 1953-73. According to the figures, 1973 was an exceptionally busy year and would have represented an increase of 150 per cent over 1953. Taking 1972 as more representative of the increase over the period, it can be seen that the volume of applications had increased by 82 per cent over 1953. This is roughly the average increase for the 1970s over the 1950s. It is half the increase in development control staff from three to eight, representing an increase of 167 per cent during the same period.

MAP 5.1 *Oxford City Development Plan – town map and programme submitted 1953, approved 1955*

164 *Planning, Production and Consumption in Oxford*

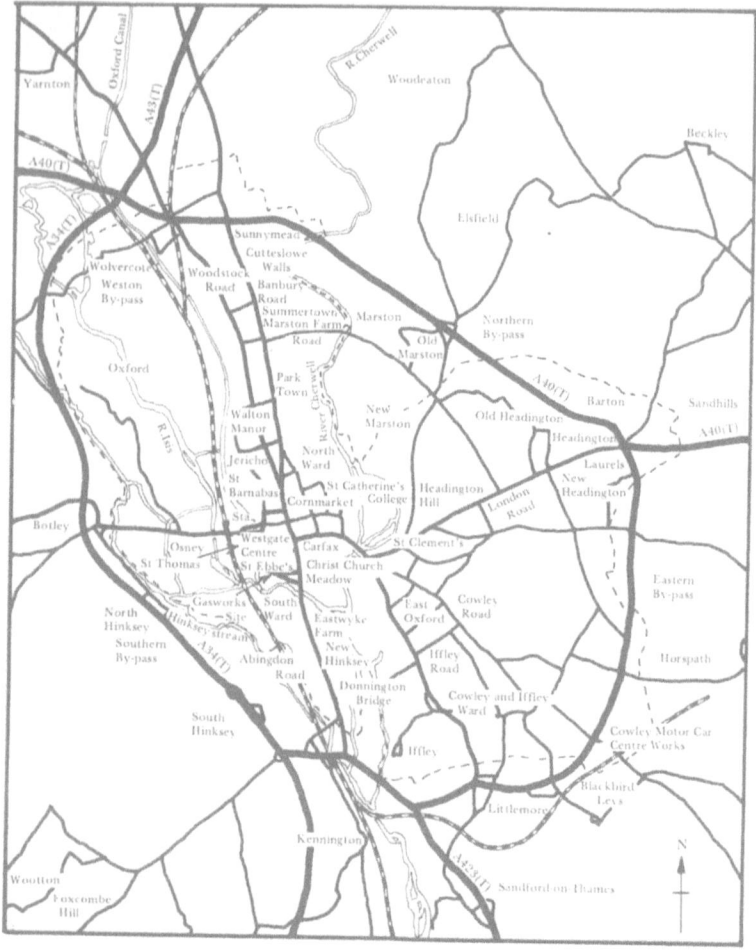

MAP 5.2 *Oxford City District – main roads, areas, landmarks and planning issue locations*

The combined apparatus of elected and appointed officials was, however, formally responsible for the production of the Development Plan shown in Map 5.1. Like all other such plans it presents in great detail the existing and proposed land uses within its area of jurisdiction. It also shows the programming of land-use changes. The most important or contentious of these are located in Map 5.2 and analysed below.

First, the areas where local bureaucrats exercised their maximum independence are analysed. Second, the goods and services largely produced by the local state itself are evaluated. Third, the relationships between the local state and private production are discussed insofar as they required the preservation of existing land uses or the designation of new ones.

Bureaucratic autonomy

The major and most frequently used reasoning employed by the local authority's planners in the objectives set in the Development Plan for the City of Oxford was based on considerations of architectural aesthetics, neatness and tidiness. This was the result of a number of mutually reinforcing factors. The first was the appointment of an architect-planner to produce the first attempt at a development plan for the city. The second was the placing of the local authority's planning function in the hands of the City Architect's Department. The third was a sympathy on the part of some groups in the city for aesthetics and tidiness. The fourth was an indifference on the part of the majority of the population to these kinds of issues.

The appointment of Thomas Sharp to produce a plan for Oxford was an important step in determining the content of that plan. His lyrical appreciation of the older, largely university parts of the city was combined with a lack of understanding of economic conditions and a lack of sympathy for the older areas of working-class housing. His plan was therefore largely concerned with civic design and the aesthetic preservation of the setting for an international university.

These considerations echoed the sympathies found in the City Architect's Department, where responsibility for the preparation of Oxford's statutory development plan came to rest. Such sympathies also formed a substantial part of the 'autonomous' professional ideology of town planners, particularly during the 1940s and 1950s. They coincided with many of the interests in favour of the *status quo*. The result was that neatness, tidiness and aesthetics formed an important part of the claim to technical autonomy from outside forces made by planning bureaucracies, not only in Oxford but also among the profession at large.

Where such considerations coincided with interest groups outside the council they could be translated into effective policy outcomes. Where they interfered materially with those interests the outcomes were less certain. Judgements of this kind are also notoriously matters of opinion. Support for aesthetic considerations was, however, forthcoming from voluntary associations like the so-called Freedom Forum. This was a group composed mainly of ratepayers. In 1962 it formed a committee to vet all planning applications. The object was to publicise those which were thought to affect the appearance of the city.

Most members of the local community were relatively indifferent to the importance attached by the planning bureaucracy to aesthetics. The two main reasons for this were, first, that many people were more concerned with obtaining basic necessities like housing and jobs. Second, the language in which such considerations was explained was obscure to many people, and its implications, particularly in terms of redevelopment, were not clear.

The net result of the interplay of these factors was that several important aesthetic considerations were incorporated in the Development Plan and later translated into statutory force. The first of these employed Section 32 of the 1962 Town and Country Planning Act to list 653 buildings, mostly in central Oxford, as being of special architectural merit, and therefore subject to stricter controls on possible future additions and alterations to them. Second, in the same year as the Act, a code was suggested which would restrict the height of new buildings in central Oxford to 60 feet. This was eventually confirmed and incorporated in the written analysis of the first review of the Development Plan. Murray, who by then had replaced Chandler as City Architect and Planning Officer, said that 'It is the intention of the Council to protect the landscape [that is, views of the city from outside] and allow nothing that would tend to mar the townscape of the City' (Oxford City, 1964a, p. 39). The views and areas to be preserved in this manner incorporate almost entirely and exclusively the original medieval area of Oxford. Third, the review suggested that a site known as 'The Laurels' on London Road should be redeveloped with 'its primary object the improvement of the entrance into the city from London' (Oxford City, 1964a, p. 292).

These aesthetic proposals were confirmed in the 1967 Amendments to the Development Plan shown in Appendix 2. The written statement explaining these amendments said 'Provision is made for the special protection and preservation of a large part of the Central Area of the City, mainly occupied by the University and Colleges' (Oxford City, 1967a, p. 4). It also affirmed that 'the Council, in order to protect the present character of the City Centre, will control development of high buildings' (Oxford City, 1967a, p. 5). The Laurels site was also designated for compulsory purchase in order 'to secure its development in such a manner as to provide an improved and worthy entrance to the City from an easterly direction' (Oxford City, 1967a, p. 11).

In the same year, the Civic Amenities Act made provision for local authorities to designate certain areas for preservation. Again, the aesthetic logic of planning may be seen in such provisions. Oxford has made extensive use of this Act, which was later consolidated in the 1971 Town and Country Planning Act. The first areas to be designated in this way were essentially middle-class housing areas such as North Oxford and the old villages which had been engulfed by Oxford's growth. The policy was confirmed in the Second Amendment to the Development Plan in 1970, as shown in Appendix 3. As Murray said in the written analysis accompanying the amendment, 'The Council intends to further its policy of protecting and preserving special areas in the City by the designation of Conservation Areas' (Oxford City, 1970a, p. 5). Included in subsequent designations, however, were streets of exactly the same type of working men's housing which Sharp had considered the ignoble nine-tenths of central Oxford. Thus parts of the Victorian suburbs, the central area and Walton Manor, all contained streets of small terraced houses, and Osney Town, the last area to be designated, was composed almost exclusively of such housing. Aesthetic taste had turned full circle. At the time of writing, Oxford has ten preservation areas. Added to this, other areas of old terraced housing like Jericho and St Clement's have been declared improvement areas, signifying a future of rehabilitation rather than redevelopment.

The most commonly employed logic base of planning could be considered both its most trivial and its main claim to autonomy from outside influences. The frequently employed aesthetic and tidiness arguments can be seen as a special preserve of architect-planners, especially as exemplified by Curl (1977), an ex-member of the Oxford City Architect and Planning Officer's Department. They are often couched in a language and contain priorities unfamiliar and inappropriate to the daily problems confronting most members of the community. They can also be followed with relative indifference by developers seeking to acquire permissions for new buildings. At the planning stage it makes only a marginal difference to such interests what colour bricks or what shape windows they should employ. The arguments do, however, echo some middle-class tastes and values and, combined with a general indifference among the community at large, leave the planners with a considerable degree of autonomy to follow their inclinations.

State production of roads, redevelopment and collective facilities

A second level of more controversial reasons for development planning centred on the arguments that the market does not produce certain goods and services, either because they cannot be charged at their full value, or because some groups cannot afford the market price, or because individual market decisions eventually impede the desires of the community. Despite this, the goods and services are, or have, become essential to the maintenance of community activities and therefore 'ought' to be provided in some form or another. It is argued that the only agency which can provide them and recoup the cost from the community at large is the state. Among the items provided in this way are roads, public housing, parks and the alleviation of congestion.

One of the most contentious of these items in Oxford has

been roads. No less than fifteen separate public and private proposals have been put forward since the Second World War. Most of them have been rejected but not without considerable conflict, which has illustrated admirably the interplay of local, national and even international interests concerned with specific local planning objectives.

Roads

The roads issue in Oxford resolved itself, in practice, into attempts to construct three sets of roads at varying distances from the city centre. The first of these, which met with least resistance and therefore has been constructed, was a proposal in 1927 to build a ring of outer bypasses. The first section of these roads was completed in 1935 around the north of the city. The need for the completion of this ring was echoed by Sharp (1948). This was the only one of his four recommendations to be completely accepted in the Development Plan.

Figures were produced to show that between 14.8 and 21.0 per cent of all vehicles in the city centre on one Friday afternoon in 1949 were merely passing through. Chandler, the City Architect and Planner at that time, argued that

> The completion of a system of outer ring roads would divert a considerable quantity of this traffic from the central area of the city and since this would include a high proportion of heavy lorries and coaches, the relief given would be greater than the figures suggest. (Oxford City, 1953, p. 15)

So a system of outer bypasses became a priority in the planning of Oxford's roads. Although they mainly passed through territory administered by Oxfordshire or Berkshire they were, in the main, approved by the government in 1955.

By 1958, the northern and southern bypasses were complete and work had begun on the western and eastern sections, as shown in Map 5.3. In 1961, work began to extend the southern bypass, to dual the link with the completed western section and, in 1963, a contract was placed to link the eastern and southern bypasses. Nearly forty years after the original

170 *Planning, Production and Consumption in Oxford*

proposal, Oxford was surrounded by a complete ring of roads. Positive local authority planning objectives had remained consistent enough over that period and opposition had been small enough to permit the translation of plans into reality.

SOURCE   *Oxford Mail* (30 November 1953) p. 4.

MAP 5.3   *Proposed outer bypasses*

The authority also proposed and was able to construct two intermediate relief roads. These were approved in principle in 1959. The following year the Conservative group on the council said that these roads should be given priority over others. They were to run from the Iffley to the Abingdon

Roads over the Donnington Bridge, and from Headington to Summertown via a link near the old Marston Ferry. Some opposition to the latter came from the Old Marston parish meeting, but the usefulness of these roads was generally conceded, and they were duly constructed.

The most controversial road proposals were those to construct a system of inner relief roads. Three factors were instrumental in the adoption of this positive objective by the local authority. First, local commercial interests were in favour of growth and development for the central business district and were strongly represented both inside and outside the Council Chamber. Second, it was assumed that ease of access for the private car was essential to support the central area, particularly in its regional commercial role. Third, the resulting and growing traffic congestion on the main radial roads to the centre, particularly High Street, could only be alleviated by building more roads. This combination of local interests favouring growth at the centre, the local authority's acknowledged responsibility for coping with traffic, and the conventional wisdom that more traffic needed more roads led the authority to its proposals for inner relief roads.

In order to maintain and develop the central business district, the Chamber of Trade proposed and supported schemes for inner relief roads and central area parking. Minns proposed the route shown in Map 5.4. In purpose, it was similar to those proposed earlier by Dale, a local architect, and Sharp. It was advocated by the Chamber of Trade. All three routes had two things in common: they passed through Christ Church Meadow and continued through St Ebbe's.

Sharp said that he did not think the Meadow was 'particularly lovely – it is just a cow-meadow – and I think the new road would increase the beauty' (*Oxford Times*, 5 March 1948, p. 5). Better still, 'more than two miles of indispensable new roads can be obtained at an almost trivial cost. For the most part the lines of these roads pass over open land or slum sites' (*Oxford Times*, 19 March 1948, p. 4). Much of the university and a number of colleges did not agree with this view.

In fact, they reserved their most vehement and persistent opposition for the inner relief road proposals. Their fight to

172 *Planning, Production and Consumption in Oxford*

prevent them was conducted inside and outside the council in the Houses of Commons and Lords and at each and every public inquiry.

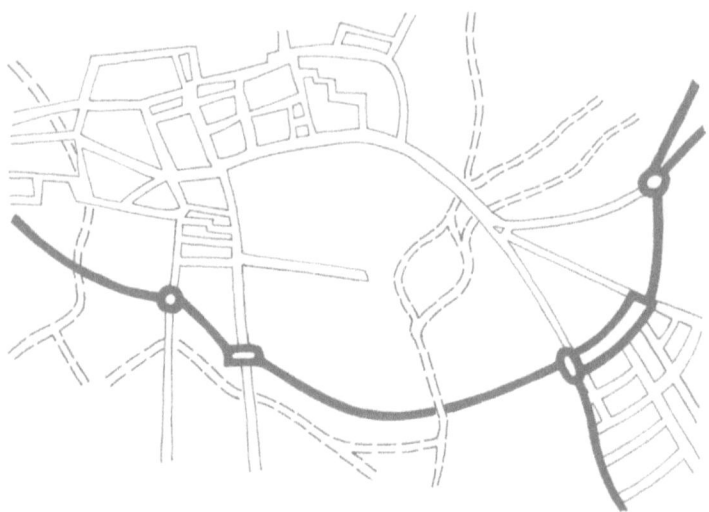

a) Lawrence Dale's 'riverside embankment mall' to the south of Christ Church Meadow

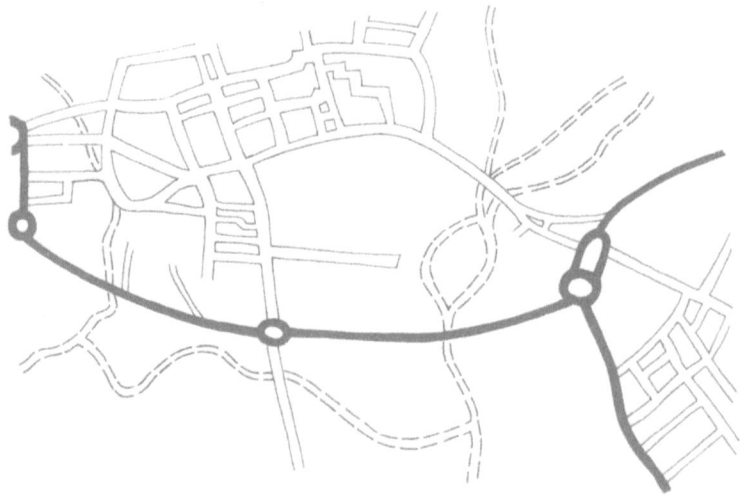

b) F. J. Minns's 'Cathedral Mall' – a shorter route through the Meadow

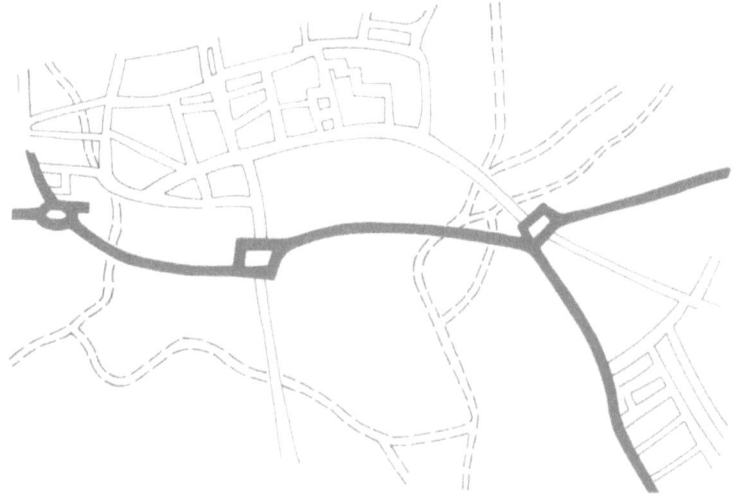

c) Dr Thomas Sharp's 'Merton Mall' - the shortest route

SOURCE   *Oxford Mail* (25 November 1953) p. 4.

MAP 5.4   *Private proposals for inner relief roads*

Inside the council, a fight was conducted to prevent the proposals being included in the Development Plan. This was often led by Councillor Brown, a university member. In supporting the motion not to include the proposals in the plan, he said that, 'The world of the planner was too often a world of make-believe in which maps, diagrams and statistics seemed to take on a life of their own and become more real than the facts of geography and population' *(Oxford Times,* 22 February 1952, p. 7). He went on to argue that inner relief roads do not relieve traffic, they merely redistribute it. He also argued that other types of policy were needed to prevent congestion, such as decentralisation, parking and delivery restrictions.

As a result of this university opposition to inner relief roads, and the section running through Christ Church Meadow in particular, the proposed development plan was modified in what proved to be a somewhat haphazard fashion.

Chandler, in the written analysis accompanying the publication of the eventual Development Plan, described that part of the inner relief roads running through St Ebbe's as 'the only line which can be taken by a new main road to ease traffic congestion at Carfax and in Queen Street and in St Aldate's Street' (Oxford City, 1953, p. 13). This argument was perhaps less conclusive in view of the fact that two pages later he said,

> The Council has given earnest consideration to many proposals for the construction of relief roads and bridges and, ... it is not yet of the opinion that sufficient evidence has been produced to support any one proposal so far considered in view of construction difficulties and the damage which might be done to the charm and character of Oxford. (Oxford City, 1953, p. 15)

Consequently the Meadow Road was not included in the Development Plan, but the section of the inner relief road proposals running through St Ebbe's was.

Duncan Sandys approved the plan in 1955 as the Minister of Housing and Local Government. He called upon the council, however, to propose a complete system of inner relief roads.

Several groups outside the council supported such schemes. The Oxford Preservation Trust said that it was essential to have a road across Christ Church Meadow, as near to the river as possible.

The Oxford Ratepayers Association also had something to say. In 1955, its committee concerned with planning said that:

1. It was wholly in favour of a road around Christ Church Meadow running on the south side of the Meadow along the river, this involving only a short bridge over the Cherwell being by far the least expensive route.
2. Carried through St Ebbe's to the station, this road would develop St Ebbe's and create here rateable values that render the initial cost ultimately profitable.
3. The Association would stress the importance of the Marston Road, representing as it does a ready made relief road. At little expense it could be connected to the Northern Bypass and take the North-East stream which now congests Carfax.

4. This being done the projected Parks Road, which is in the nature of a causeway across Mesopotamia, costly and destructive of many amenities, might be rendered quite unnecessary.
5. The Association would protest at the alarming expense and the little advantage of the projected Donnington Bridge. *(Oxford Times,* 14 October 1955, p. 8)

It was therefore in favour of minimising possible ratepayers' expenses by redeveloping working-class housing in St Ebbe's for higher rateable values, putting in a relief road where many of its members lived and not providing one where it did not have many members.

The council suggested a route through Christ Church Meadow favoured by a minority of the planning committee. This line was essentially that advocated by Councillor Minns and the Chamber of Trade shown in Map 5.4. They also suggested a road through the university parks.

The Vice-Chancellor, A. H. Smith, immediately voiced the university's opposition. He said that,

The siting of roads which has been selected appears calculated . . . to provoke the maximum opposition not only from the University but from all who care about the City of Oxford. A road has been suggested across Christ Church Meadow which seems calculated to destroy, as far as possible, the great stretch of the Meadow and the sense of space which it gives. In this respect it seems the worst of all the roads which have been proposed across the Meadow. (*Oxford Times,* 1 July 1955, p. 13)

The debate raged in *The Times.* Twelve college heads came out in favour of the inner relief roads. Eleven were clearly against: these were Balliol, Merton, Exeter, Corpus Christi, Christ Church, St John's, Worcester, Hertford, St Edmund Hall, Keble and St Hugh's. Robert Blake, Tutor and Senior Censor at Christ Church, said, in a letter to *The Times,* that the college would fight by every legitimate means at its disposal all plans for a road through any part of the Meadow.

These conflicting views and those of the council were put

176 *Planning, Production and Consumption in Oxford*

before Duncan Sandys at secret meetings in the Town Hall. Other groups who met the Minister in secret were the Preservation Trust, the Hebdomadal Council, the Chamber of Trade, the Trades Council and St Hilda's College. No representatives of the residents in St Ebbe's were present, though the Preservation Trust was pressing for the speedy redevelopment of the area, and the Meadow Road was to continue through that place.

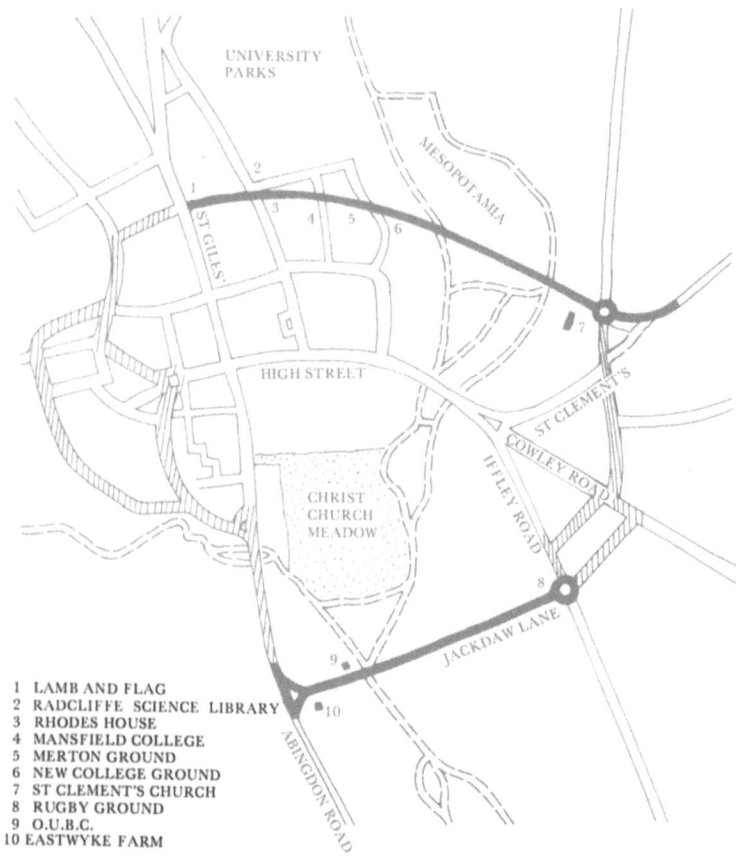

1 LAMB AND FLAG
2 RADCLIFFE SCIENCE LIBRARY
3 RHODES HOUSE
4 MANSFIELD COLLEGE
5 MERTON GROUND
6 NEW COLLEGE GROUND
7 ST CLEMENT'S CHURCH
8 RUGBY GROUND
9 O.U.B.C.
10 EASTWYKE FARM

The proposed north relief and south relief roads are marked on this map in black. The shaded roads linking the ends of the relief roads were possible routes which remained to be decided upon by the General Purposes Committee.

SOURCE   *Oxford Times* (4 November 1955) p. 7.

MAP 5.5   *General Purposes Committee proposed inner relief roads*

After the meeting with Duncan Sandys, the General Purposes Committee of the City Council proposed two new inner relief roads, shown in Map 5.5. The St Ebbe's section of the old plans was included even though it no longer connected directly with the new southern route passing through Eastwyke Farm. The Chamber of Trade, although still in favour of a road across the Meadow, supported the new proposals. Minns also said that the plans had to be 'accepted as a whole or not at all, for the south road is useless without the north road, and vice versa' *(Oxford Times,* 4 November 1955, p. 7). From that time the Chamber consistently supported suggestions for an Eastwyke Farm route, combined with a northern relief road not passing through commercial premises.

Blake deplored the new proposals and said that he did not think that 'the case for inner relief roads ... [had] been made out' *(Oxford Times,* 4 November 1955, p. 7). Alderman Smewin (Labour) said that the matter was developing into university versus the city. By the latter he meant those interests seeking to improve the roads leading to an expanding commercial centre. Councillor Ford (Labour) went further and alleged that,

> The Hebdomadal Council considers it essential that the University area be converted as quickly as possible into a National Trust Sanctuary for dons, in order to preserve the more eccentric, academic specimens whose extinction is threatened by the close proximity of commerce and traffic. *(Oxford Times,* 2 December 1955, p. 7)

Nevertheless, the university remained largely against the inner relief roads. They were joined by twenty-six members of the council itself who declared their opposition to the roads.

An inquiry was duly held in 1956. Sandys rejected the council's proposals and took the unprecedented step of proposing his own route, shown in Map 5.6. It involved closing Magdalen Bridge, putting a road through Christ Church Meadow, and passing through or above several commercial, government or college properties on its way north to St Giles'.

The University Congregation promulgated a decree instructing the Hebdomadal Council to sustain unreserved opposition

178 *Planning, Production and Consumption in Oxford*

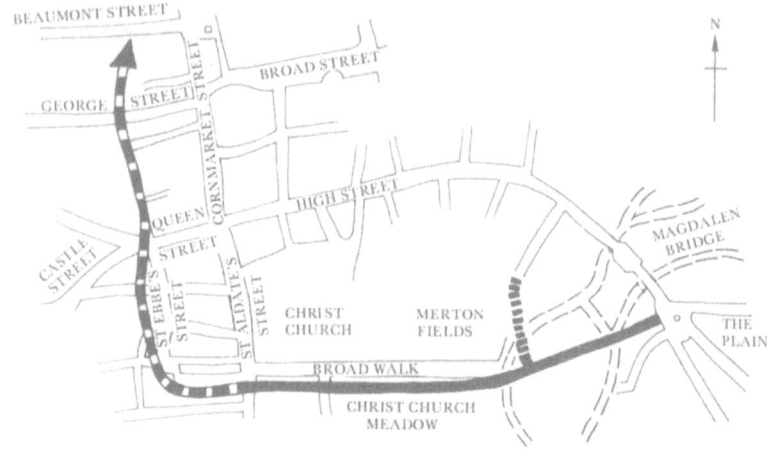

This sketch plan, not strictly to scale, shows the route of the proposed road across Christ Church Meadow, with the Rose Lane link, and an approximate route from St Aldate's to Beaumont St on the way to St Giles'.

SOURCE   *Oxford Times* (28 September 1956) p. 11.

MAP 5.6   *Duncan Sandys' proposals*

to the road. The Dean and Chapter of Christ Church issued a writ against the Minister, challenging the validity of his proposals. Lord Beveridge, an Oxford resident, initiated a debate in the House of Lords, which decided in 1957 that the city was under no obligation to follow Sandys' advice. It was agreed that the whole question would be the subject of a public inquiry to be conducted by an independent person instead of by one of the Minister's inspectors; that the report on this inquiry would be published; and that the matter could again be raised in the House of Lords. Henry Brooke, who had by this time replaced Duncan Sandys as the relevant Minister, assured interested parties that the inquiry would be of the widest scope.

As a result of this the council undertook a traffic survey. In 1959 the results were published and a new Meadow Road was proposed. Various proposals were also made the following year as to how it should proceed north to St Giles'. Opposition to specific routes continued so, in 1960, the Planning Committee submitted a report containing three schemes

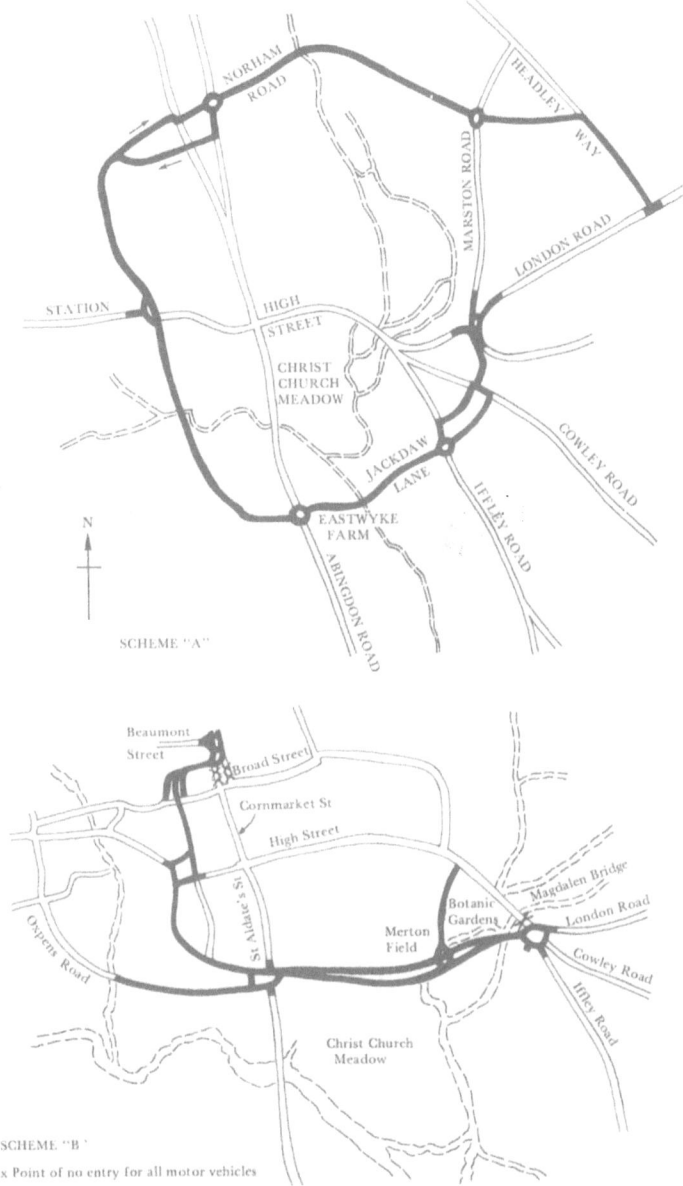

SOURCE   Oxford City Council.

MAP 5.7   *Council alternatives A and B*

180 *Planning, Production and Consumption in Oxford*

SCHEME "C"

Possible point of no entry for all motor vehicles, except certain bus routes.

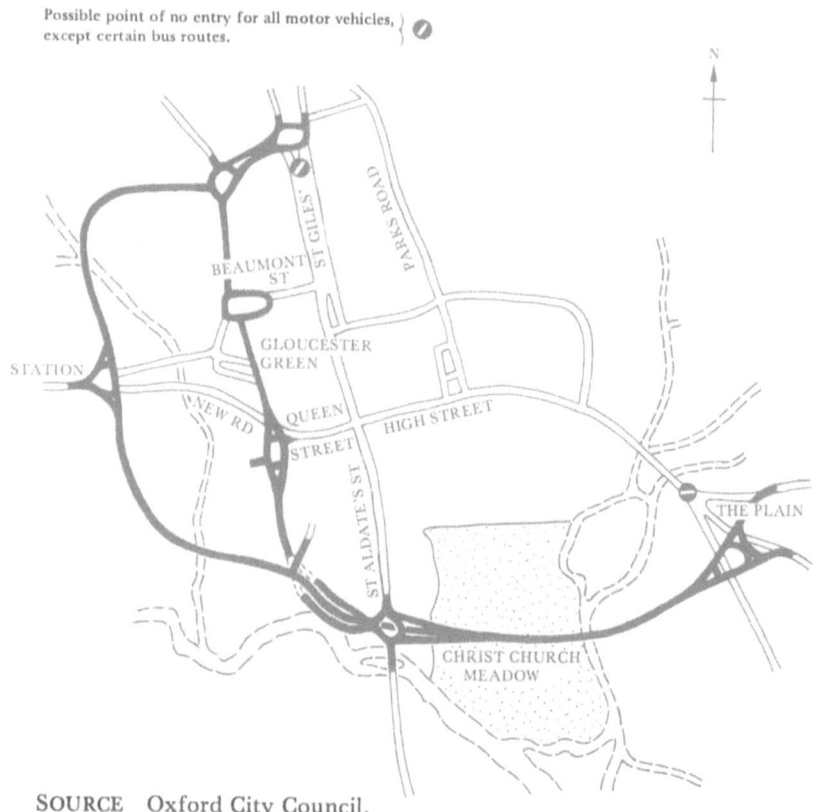

SOURCE   Oxford City Council.

MAP 5.8 *Council alternative eventually preferred in modified form*

which it suggested should be the subject of an inquiry at large. Sir Frederick Armer was appointed by the Minister to conduct the inquiry.

The three alternatives are shown in Maps 5.7 and 5.8. Essentially, they consisted of:

1. The Abercrombie intermediate road, circling central Oxford at a radius of about a mile from Carfax (scheme A).
2. The Duncan Sandys road across Christ Church Meadow, swinging west and north to the southern end of St Giles' (scheme B).

3. A modification of the Council's Meadow Road with the spur going to the Oxpens and the main road to MacFisheries' Corner, this to be extended along Bulwarks Lane to a roundabout at the western end of Beaumont Street, and then along a widened Walton Street to a roundabout at the northern end of St Giles' (scheme C).

In practice, they were not real alternatives as all accepted the basic assumptions concerning the central business district, the importance of radials and that more cars need more roads. All the proposals therefore represented variations on the same theme.

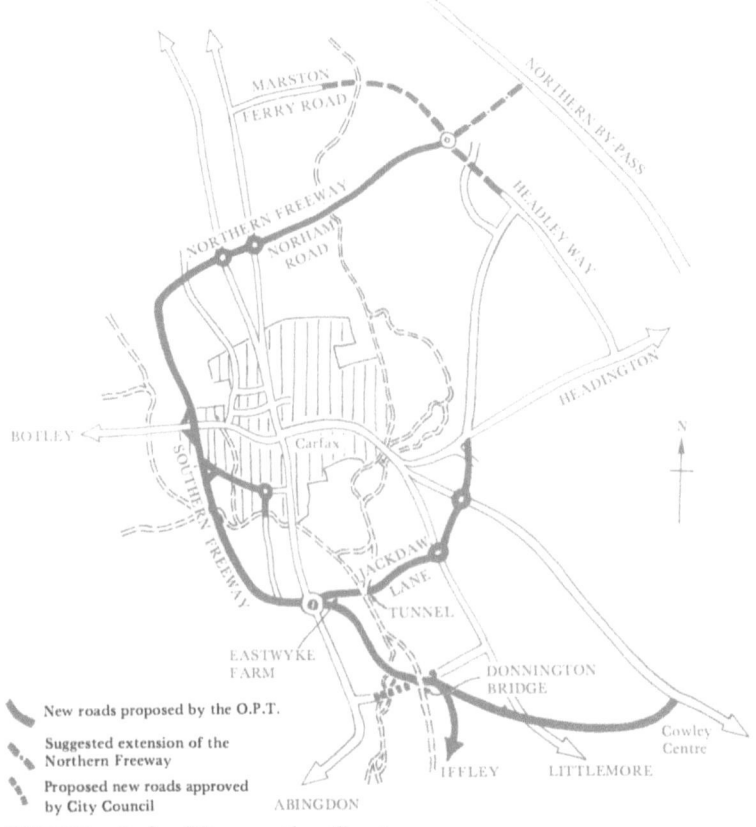

SOURCE   Oxford Preservation Trust.

MAP 5.9 *Preservation Trust scheme*

182 *Planning, Production and Consumption in Oxford*

SOURCE *Oxford Times* (23 March 1962).

MAP 5.10a *The routes of the relief roads favoured by the Minister of Housing and Local Government*

The inquiry was held in December 1960. By that time, even the Oxford Preservation Trust was against a Meadow Road. Instead, they advocated the Eastwyke Farm route south of the river, together with an extensive and costly collection of other roads shown in Map 5.9.

The University Congregation voted against the construction of inner relief roads before the effects of the completion of the outer bypasses, intermediate relief roads, decentralisation

History of Planning of Development and Production 183

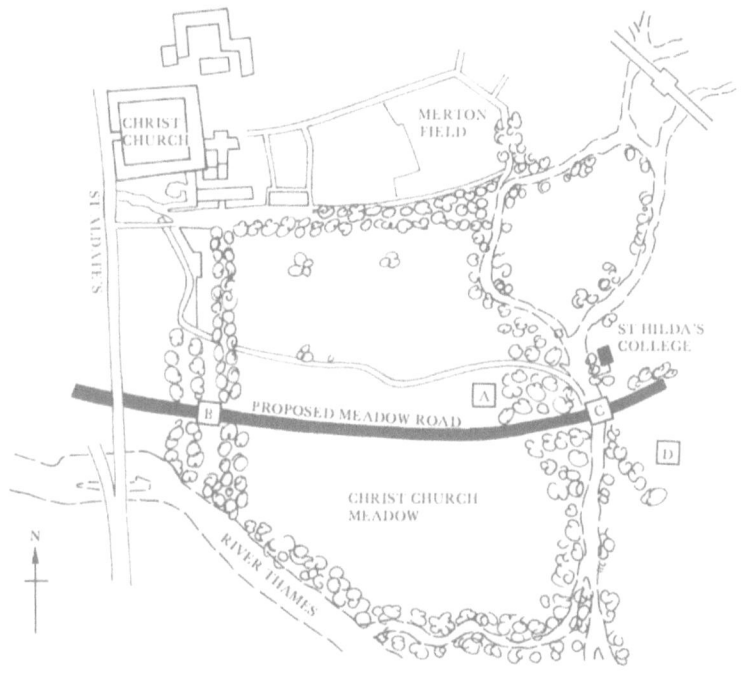

A	An artificial hill, planted with trees, to be created between the old Cherwell and the new.
B	Bridge taking the New Walk across the road.
C	Bridge taking the road across the Cherwell.
D	Christ Church cricket ground.

SOURCE *Oxford Times* (11 October 1963).

MAP 5.10b *The 'Jellicoe Plan' for a sunken Meadow Road*

to Cowley, and better parking facilities in the centre were known. Nevertheless, the Inspector recommended a slightly modified version of the city's proposals, scheme C, which included a road across Christ Church Meadow, shown in Map 5.10a.

This recommendation was followed by a storm of protest from the university and its representatives in the council.

Lord Lucas of Chilworth described the road as 'vandalism for the sake of vandalism' *(Oxford Times,* 23 March 1962, p. 16). Alderman Brown (University) said, 'The proposed roads are . . . fundamentally inconsistent with the City's policy of decentralisation and development of the Cowley Centre' *(Oxford Times,* 23 March 1962, p. 16). The warden of Merton College said, 'The decision is aesthetically barbarous and as a planning measure quite fatuous' *(Oxford Times,* 23 March 1962, p. 16).

The proposals were unanimously condemned in the House of Lords, especially by past and present university members sitting there. Despite this, Dr Charles Hill, who was by this time yet another Minister of Housing and Local Government, accepted the recommendations in 1962. This was by no means the end of the matter.

The Minister's acceptance of the council's proposals necessitated possibly two further public inquiries. One would be needed to hear objections to the incorporation of the roads into the Development Plan and, if that was successful, another inquiry would have been needed to hear objections to the necessary compulsory purchase orders. While the bulldozers were busy in St Ebbe's, a plan was drawn up to minimise the possible effects of a road in the Meadow.

In 1963, the plan for a sunken relief road across Christ Church Meadow was unveiled (Map 5.10b). The city had employed Jellicoe, a consultant landscape architect, to produce a plan which would make the road invisible from the Broad Walk. This he proposed to do by sinking the road into a cutting.

This cosmetic treatment did not placate opponents of the scheme. They were also encouraged by a report from Riddell, the City Engineer and Surveyor, which said that Oxford's central area traffic had increased by 2½ times less than the national average in the six years preceding 1964. Nevertheless, the proposals for an inner relief road running through Christ Church Meadow at St Ebbe's were included in the Development Plan Review published in 1964. The council voted 56-3 in favour of the modifications. Two university members and one Conservative voted against. Opposition outside the council was greater and began to focus on the necessary public inquiry.

The Dean of Oriel College called the colleges to battle when he said that 'The University and Colleges must spare no pains but fight, fight and fight again to prevent a road being built across Christ Church Meadow' *(Oxford Times,* 21 February 1964, p. 11). Their fight was spearheaded at the public inquiry in 1965 by Professor Buchanan, author of a seminal report on *Traffic in Towns* in 1963. He summarised the case against the Meadow Road as

> that the relief road scheme which the inspector recommended after the 1960 inquiry was seriously damaging to Christ Church Meadow, prejudicial to the effective redevelopment of St Clement's and St Ebbe's, ruinous for St Hilda's College and Magdalen College School, was conceived in isolation from the problems of the radial roads and was in any case an extremely doubtful proposition for its primary function of protecting the University area from excessive traffic. *(Oxford Times,* 22nd January 1965, p. 15)

Lewis Mumford was also induced to give written evidence against the road from the United States.

In 1967, Richard Crossman, now Minister of Housing and Local Government, approved the redevelopment of St Ebbe's and refused to allow the Meadow Road. Crossman, an Oxford man himself, suggested that the city appoint consultants to make a new examination of possible routes across the Meadow and further south *(Oxford Times,* 28 January 1966, p. 18).

Accordingly, Scott, Wilson, Kirkpatrick and Partners were appointed as consultants to the Development Plan Review. In 1968 they proposed a relief road south of the Meadow, the closure to traffic or restriction of many streets in the central area, a new attitude towards parking, and a new north-south urban motorway alongside the railway line. This motorway could be extended to the bypasses, as shown in Map 5.11. The scheme was adopted by the council in 1969, not without opposition both inside the chamber and out. East Oxford residents, for example, started a 'stop the Eastwyke Farm Road' campaign. Two women walked from Oxford to Downing Street to ask the Prime Minister to hold an inquiry into the

186 *Planning, Production and Consumption in Oxford*

SOURCE   Oxford City Council.

MAP 5.11   *Oxford roads: showing proposed modifications to town map amendment No. 2*

road scheme. Residents were advised not to co-operate with the council in completing the paperwork involved in determining who would be affected by the road. A new note of passive resistance had emerged.

Yet another inquiry was held in 1970. The following year, 1971, the Secretary of State for the Environment, Peter Walker, approved the council's road plans with the exception of the extensions to the bypasses. These proposals were duly incorporated in the Second Amendment to the Development Plan in 1971, shown in Appendix 3. In 1972, a mass campaign was organised against the decision to insist that the Eastwyke Farm Road remain on the Development Plan. Such action arose from the lessons learned over the previous two decades.

Throughout this period, local working-class residents complained that they were not being consulted on the future planned for their areas. They were also against the fact that many important decisions were not even taken in the open. Many covert bargains were struck behind closed doors. Jenner, Secretary of the Trades Council, told one of its meetings that, 'from my own experience . . . things are shaped in this city over the phone without going to the Council at all' *(Oxford Times,* 26 April 1968, p. 18).

In 1973 the Labour-controlled council voted not to implement the road proposals contained in the Second Amendment. Instead they proposed a 'Balanced Transport Policy'.

> Two important parts of [this] approach are firstly traffic management measures to give public transport priority over private cars on the existing radials and in the City Centre . . . and secondly alterations in the amount, location and cost of public parking space in the central area to make the use of the private car for access less attractive. (Oxford City, 1973c, p. 4)

In this way the council moved to a different set of positive planning objectives as far as inner city transport was concerned.

The following year brought local government reorganisation. This placed responsibility for strategic planning and main roads into the hands of the County Council. Commuters living in the county like to be able to drive to work in the central business district. The planning authorities, as they now are, have reduced parking charges there, called into question the balanced transport policy, and proposed to implement the Second Amendment road plans.

The inner relief road issue in Oxford thus illustrates visibly all the political forces that may be brought into play over local planning issues. The different fates of Christ Church Meadow and St Ebbe's, which will be discussed next, also illustrate the variations in power between an international university and local, working-class residents.

The continued and currently unthreatened existence of Christ Church Meadow shows how powerful organisations may mobilise critical support at different political levels, such as the central government and international support, to achieve their ends. The organisations concerned mobilised their existing power, resources and connections to ensure that no relief roads were built through their property. In analysing this outcome it is difficult to disentangle the 'real' merits of their case from the sheer use of power to achieve their ends irrespective of the 'technical' validity of their arguments. On the whole, it seems fair to say that the various merits and demerits of the case for a road through the Meadow were fully aired and were reasonably balanced; what finally tipped the balance against the road was the power of the organisations who were opposed to it. This outcome should be directly compared with that for St Ebbe's, which is both adjacent to the Meadow and a possible route for relief roads.

St Ebbe's

Sharp had described St Ebbe's as part of the ignoble nine-tenths of Oxford. He looked upon it as an area to be tidied up by replacing workingmen's houses with relief roads, public and commercial buildings. This view was echoed in the Development Plan which described the area as 'an integral part of the central area of Oxford and the only natural line of expansion left to the central business area' (Oxford City, 1953, p. 13). In the same written analysis, accompanying the Plan, it was also argued 'that the only way of achieving a proper plan for St Ebbe's is to deal with it as an area of comprehensive redevelopment and . . . [the local authority] will seek . . . to designate the whole, or at least major parts, of the area, for compulsory purchase' (Oxford City, 1953, p. 13).

The Chamber of Trade was in favour of these proposals. Minns (Conservative), who was also a member of the Chamber, Lord Nuffield's nephew, a local builder and, at various times, a member of the planning and housing committees, argued that, 'The redevelopment of St Ebbe's was perhaps the only chance of expanding the commercial centre of Oxford for the next 500 years' *(Oxford Times,* 7 January 1955, p. 16). It was this alone, in his opinion, which prevented the proposals contained in the Development Plan from 'being an almost complete fiasco' *(Oxford Times,* 15 May 1953, p. 9).

Detailed plans for the redevelopment of St Ebbe's were not revealed until 1954. In the Council Chamber, Alderman Gill (University) objected to the rehousing of 2000 people from the area. He said, 'I believe a town is a place where people should live, and not a place where planning people build grand boulevards' *(Oxford Times,* 5 November 1954, p. 9). During the same debate, Councillor Spokes (Conservative) said that a survey had revealed that two-thirds of the population wanted to stay in St Ebbe's.

The physical, aesthetic, transport and commercial objectives of the plan did not provide for this. The stated objectives were:

1. Redevelopment to be of a high visual standard and a credit to the old City.
2. The river frontage to be opened up and improved.
3. The main communications to be improved so as to ease traffic conditions in the central area.
4. Living conditions to be brought up to modern standards while retaining the community spirit.
5. Views of prominent features of the old City to be opened up and street scenes up to the standard of the old City, though not necessarily in the same style, to be provided.
6. Buildings of historic and architectural interest to be retained.

7. Provision of space for car parking, offices, public and semi-public buildings to be provided. *(Oxford Times,* 5 November 1954, p. 9)

Local residents were not satisfied.

Details of rehousing were still vague in 1955. Councillor Foot (Labour) argued that it was widely agreed, especially among the Labour group on the council, that it would be wicked 'to clear away the very long established community that lived in St Ebbe's *(Oxford Times,* 28 January 1955, p. 12). A large public meeting was held in July which endorsed this view. When asked for a show of hands, only six people at the meeting voted for leaving St Ebbe's.

Unfortunately the people of St Ebbe's did not form a residents' association until after the Development Plan became a statutory document. The chairman, Higgins, said that one of the most immediate problems confronting the Association was shortage of funds. He proposed that the subscription should be one shilling per family per month in order to fight the combined might of the city's commercial and governmental interests. Perceptively enough, he said that the battle might be a long and expensive one.

Having formed an association, the residents asked if a number of city and university officials might come and discuss with them their planning proposals for St Ebbe's. The mayor said that he hoped the proposed meeting would be carried out in a spirit of goodwill so that the future of St Ebbe's might be discussed to the benefit of all concerned. What happened tomorrow, he explained, was problematical and, after a public inquiry, still subject to a ministerial decision, but the City Council would take care of their interests *(Oxford Times,* 16 September 1955, p. 11).

Eventually, in 1958, Chandler spelt out what was to be substituted for the close-knit community of mixed working-class housing, industry and services that was St Ebbe's. It was to be used for

> the improvement of principal communications to ease traffic conditions in the central area, the retention, where possible, of buildings of architectural and historic interest,

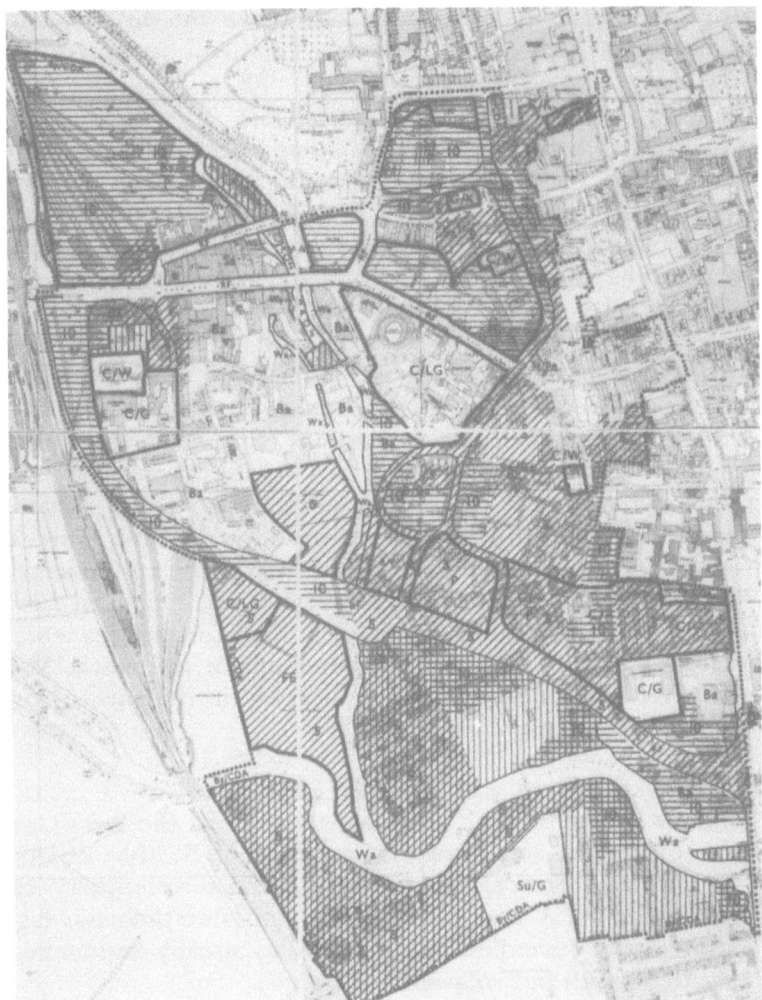

MAP 5.12 *Oxford City central area comprehensive development area: programme map submitted 1964, approved 1967*

after the completion of the programme. Generally, those areas to the north of the new road line sweeping from the northwest to the south-east of the area were designated for commercial, car parking or public building uses. Most of the area to the south was zoned for accommodation. It followed from the opening-up of prominent features of the old city and achieving a high visual standard which will be a credit to the City. *(Oxford Times,* 8 August 1958, p. 11)

This provides a good example of some of the implications of the adoption of architectural values as a basic logic for development planning.

Councillor Ingram (Labour and later Conservative) assured residents that redevelopment would begin the following year. Chandler, City Architect and Planning Officer, assured the same local meeting that there would be no need 'for anyone who is living in St Ebbe's at the moment to move elsewhere if he wants to stop' *(Oxford Times,* 19 September 1958, p. 15). Concern was voiced, however, that apart from planning blight gripping the area, rent levels proposed by the council would make St Ebbe's unattractive to its existing residents. In the end, these two insidious features were as effective in forcing people out of the area as the bulldozers.

Despite assurances to the contrary, it was not until 1966 that the planning authority unveiled plans for the area which were incorporated in the First Amendment, shown in Map 5.12. Five main proposals were included in the then £5.5m scheme. They were:

A new shopping and commercial centre with a central library would be built in what is known as the West Gate complex – the area between Castle Street, St Ebbe's Street and Charles Street. There would be new temporary car parks nearby. A new office block alongside the new Magistrates' and Juvenile Courts which, as already announced, are to be built in Bridewell Square.
The new College of Further Education in Oxpens.
A new central fire station and a three storey demountable car park for 450 cars on the Rewley Abbey site . . .
A new road system in St Ebbe's, which will ultimately form part of the road pattern for central Oxford. *(Oxford Times,* 2 December 1966, p. 15)

Map 5.12 also shows the programme for this redevelopment. Only those areas not shaded were planned to be left intact this decline in the total area available for residential purposes that housing densities would have to be increased by the construction of flats and maisonettes rather than houses. Subsequent policies have taken a different view of the value of the type of housing once found in St Ebbe's.

Working-class residents of areas like St Ebbe's, Jericho, St Clement's, East Oxford and Cowley started forming local associations to protect themselves against redevelopment. The late 1950s and early 1960s saw residents' associations formed in all these areas. One of the main stimuli to their formation was the perceived lack of consultation by the local planning authority before proposals for redevelopment and compulsory purchase orders were drawn up. Talking about the Cowley Centre development, for example, Morris, chairman of the Cowley Community Association, said that the people of Cowley had never been consulted whether they wanted it. Mitchell, the treasurer of the association, went further and said that perhaps the time had come for the people of industrial Oxford to govern their own affairs *(Oxford Times,* 28 June 1957, p. 11). Eventually, in 1972, the East Oxford Association put forward its own positive policy document. This was the first such document put forward by a substantially working-class area in Oxford.

Feelings of lack of consultation in such matters as proposals for redevelopment were common in other parts of Britain. The Skeffington Report (Ministry of Housing and Local Government, 1969) was tantamount to an official recognition that some of these interests had not had much of a hearing, let alone action, in the past. A right to participate was enshrined in the 1968 Town and Country Planning Act. By the time this right was extended to St Ebbe's there were few residents left to participate. The list of levels of participation contained in a document for discussion is revealing as it puts into perspective not only the likely weighting of local residents' views, but also the interests that had always participated, Skeffington or no. The paper said that,

Participation in the Central Area Local Plan is . . . a complex matter which needs to be approached at several different levels:

194 *Planning, Production and Consumption in Oxford*

(a) overall strategic participation with the public at large
(b) overall strategic participation with interest groups
(c) strategic participation with local groups
(d) local participation with local central area groups
(e) local participation with international, national, regional, University Collegiate and other groups, and with land and property owners. (Oxford City, 1974a, p. 26)

In St Ebbe's, category (d) was continually outweighed by category (e).

Practically the only parts of St Ebbe's to be left were those owned by category (e) groups such as public houses or those where category (e) groups eventually championed their retention. One such group was the Oxford Preservation Trust.

Its attitude to St Ebbe's changed over the period. In 1955 it said that there was an 'urgent need for proceeding with the redevelopment of St Ebbe's without delay' *(Oxford Times,*

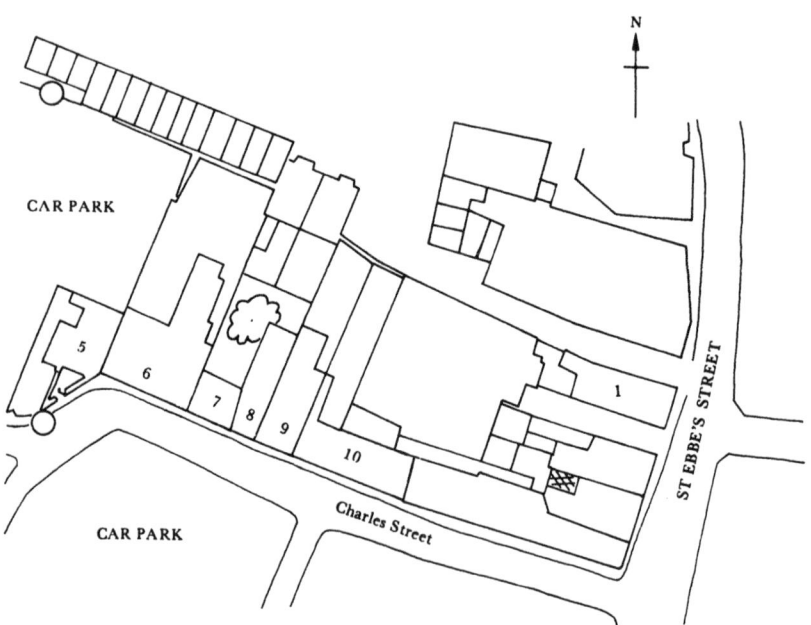

MAP 5.13 *Charles Street*

14 October 1955, p. 8). In 1959 it appointed Holford as its adviser on the redevelopment of the area. By 1970, however, it had come to the conclusion that some parts of St Ebbe's were worth preserving. Specifically, it objected to a proposal by the council to demolish numbers 8, 9 and 10 Charles Street, which were all that remained of a listed terrace of seventeenth-century cottages, shown in Map 5.13 and Figure 5.5.

An inquiry was held in 1970. The *Oxford Mail* (18 September 1970) summed the situation up as one where local and national amenity groups wanted to preserve the three buildings and were fighting a property company (Hume Holdings Ltd or one of its subsidiaries) which wanted to use the site for offices and shops. The council would seem to have taken the side of the property company by virtue of its having applied for listed building consent to demolish.

At the inquiry, the Oxford Preservation Trust made an offer to buy the dwellings for £8500 and then restore them. This offer to purchase came as a surprise to the council, but was based on reports prepared for the Preservation Trust by Messrs Buckell and Ballard and Swan, King and Partners, both of which estimated that restoration of the properties would cost between £9000 and £10,000, rather than the £15-£20,000 estimated by the City Estates Surveyor. The result of the offer made at the inquiry was that the latter was adjourned (and later dismissed) so that the council could assess the situation.

The Preservation Trust subsequently purchased and restored the properties. It now uses one of them as its Oxford headquarters.

Despite this small victory, by 1974, when a further discussion document was produced concerning the future of St Ebbe's, much of the redevelopment had been completed in the northern part of the area, and some maisonettes had also been built near the river. Nevertheless, as the document pointed out, 'it is over ten years since the greater part of the houses in the area were demolished for redevelopment and the land has lain unused or used for car parking for that time' (Oxford City, 1974a, p. 25). Even after the passing of this length of time, the local authority was still undecided what its positive objectives were for the area.

196 *Planning, Production and Consumption in Oxford*

1962

SOURCE   Spokes.

1977

SOURCE   Spokes.

FIGURE 5.5   *Charles Street, 1962 and 1977*

The planners said at this time that,

> three major directions of development seem to be most sought after and most acceptable within the agreed constraints. These have as the dominant use for the area:
>
> (1) dwellings
> (2) recreation
> (3) open space activities (Oxford City, 1974a, p. 21)

Despite this, the same document argued contradictorily 'that the southern end of St Ebbe's probably provides the last opportunity for a long time to construct or preserve land for the construction of any large scale Council sponsored project' (Oxford City, 1974a, p. 18). So having become a, if not the, major landowner in the city centre, the council turned its attention to such possibilities as 'commercial or large scale community needs . . . churches, clubs, University teaching and government offices' (Oxford City, 1974a, p. 16). Of dwellings there was little further mention. In this way the council sought to satisfy the interests of the major power groups in the city centre. The university, commerce and the state itself were provided with actual or possible developments there. For the original residents, the plan remained silent.

At the time of writing, 1979, plans have been made, and some contracts signed, to build houses in the southern part of the area. Half of these houses will be relatively expensive and privately owned. The other half will be publicly owned, but far too late for the original residents of St Ebbe's who wished to remain there (see Appendix 4 for these plans).

Housing

Sharp devoted rather less attention to housing than he did to civic design. He did recognise, however, that

> more than eight thousand new dwellings are required to make this city of 100,000 inhabitants a reasonably satisfactory living place. At least half of these dwellings are of a kind which it is unlikely that the private builder will ever consider making an effort to supply' (Sharp, 1948, p. 55).

Despite the recognition that the market does not produce cheap working-class housing, he was happy to see much of what existed demolished, and made few suggestions for the provision of the 4000 houses which he himself had identified as being the likely market shortfall.

Chandler made similar remarks in the written analysis which accompanied the Development Plan. There he said that 'about 9000 or just over a third of the residential properties in the City were constructed before 1900 and very nearly half of them are outmoded and inconvenient or insanitary by modern standards' (Oxford City, 1953, p. 12). The worst of them, he said, were to be found in St Ebbe's, St Thomas' and St Barnabas'.

At the time of the production of the Development Plan, the 'correct technical solution' to the problems of old housing areas was redevelopment. This was considered by the local architect-planners to be the best way to deal with most of the areas of Victorian working-class housing in the city. In the central area this view accorded well with the local commercial interests in expanding the central business district and the local authority's interest in maximising its rate revenue by substituting commercial for housing values.

As early as 1948, however, some doubts were voiced about this view and treatment of a Victorian working-class housing area. John Betjeman, a local resident and then secretary of the Preservation Trust, said that there were 'many buildings in the St Clement's area which were well worth preserving' *(Oxford Times,* 16 April 1948, p. 8). Nevertheless, the planning authority insisted on zoning parts of the area for redevelopment by the university. Working-class housing was once again to be replaced, this time by university buildings.

Eventually, council objectives with respect to Victorian working-class housing other than St Ebbe's did change. Some of the change can be attributed to pressure from local residents, particularly with the example of St Ebbe's before them, and also as a result of the machinery and levels of compensation for compulsory purchase. The council's first setback came when the Minister refused to designate St Thomas' and St Clement's for compulsory redevelopment in the First Amendment to the Development Plan. At the same time, the same policy was reversed in Jericho. Instead of redevelopment, the Planning Committee recommended a policy of restoration. The aim was

> to urge householders and landlords to improve all the houses that are worth keeping with the aid of Council grants and loans; to demolish only the houses that are unfit; to rebuild where necessary, with small blocks of flats and houses, garages, and play spaces for children; and to devise a new road system which would turn many of the streets into quiet cul-de-sacs. *(Oxford Times,* 4 November 1966, p. 15)

Even so, uncertainty lingered in Jericho as late as 1968. The newly formed residents' association demanded a meeting with the Housing Committee. They complained that the council had said that the houses were going to be renovated but that so far only two had been completed and no one was living in them. They said that, 'If it goes on like this soon there won't be any Jericho people left to go into the new flats and houses' *(Oxford Times,* 2 June 1968, p. 17).

When the threat of redevelopment was lifted from Jericho, competition developed for the type of housing there. Not only had the numbers of this form of housing been reduced by demolition there and in St Ebbe's and St Clement's, but now middle-class groups started to compete for it. The process of gentrification began. The residents' asociation complained that 'Rents of private houses in Jericho are going up so fast that the whole area is in danger of becoming a rich man's paradise' *(Oxford Times,* 18 June 1971, p. 9). Sir Michael Rowe, President of the Land Tribunal, said that, 'Parts of the Jericho area of Oxford, earmarked for clearance, had been turned now into a miniature Chelsea and terraced houses were much in demand as small town- or mews-type homes' *(Oxford Times,* 14 April 1972, p. 2). So, even when working-class residents of some areas successfully resisted the complete demolition of their housing, this did not necessarily save it for their own future use.

By 1973 the same planning objectives that had been instituted in Jericho were proposed in East Oxford. The preliminary local plan advocated,

To cope with pressing problems of overcrowded houses without basic facilities like a fixed bath, a programme of general improvement of houses is suggested, starting in St Clement's, moving on to the Rectory Road area, then Leopold Street/Randolph Street, and the area round Charles Street. (Oxford City, 1973m, p. 1)

The discussions centred on St Thomas' were even more revealing.

St Thomas' is an area adjacent and similar to St Ebbe's. In the 1940s it was considered to be in a similar condition to St Ebbe's and therefore 'ripe' for the same treatment meted out to its neighbour. The local authority's 1975 description of St Thomas' could equally have applied to St Ebbe's before the area was razed. As the planners said,

> Although in places St Thomas' is run down in appearance, it has many interesting features, the loss or deterioration of which should be avoided. These features include: interesting historic streets, their corners and curves, old walls and building lines - in particular St Thomas' and Paradise Streets; - the many old buildings, from the obvious ones of historic and architectural interest such as the Castle, St Thomas' Church and some older domestic buildings, to buildings that give the area 'character' such as St Thomas' old school and Christchurch Old Buildings; - the waterways - the Castle Mill Stream, its backstream and the canal and the relationship of these to their surroundings. There is much scope for improving these features of St Thomas'. (Oxford City, 1975, p. 2)

The positive objectives derived by the council from this analysis were:

(1) the need to avoid as far as possible disturbing local residents
(2) the need to safeguard cheaper housing for rent, and
(3) the need to hold down the growth of jobs and traffic in the city centre by encouraging housing rather than business development. (Oxford City, 1975, p. 3)

These objectives represent almost the exact reverse of what had been done in neighbouring St Ebbe's.

Again this shows a change of local development plan objectives over the period under study. This time the change was partially the result of growing organisation and power of local residents inspired as a reaction against state activity in their own and other areas. It also illustrates once more the role of the local state as a focus of political activity with its objectives set or altered according to the balance of power between contending interest groups.

A further contradictory and changing aspect of the proposals concerning housing contained in the Development Plan was the objective of restricting population growth in the city. On the one hand, the plan said that the total number of dwellings within the city boundaries should be restricted to 27,765 in order to contain the growth of population. In the same document, however, Chandler said that

> after having regard to all the other uses to which land must be put with full facilities for schools, allotments, open space, commerce and industry, and without destroying the existing open character of the city or losing the existing green links between its various developed parts, every suitable piece of land available for housing development should be put to that use. (Oxford City, 1953, p. 9)

This latter proposition accorded much more with an earlier demand from Sir Miles Thomas, of the Morris Motors Company, that the council should build houses for the Nuffield workers because the availability of labour was conditioned by the availability of houses for workers to live in.

In order to restrict the growth of Oxford's population and remove the type of housing found in St Ebbe's, the shortfall, especially of working-class housing, was exacerbated. The solutions proposed were to concentrate new public authority housing in Cowley, Iffley and Littlemore, to plan for increased densities in St Ebbe's, and to house the resulting 16,000 overspill on an old sewage farm site owned by the city but outside its 1953 boundaries. This site was eventually incorporated within the city's jurisdiction in 1957. The tendency has been, therefore, to alter the location of working-class housing by demolishing some of it in the centre and building public authority estates on the periphery of the city near the Cowley industrial complex.

The number of accommodation units owned by the council rose by 4068 from 4996 in 1952/3 to 9064 in 1972/3. In addition, it sold off or demolished a further 2049 units in the same period. Although this shows a consistent increase over the period, it masks power struggles over the objectives concerning council housing.

The main debates focused on council housing were about where it should be located, how much of it should be built and how it should be paid for. The adjoining authority, Oxfordshire, for example, did not want the housing to be located at Blackbird Leys. The Conservative-dominated council was not wholly enthusiastic about building public housing and also favoured selling what existed to minimise the short-term costs to the authority. The numbers of houses actually built or sold therefore tended to fluctuate over the period according to various factors like the rise and fall of different power groups inside the Council Chamber, and the vagaries of the economic climate and central government policies outside.

The net result of these struggles was that those with money and the inclination increasingly had to purchase accommodation outside the city. For those without sufficient economic power and unable to acquire a restricted supply of council housing, overcrowding increased. By 1973 this was a sufficiently large issue for the council to seek to prevent it by requiring houses in multiple occupation to be registered. This placed the council in the position of being against both the growth of accommodation within the city and the overcrowding which inevitably resulted from such a policy.

Collective facilities

A further middle-level reason underlying the justifications made by the state for development planning was that people should be encouraged to engage in healthful behaviour. For Sharp, this meant social health and, for the city, parks and allotments.

Sharp argued that the social health of the city would be improved by the provision of new libraries, art galleries, museums, health and social welfare centres, educational establishments and so on. He also advocated neighbourhood planning to promote the social health of the city. In this he reflected the conventional wisdom among architect-planners of the time. He said that the purpose of neighbourhood units

> is to overcome the social difficulties and dangers which almost inevitably occur when a town grows big. The unorganised great cities of today are far too big to be apprehended as a whole; personal contacts and group contacts are made difficult; interest in the city and in civic affairs and their management is lost; people tend to get segregated into large single class quarters. (Sharp, 1948, p. 158)

He advocated the creation of fourteen neighbourhood units of about 10,000 population each to overcome these difficulties. The bulk of these proposals have not been adopted.

Instead, the city's Development Plan concentrated on the provision of parks and allotments. In preparing the plan, the council

> had in mind three principal objectives: first to secure whereever possible a sufficient number of playing fields and recreation grounds for every neighbourhood at a rate of four acres per thousand inhabitants; secondly, to preserve . . . open character and maintain the green divisions . . . thirdly, to encourage owners of land, who have in the past generously permitted the public free access over their land . . . to continue to do so. (Oxford City, 1953, p. 18)

Taken together, these measures provided for the retention as public open space of one sort or another of 1827 acres either within or adjacent to the city boundary.

This policy was continued in the first amendment. At this time,

> The Town Map [showed] two kinds of open space-private open space and other open space - whether in municipal

or private ownership, to which the public has access or it is considered should be available to the public. The total area of public open space is 1227 acres. (Oxford City, 1967a, p. 6)

Despite a continuing official commitment to public open space, these figures show a reduction of 600 acres from their 1953 equivalent.

The other main planning issue concerned with healthful behaviour was allotments. Sharp (1948) had suggested using some allotment land for housing. This was partly a corollary of suggesting the demolition of central area working-class housing and its replacement with commerce and public buildings. The Oxford and District Federation of Allotment Associations, representing 5000 members, urged the council not to adopt the Sharp Report in this respect. They were supported by Councillor Meadows, chairman of the Allotment Committee, who said that the land of the East ward and Donnington allotments should not be used for building (*Oxford Times,* 20 March 1953, p. 7).

The plan provided for '554 acres of which 375 acres [were] within the City and the remaining 179 acres just beyond the boundary' (Oxford City, 1953, p. 25). Even so, much heat was generated by the proposal to use some allotment land for housing.

This was reflected at the inquiry into the Development Plan where considerable time was devoted to arguments about the allotments. In reply, Chandler said that allotment sites could be easily and economically developed for housing purposes, and the 4000 people on the housing waiting list were suffering much greater hardship than were the allotment holders (*Oxford Times,* 4 December 1953, p. 5). He neglected to mention that council policies for redevelopment and restriction of the city were contributing to the length of the waiting list.

Over the next decade, however, the demand for allotments seemed to slacken so that Murray argued in the Review of the Development Plan that 'This is a declining demand and there is no indication that this trend is likely to be reversed' (Oxford City, 1964a, p. 93). Consequently, the first amendment

History of Planning of Development and Production 205

showed 'an area of 205 acres within the City and, with the concurrence of the adjoining planning authorities, other allotments are provided beyond the present boundaries of the City, making a total of 342 acres' (Oxford City, 1967a, p. 5).

The arguments rumbled on as, bit by bit, allotments were taken for building purposes. In 1969, for example, Murray faced a stormy public meeting to tell residents of east and

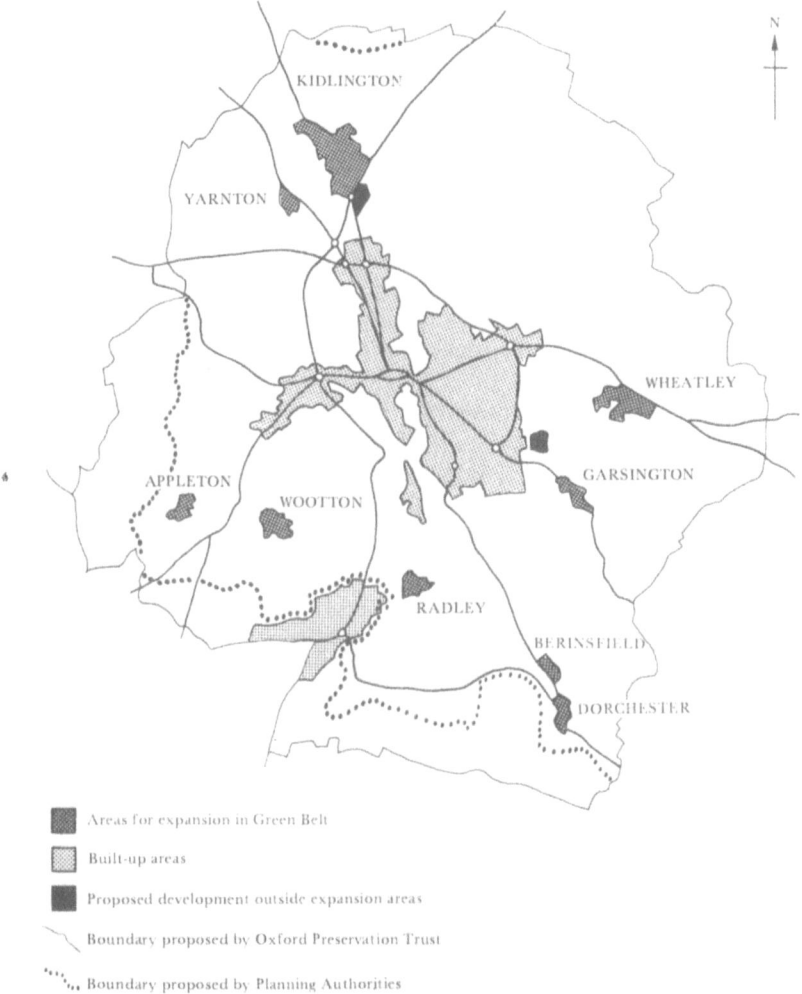

MAP 5.14   *Oxford City green belt: submitted 1958, approved 1975*

south Oxford affected by the current road schemes that they could all be rehoused on the Donnington allotments and the old gasworks site. In the event, despite a renewed interest in allotments as the price of food soared in the 1970s, allotments little by little came to be used for housing and other building purposes. So that by 1970 the second amendment showed a total of 327 acres of allotments and 1205 acres of public open space (Oxford City, 1970a, p. 4).

It can be seen, therefore, that in terms of acres designated in the Development Plan, the local authority had a declining commitment to healthful behaviour as pursued in parks and allotments. The results can be seen in such features as the growing queues for football pitches and allotments.

Conversely, considerable attention has been devoted to the regulation of individual rights in order to minimise their undesirable effects on the existing community, particularly the university community found in central Oxford. Containment, consolidation and decentralisation have all been aimed at preserving a compact university town and minimising congestion in its centre.

Containment was achieved by the long process of establishing a green belt around the city. Part of the problem associated with doing this was that most of the land forming such a belt fell under the jurisdiction of either Oxfordshire or Berkshire and not the city. Eventually some agreement was reached, and a sketch plan of a green belt for the city was submitted to the Minister of Housing and Local Government for his approval in 1958. A public inquiry into the proposal was held in 1961. The chief objections came from Kidlington and Garsington, who wanted less restrictions, and the Oxford Preservation Trust, who wanted more. Their respective proposals can be seen in Map 5.14.

Delay followed the inquiry. Three years later, the *Oxford Times* complained that 'there is still no prospect of a decision on it by the Minister' *(Oxford Times,* 30 October 1964, p. 27). Seven years later, the same complaint was still being made, and it was remarked that 'green belt land in Oxfordshire . . . has only been proposed and never formally ratified' *(Oxford Times,* 21 May 1971, p. 9). Confirmation eventually arrived in 1975. This delay did not prevent its operation and consequent containment of development in and around the city during the post-war period.

Within the contained city, relief from congestion at the centre was planned to be given by decentralisation to Cowley. The Development Plan proposed not only to concentrate public authority housing in or near that area but also to provide a district shopping centre there so as to dissuade some shoppers from crossing Magdalen Bridge for their daily requirements. This, it was hoped, would reduce traffic flow in the central area. Accordingly, some 23 acres of land in Cowley were designated for compulsory purchase in the Development Plan in order to provide this district centre.

Again in a contradictory fashion, the Development Plan objectives of the local state were positively in favour of commercial growth at the centre and decentralisation to Cowley. Consequently, the other main commercial development favoured by the local authority was established to siphon off some of the potential growth of and travel to the centre. Like the central area, commercial developments predominated. Some residential accommodation was included in the Cowley Centre plans, but proved to be unsuitable for families on the housing waiting list and was let at market rents. Taken together, however, the central area and Cowley Centre developments meant that under pressure from conflicting interest groups the local state came to be positively in favour of both centralisation and decentralisation.

One other example of the local state seeking to curb individual rights in the name of the community is that of the Cutteslowe Walls (see Figure 5.6). This saga is well documented by Collison (1963). Briefly, as Chandler pointed out in the written analysis accompanying the Development Plan,

> before the war, the Urban Housing Estate . . . was developed on the east side of the Banbury Road near its junction with the Northern Bypass, two walls were erected, one across the carriageway of Carlton Road and one across the carriageway of Wentworth Road . . . to prevent any connection through this estate between the Council's Cutteslowe housing estate and the Banbury Road. (Oxford City, 1953, p. 28)

208 *Planning, Production and Consumption in Oxford*

The wall in Carlton Road seen from the urban housing estate

City councillors watch the final demolition, March 1959

SOURCE P. Collison, *The Cutteslowe Walls* (London: Faber) pp. 62 and 99.

FIGURE 5.6 *The Cutteslowe Walls*

The council, however, did not couch its opposition in terms of social class, but of administrative convenience. At the inquiry into the Development Plan, the authorities argued that the Walls were, from the point of view of local security, a nuisance to the police. They were also said to cause additional costs in the collection of house refuse and street-cleaning services. Special arrangements had to be made to provide residents of the council estate with a bus service. The Walls were also undesirable from the point of view of the ambulance and fire services.

In order to remove the Walls, the council had to purchase compulsorily the land on which they stood. In doing so they clashed with middle-class residents. The two things this social class was against were the removal of the Cutteslowe Walls and the parts of road networks which affected them in one way or another.

Out of 281 objections to the original Development Plan, 165 came from middle-class groups protesting at the removal of the Walls. Petitions were handed to the Inspector. Representatives argued that property values on the private estate would fall if the Walls were removed. The council was said to be showing partiality in favour of its own tenants. Despite this opposition, the Walls eventually came down.

To summarise this middle level of local state logic and consequent planning objections, the Development Plan has had some success in providing land for developments which the market would not have produced, such as working-class housing. Its efforts to provide amenities like parks and allotments have been generally accepted, although the provision of these amenities within the city has actually declined. It has also established a legitimate though controversial concern with the provision of transport facilities and the containment or urban sprawl and congestion. In terms of really significant output effects, this middle range of logic and activity may be considered to have had the most important results of post-war development planning in Oxford.

Profitability, externalities and public health

The final level of reasons underlying the Development Plan

does not feature strongly in its logic either because the Planning Department was only concerned with designating land for services which other departments provided or because it had the power to alter public but not private short-run profitability criteria. The provision of water and sewage services, for example, required land to be designated in the Development Plan, but execution was effected by other departments of the local authority. The prevention of self-harming actions like road accidents was very much the preserve of the City Engineer.

Private and public profitability

Development planning in Oxford was indirectly and directly concerned with the short-run profitability of private entrepreneurs and local authority commercial ventures. This was expressed in concern over the city's dependence on the vehicle manufacturing industries at Cowley and with shopping facilities.

Sharp focused attention on the city's dependence on the Nuffield Organisation and the Pressed Steel Company which, in 1939,

> represented 30 per cent of the total insured workers in the City, 66.5 per cent of all those employed in the manufacturing industries, and 97.8 per cent of those engaged in the production of motor vehicles and aircraft. These figures are not merely illuminating: they are alarming. (Sharp, 1948, p. 57)

The university authorities were also against further industrial expansion at Cowley. They welcomed the parts of the Sharp Report which suggested removing or precluding the further development of industry at Cowley. Sir Richard Livingstone, Principal of Corpus Christi College, 'regretted that industry ever came [to Oxford] and thought the City Council was right in its attempt to keep the population down, for if it made mistakes in planning it could never get rid of them' *(Oxford Times,* 4 February 1949, p. 5).

Faced with this combined threat, the Pressed Steel Company offered the university £10,000 per year for seven years to encourage research in the physical sciences. In accepting the gift, Professor Plaskett said, 'The company has taken a selfless and enlightened course in attempting to build, not for themselves but for the country as a whole, a sound foundation of academic research' *(Oxford Times,* 4 March 1949, p. 5). Lord Nuffield, founder of the Morris Motors Company, went further and gave a site and £900,000 for the financing of a new college named after himself. The foundation stone for this was laid in 1949. After these gifts, little more was heard in public of university opposition to the Cowley industries.

The Chamber of Trade was worried that removal of the car works would damage spending power in the city *(Oxford Times,* 26 March 1948, p. 4). The industrialists negotiated quietly behind the scenes. Their negotiations bore fruits when, after a public relations visit to the works, Councillor Grant (Conservative) said that, 'so far as he could find out there was no organised body of opinion in the City Council which supported the recommendations of the Sharp Plan, so far as the removal of the works at Cowley was concerned' *(Oxford Times,* 1 April 1949, p. 8). After that the Cowley firms went quietly on their way as far as town planning was concerned.

Despite these negotiations, which precluded serious attempts to remove the Cowley works and excluded such proposals from the Development Plan, the local planning authority continued its concern with restricting the size of Oxford's population. Thus, according to the Development Plan,

> It is the Council's policy to make every endeavour to prevent the City's population from increasing, and it is estimated that by 1973 – the end of the 20 year period of the plan – the population within the present City boundaries will, by means of redevelopment and abatement of overcrowding have been reduced to 102,500. *(Oxford Times,* 13 March 1953, p. 8)

The main source of population growth was identified as jobs in manufacturing industry, so an agreement was reached with the main employers not to increase their workforces. Such an agreement could not be enforced effectively by land-use planning machinery. Only new or physically expanding industries could be regulated by the mechanisms of development control. Little or no control could be exercised over tertiary employment in this way. Eventually, in the review of the Development Plan, Murray was forced to admit that 'the restriction contained in the Development Plan, where no additional land was allocated for industry, apart from that necessary for dealing with re-location, has not succeeded in preventing a large and continuing increase in employment in industry' (Oxford City, 1964a, p. 13). It also had little or no effect on the structure of the economy, as will be shown later.

In addition, tertiary employment grew much faster than manufacturing jobs after 1961, but the council did not revise or restate its restrictive policies on employment until 1972. Then, the Planning Committee

> accepted that there is now an overwhelming need to make the restrictive policy which has applied to industrial growth for some years applicable to service industry and office development to avoid further overstraining of the City's transportation system and excessive pressure on the already hard-pressed housing stock. (Oxford City, 1972e)

It also went some way to admitting that land-use regulation is not a particularly effective way of restricting such growth. The committee said that, 'there will be difficulties in administering the policy because control by land use zoning is being replaced by control based on interpretation of good planning principles and inevitably any decision is now open to argument' (Oxford City, 1972e).

Land-use planning did not, therefore, prove an effective tool in controlling the industrial and commercial decisions of existing, local uses of land. It did, however, prevent some new users from entering the area.

Another area in which the Development Plan sought to alter private profitability criteria in the name of the community was commerce, especially shops. It was clear that, if left to their own devices, commercial operators did not produce shops and offices in line with the planning authority's requirements. Shop operators in particular had some interest in restricting the supply of the particular type of shop they owned, as well as minimising the overhead costs of their operations.

Commercial institutions, as represented by the Chamber of Trade, were against decentralisation to subsidiary shopping centres but, at the same time, they were also against the traffic congestion caused by centralisation, mainly on the grounds of its possible interference with trade and commuting by the private car. Councillor Minns (Conservative), for example, said that the Chamber opposed the Development Plan for vigorous decentralisation of the central shopping and business area . . . for failing to provide more car parks and in particular relief roads *(Oxford Times,* 15 May 1953, p. 9).

At the public inquiry into the Development Plan, the Chamber of Trade's contradictory position became even more evident. Councillor Iliffe (Conservative), representing the Chamber, said that it approved the Cowley Centre in principle but was opposed to the council's policy of decentralisation. This was marked by its objection to the further development of a subsidiary shopping centre in north Oxford at Summertown *(Oxford Times,* 4 December 1953, p. 7). In 1955, the Chamber raised more objections to a proposal to decentralise (a little) the large covered market in Oxford.

This opposition to decentralisation was the reverse of the coin of central business district growth. Commercial interests approved of the latter. They did not, however, support the local building industry when it came to handing out contracts for the construction of the Westgate. Local builders were unavailingly against giving the contract to Taylor Woodrow Construction, but they were not supported by commercial representatives in the council.

In the event, the planning authority pursued both the ends of central business district growth at the Westgate and decentralisation to the Cowley Centre. Some of its other policies entrained difficulties in the pursuit of both these objectives. Thus, having constrained the size of the city and its internal growth by such policies as the green belt, zoning, high building restrictions and conservation, the planning authority had increased the costs of entering the field to prohibitive levels. This, as Murray admitted, led to 'a virtual monopoly of new development by the big multiple shops, insurance companies etc.' (Oxford City, 1964a, p. 116). When the authority decided that more shops were needed in Cowley to further the policy of decentralisation, and more were needed in the centre to fulfil Oxford's regional role, it followed that the only institution prepared to fund the infrastructure and construction required was the local authority itself. It was also thought that the authority was the only institution capable of assembling the sites required into one single holding. The net result of these beliefs was that the local authority compulsorily purchased the land for new shopping centres, put in the infrastructure, built most of the commercial premises and enticed the big multiple shops to use them by highly favourable rents. In this way the planning authority aided the private profitability of some private entrepreneurs at the direct expense of the local community.

Externalities

The prevention of undesirable externalities presented the planners with considerable difficulties. The biggest of these was the gasworks, originally sited in St Ebbe's and later extended south of the Thames. Such nationalised industries were, and are, subject only to voluntary planning control. The result was that although the gasworks contributed considerable air pollution to St Ebbe's, the city could only negotiate for its removal. The gasworks was inextricably tied up in the planning mind with St Ebbe's and, as a result, contributed to the unfortunate feeling that the whole area should be demolished. The close relationship between the two can be seen in Figure 6.3.

Despite the fact that a site was set aside for the gasworks in Cowley, it continued to expand on its existing site. Eventually it took a decision by the House of Lords to prevent its further expansion. By the time it started to move to Cowley, new developements such as regional supplies and North Sea gas were on the horizon, and the whole saga proved largely to have been a waste of time and effort. At the same time, the presence of the works had taken its toll in blighting St Ebbe's and contributing to its eventual demolition.

The above discussion has shown that the logic of development planning is varied and complicated. It varies according to time, level and achievements. It is complicated in the sense that a number of different reasons are used for its justification *vis-à-vis* different activites. No monocausal explanation of the role of the state, however sophisticated and disguised, can do justice to this variety and complexity.

During its post-war existence, however, development planning in Oxford, and indeed many other places, exhibits certain key characteristics. Its logic has proved weak in persuading, or getting the power to force, entrepreneurs to modify their profitability criteria in the name of the community at large. Development planning has been something of a blunt instrument when it comes to altering commercial and industrial decisions of what to build where, and how to use existing development. To be fair, it has not been entirely without effect, and a different kind of planning was probably required to effect changes in these types of decision.

Conclusions

The preceding historical analysis shows that, at least in the case of one local planning authority, the location and role of the state involves a degree of autonomy for its bureaucrats, inter-organisational conflict over its own production objectives and a modest degree of control over the production objectives of other organisations. In general, bureaucratic autonomy was related to administrative claims to possess special and scarce skills and knowledge. State production objectives were concerned with supplying goods and services not forthcoming from the market to industrial consumers, and providing facilities for private organisations at lower costs than they themselves would have had to pay in a free market. State control of the production objectives of these organisations was modest either because they used their power to modify state objectives or because they had sufficient room for manoeuvre within the limits of state planning powers.

During the post-war period, the state extended its interests in the direct production of goods and services. In particular, it acquired increased powers of land uses and development at the local level. Prior to local government reorganisation in 1974, the local authority studied here was particularly concerned with the production of schools, commercial precincts, roads, amenities, libraries and housing. This is exemplified by its capital expenditures on these items which totalled nearly £2.5 million in 1970/1. This was a large investment by any local standards.

The evidence described above therefore shows that a quantitative and qualitative change has taken place in the role of the state with respect to the local planning and production of land and buildings. This change is marked by an increasing involvement in the direct production of generally necessary though unprofitable physical goods. Partly as a result of this involvement, the local state has become one of the largest single landowners, particularly in those areas of the city which generated little or no profit before the introduction of mandatory land-use planning.

The most significant action requiring some modification of this general statement was central area development. In this instance the local state assembled a large site, often by the use of its powers of compulsory purchase. The costs of assembling this site were therefore less than the eventual private users of it would have had to have paid on the open market. In this case the objectives of the local authority were integrated with those of private commercial interests. To some extent this was the result of joint membership by particular individuals of the council, business organisations and various clubs.

Local business interests therefore enjoyed a fairly high level of integration with the local council. This was responsible for their ability to influence the local planning authority's objectives in the control and production of land uses and buildings. These interests were by no means always dominant in the production activities of the local state. Both traditional landowning interests and the new bureaucratic order had important effects on local development planning.

Traditional landowning interests, mainly in the shape of colleges and the university, were adept at thwarting the local planning authority's road plans and at following their own land-use objectives. The Christ Church Meadow road plans provide a vivid example of the ability of traditional landowners to prevent incursions into their ancient property rights.

These abilities do not depend primarily on the ownership of capital. Rather, they rest on a combination of landownership, political skill, knowledge and personal contacts. The latter, as much as anything else, were responsible for university successes in preventing state interference with their traditional land holdings.

Similarly, the autonomy or independence of local planning bureaucracies does not rest on capital ownership. It rests first on claims to independent knowledge and skills which are often associated with relatively closed professional organisations. It also rests on the combination of these skills into large, and often growing, hierarchically structured formal organisations. These characteristics create both internal and external power relationships. Externally, the bureaucracy presents a relatively uniform claim to authority on the basis of its claims to exclusive knowledge and skills. To some extent these are ceded as a result of public indifference or a lack of the ability to evaluate these claims. Internally, the hierarchical structure of the bureaucracy as illustrated in Figures 5.3 and 5.4 creates its own power structure. In general, those towards the higher echelons have more power than those in the lower levels.

Externally, the local planning authority studied exhibited quite high levels of power in its ability to institute and maintain objectives concerned with neatness, tidiness and aesthetic value judgements. Indeed, as far as many individual contacts with the planning authority were concerned, these kinds of powers and judgements would appear to be its main function. In so far as these judgements extend into an understanding of areas like St Ebbe's, they form an important ideological and theoretical basis for much of what is done in the name of land-use planning. They therefore have ramifications well beyond their immediate concern with what is visible.

The internal power structure of the local planning authority exhibits a fairly typical tension between the very top political and administrative echelons and those below this level. The objectives of the two groups are often different. At the top are found considerations concerned with the acquisition or retention of political power. As a consequence of this, many activities are not so much concerned with 'rational' planning as with political conflicts, machinations, bargains and compromises. Lower in the hierarchy, traditional allegiances to professional or technical codes of action may be found. These tend to emphasise the 'special' skills involved in planning and the technical 'expertise' of its purveyors. These two sets of objectives often result in tensions within local planning departments themselves as to what the proper and legitimate objectives of the administrative exercise should be.

Taken together, the characteristics exhibited by land-use planning in Oxford since the Second World War show the extremely complex nature of the location and role of the state. To generalise, these are a mixture of various objectives which include those of the administration itself, traditional landowners, business and commerce. Negotiations between these interests are carried on by formal organisations whose members also have high levels of informal contacts and overlapping roles. These relationships are fairly continuous and exhibit many of the characteristics associated with a corporate state.

Chapter 6

The Distribution and Consumption of New Physical Development

Introduction

Chapter 6 examines the distribution and consumption of new physical development by different organisations and groups in Oxford during the period covered by the 1955 Development Plan. The mechanism by which these distributions were controlled by the local planning authority was development control.

Most of the work of development control is concerned with private sector developments or works by the local authority itself which normally conform to the local development control requirements. Central to this activity is the statutory definition of development. This has been repeated verbatim in all the post-war planning acts and appears as Section 22(1) in the 1971 Act. There, development is defined as 'the carrying out of building, engineering, mining or other operations in, on, over or under land, or the making of any material change in the use of any buildings or other land'. Some specific exclusions from control are also made in the Act. These include minor activities such as interior maintenance, roadworks, incidental uses, agriculture and changes of use within certain categories of activity specified by the Use Classes Order. The main exclusions as far as private developers are concerned arise from the provisions contained in the General Development Order. This document, which is updated and consolidated from time to time, is designed to reduce the numbers of relatively trivial applications coming before local planning authorities for development control decisions. As a result, certain specified developments are permitted without the need to follow the full planning application procedures. They include the extension of a dwelling house by up to 50 cubic metres or one-tenth, whichever is the greater, porches, uses incidental to the enjoyment of the dwelling, fences and some changes of use.

Potential developers may make a number of different types of application to local planning authorities. Six main categories are listed in Oxford City's current application form. They are:

1. Outline planning permission.
2. Full planning permission.
3. Approval of reserved matters following the granting of outline permission.
4. Renewal of a temporary permission or permission for retention of building or continuance of use without complying with a condition subject to which planning permission has been granted.
5. Listed building consent.
6. Development by a Government Department under Circular 80/71.

Other minor applications can be made to obtain permission for advertising, established use certificates, and Section 53 determinations which confirm whether proposals are permitted development or not.

The volume of applications can be quite considerable. In the three wards – Cowley and Iffley, North and South – chosen for special study in Oxford, the number of applications between 1953 and 1973 is estimated to have been 9421. Of these, 84 per cent were for developments of less than 1000 square feet, defined as 'A' types. Among this type of application, nearly half turned out to be permitted development or other activities not requiring a major planning decision. Thus, while A type applications contributed the lion's share of the development control workload, half of them did not require planning permission, being permitted development, and the other half usually only invoked aesthetic and architectural value judgements.

In contrast, B type applications of 1000 square feet or more required more significant decisions. Table 6.1 shows the tendency to submit them in outline first, 28 per cent, followed by an application for full approval later, 55 per cent. While these types of application have greater significance in their

TABLE 6.1 *Number and type of applications*

Type of application	Size of development	
	A (%)	B (%)
Outline	2	28
Full	43	55
Approval of reserved matters	–	1
Renewal/retention of permission	–	1
Temporary approval	6	12
Other	49	3
Total files (= 100%)	795*	1 495

*10 per cent sample.

effects on the distribution of development, they were often swamped in the sheer volume of A type applications. By the time they reached the Planning Committee for ratification of the departmental recommendations they often acquired a disproportionately small amount of decision-making time. Sometimes their significance could be lost altogether. Councillor Nimmo (Labour), for example, complained that from the number of items which came before each meeting of the committee it was clear that no great attention could be given to any individual item (*Oxford Times*, 10 May 1963, p. 15).

The undifferentiated volume of work establishes a potential degree of autonomy for development control staff insofar as the size, complexity and information flows surrounding the activity become impenetrable by many outside influences. McLoughlin (1973) has documented both the complexity involved in making a development control decision, and the numerous flows of information to and from the development control officers. Among these flows and counter-flows of information, both documented and verbal, ample opportunity is provided to the bureaucrats to fragment, channel, neglect, alter, ignore and colour them in such a way as to influence the eventual local planning decision. In this area, the opportunities for the mixture of planning ideologies and practice are numerous.

The predispositions of development control officers, especially in matters of aesthetic judgement, can come to be reflected in actual developments. *Cognoscenti* are said to be able to recognise the effects of individual officers in some areas. Nevertheless, the margin of autonomy is limited. It affects A rather than B type developments and, if exercised to a significant degree, can result in appeals and public inquiries where the ultimate decision can be taken out of the local planning authority's hands.

The degree of autonomy exercised by local officers, or indeed the level of influence by outside interests, is also limited by inefficiencies in the system. Many of these relate to the undifferentiated volume of work which means that a great deal of time and effort is devoted to applications which never result in development of any kind. Among B applications, bearing in mind that 28 per cent were only outline requests anyway, of the 1495 submitted in the three study wards only 728 resulted in actual development by 1977. Among A types, of which only 2 per cent were outline applications, 5440 of the estimated 7950 applications resulted in development by 1977. To avoid the continuation of this wasted effort and possibly to reduce private speculation in planning permissions, the 1968 Town and Country Planning Act stated in Section 65 that permissions should lapse if the development was not carried out. These provisions were introduced in Oxford in 1969. They imposed a general time limit of five years between the granting of outline or full planning permission and the commencement of development.

Nevertheless the system continued to creak under the strains imposed upon it. As a result, George Dobry was appointed to conduct a review of development control procedures in 1973. The terms of reference of his committee were:

1. To consider whether the development control system under the Town and Country Planning Acts adequately meets current needs, and to advise on the lines along which it might be improved, bearing in mind the forthcoming redistribution of planning functions between local authorities and the new system of structure plans.
2. To review the arrangements for appeals to the Secretary

of State under the Planning Acts, including rights of appeal and the handling of appeals in the Department of the Environment, and to make recommendations. (Department of the Environment, 1975a, p. III)

His report acknowledged deficiencies in the system of development control and produced recommendations which aimed to:

1. Give greater freedom to harmless development.
2. Guard against harmful development by retaining applications for all cases, as at present.
3. Separate from the main stream all applications which might cause harm.
4. Dispose of applications in the main stream by rapid and routine procedures.
5. Apply the same approach to appeals. (Department of the Environment, 1975a, p. 10)

In order to achieve these desirable objectives at the local level, he recommended dividing all applications into two categories. Category A was to comprise:

1. All simple cases.
2. All applications conforming with an approved Development Plan.
3. Development which only just exceeds that permitted by the General Development Order, even when not allocated for that use in the Development Plan.
4. The approval of reserved matters relating to cases classed as A when outline permission was sought.

Category B was to comprise all other applications. (Department of the Environment, 1975a, p. 10)

The former would be dealt with by streamlined and quicker procedures than before. Category B applications would be treated in much the same way as previously.

Despite the fact that a number of local authorities, including Oxford, already operate a system similar to that outlined above, development control procedures have not generally been reformed along the lines recommended by Dobry. One of the main reasons for this is the importance attached to aesthetic value judgements as the *raison d'être* of local authority planning departments. Many were reluctant to see their major concerns with neatness, tidiness and the cosmetic appearance of property apparently downgraded and dealt with more swiftly.

As a result, planning committees are swamped with large numbers of undifferentiated applications to consider. This decreases their ability to devote sufficient time to applications having major consumption and distributional consequences, even if they so desired. Where they do not desire to consider such issues, political conflicts are minimised or hidden altogther. This again has the effect of distributing a degree of autonomy and apparent political neutrality to planning bureaucrats. Few real political divisions exist on questions of the cosmetic appearance of property. Planners therefore have some autonomy to pass judgements on these issues with relative impunity. The undifferentiated volume of applications means that too much time is devoted to permitting development as a result of doubtful aesthetic arguments, while significant distributional consequences go unnoticed.

Development control is one channel through which all attempts to acquire new property rights must pass. It is therefore a critical focus of potential struggles and conflicts in state regulation of new property rights and subsequent physical properties. In combination with development plans during the period between 1947 and 1973, it provided the main machinery for the regulation of physical developments.

Chapter 6 starts with an analysis of the changing residential social composition of the wards selected for study. This shows that the distributions of physical property were being made to areas with changing residential compositions over the study period. Some of these social changes were the direct result of physical developments. The residential changes may be summarised as a movement away from the city centre by all social classes to the suburbs and beyond. This is shown by the absolute population numbers and the proportionate social class figures. The processes of gentrification and increased social polarisation at the centre are also indicated by the rising proportion of non-manual heads of households in South ward.

Next, the chapter examines who was trying to get what in terms of developments in these wards. This analysis shows that although private individuals made a majority of all applications for development, 4598 applications out of a total of 9377 for which information was available, most of these were deemed permitted development and involved relatively trivial gains. In contrast, organisations, particularly feudal landowners, the state, industry and commerce, made fewer applications for more significant developments involving large potential gains. Their abilities to acquire these developments within or outside the provisions of the Development Plan are evaluated.

Finally, the distribution of the outcomes of development control decisions in terms of properties, their costs and values to local areas is analysed. This shows that the most valuable properties were acquired by major organisations, sometimes at minimal cost to themselves and sometimes at the direct expense of lower social class residents. On the other hand, it also shows that state action brought about improvements in housing, education and other amenities for some skilled manual workers and increasingly for lower social class residents as well.

The total picture of the distribution of property rights and properties is therefore a complex one. It could be summed up as one of major gains accruing to existing local organisations; significant, though less valuable, gains accruing to successively lower social classes among manual workers; the preservation of the existing rights and properties of non-manual workers; and the extension of transportation and commercial properties into poorer working-class areas unnecessarily and without adequate compensation.

Residence and social class

The city as a whole changed its social composition between 1951 and 1971. Table 6.2 shows that the social class composition of the city changed as it became increasingly the inner area of functionally much larger settlement extending beyond its administrative boundaries. In outline it followed a descriptive pattern somewhat similar to that predicted by Burgess (see Park, Burgess and McKenzie, 1925). The tendency

TABLE 6.2 *Residence and social class*

	Socioeconomic groups					
	Professional employers and managers (%)	Skilled manual and foremen (%)	Other non-manual (%)	Semi-skilled personal service (%)	Un-skilled armed service (%)	Total numbers = 100%
Oxford						
1951	20	41	10	18	11	32 689
1961	15	35	19	19	12	31 39x10
1971	17	32	19	21	11	33 70x10
Cowley and Iffley ward						
1951	14	48	9	17	12	8 609
1961	10	39	19	21	11	8 75x10
1971	8	25	28	21	18	13 37x10
North ward						
1951	47	23	8	16	6	2 372
1961	41	15	21	13	10	2 12x10
1971	40	11	22	15	12	2 15x10
South ward						
1951	12	40	9	21	18	3 457
1961	14	33	13	20	20	2 42x10
1971	15	26	18	21	20	2 20x10

SOURCE Census 1951, 1961, 1971
NOTE The figures for 1961 and 1971 are a sample of 10 per cent drawn from all residents in private households.

was for better-off groups to move to the periphery and out into the towns and villages of the green belt and beyond. The building of council houses on peripheral sites or the expansion of adjacent villages with less expensive private housing also drew skilled manual workers in the same direction. The functional city therefore extended beyond its administrative boundaries to include a more extensive local labour market at least as large as the whole of its green belt territories shown in Map 5.14. Its functional population was in excess of 154,500 by 1974 (Oxfordshire, 1975). The main physical difference between the city as it was at that time and as it might have been without the green belt was that its surrounding villages remained separated by open agricultural land. Instead of being engulfed in urban development as had Old Marston, Old Headington, Headington Quarry, Hinksey and Iffley villages, they remained free-standing. They were nonetheless part of the functional City of Oxford for all that.

The inner part of this wider functional city lost professionals, managers and skilled manual workers between 1951 and 1971. It gained in proportions of less skilled non-manual and manual workers. The proportion of unskilled workers remained the same.

Cowley and Iffley ward, which had been 48 per cent skilled manual workers in 1951, became predominantly low-skilled, non-manual and manual workers who made up 67 per cent of the occupied residents in 1971. To the extent that council and cheaper private housing was being built in the ward during the same period, then some of it must have been allocated to these social groups. Indeed, the building of council housing in the area and its allocation to these groups may have been primarily responsible for changing the social composition of the area.

North ward had 47 per cent professional and managerial residents in 1951 and this declined slightly to 40 per cent by 1971. The proportion of skilled manual workers declined by more than half, while the proportion of less skilled, non-manual workers nearly trebled and the proportion of unskilled manual workers doubled. This indicates a remarkable increase in social polarisation in part of Oxford's functional inner city area. Thus, the proportion of non-manual residents increased from 55 to 62 per cent and the proportion of semi- and unskilled manual residents also went up from 22 to 27 per cent. No council housing was built in this ward and so the social polarisation probably also reflects a difference between private ownership and private renting. Together, these indicate the maintenance of existing property rights in North ward and the resettling of the poorest groups into the next nearest privately rented accommodation after demolition in St Ebbe's and gentrification in places like Osney and Jericho.

South ward also became more polarised during the period as a result of declining numbers of skilled manual workers and increasing proportions of less skilled non-manual and unskilled manual workers. This trend was heightened by the process of gentrification. Professional and managerial workers increased from 12 to 15 per cent of residents between 1951 and 1971. This was the only ward studied to show such an increase. St Ebbe's would probably have been a prime target for this process had it survived in its original form without the gasworks. As it was, the proportion of less skilled non-manual and manual workers in South ward as a whole increased from 48 per cent in 1951 to 59 per cent in 1971. Insofar as this meant that residents became relatively, though not absolutely, poorer during the study period, the distribution of property to the area was more rather than less regressive.

Taking Oxford as a whole and comparing its social composition with those for the wards studied, a slightly different picture emerges. Examining the residential distribution of the poorest social classes, namely semi- and unskilled manual workers, they formed 18 and 11 per cent respectively of the population of Oxford resident in private households in 1951. In the same year, they represented 17 and 12 per cent of the population of Cowley and Iffley ward, 16 and 6 per cent of North and 21 and 18 per cent of South ward's population. In other words, they were disproportionately concentrated in South ward.

By 1971, semi- and unskilled manual workers constituted 21 and 11 per cent of Oxford's private resident population. In Cowley and Iffley ward they represented 21 and 18 per cent of the population. Insofar this was the ward studied in which most council housing, educational facilities and other collective amenities were built, this represents a movement, particularly of the lowest social class, into state-provided accommodation. Insofar as this was better quality than they might have enjoyed in the private sector, this represents a gain for this group.

A similar movement, however, may be seen into North ward. Thus, in 1971, semi- and unskilled manual residents represented

15 and 12 per cent of the population. The doubling of the proportion of the lowest social class from 6 to 12 per cent between 1951 and 1971 indicates movement into the private rented housing of that area. Insofar as the cost and quality of that type of housing was probably higher and not much better than that of South ward, this represents a financial loss to this group in comparison with the relationships they might have had between housing cost and quality had they lived in South ward.

A similar picture emerges in South ward itself. There the proportion of semi-skilled manual workers remained high at 21 per cent and the proportion of unskilled manual workers rose from 18 to 20 per cent compared with the average for the city of 11 per cent. Insofar as a substantial amount of demolition of the type of housing that these groups required took place in South ward during the study period, then this must have increased overcrowding there and taken a basic requirement away from them. This represents a regressive redistribution of property.

These figures illustrate the difficulties of trying to relate changing distributions of property to territories whose social compositions were themselves changing. Some of these social changes were also the direct result of property changes such as the building and demolition of housing.

The tables in subsequent parts of the chapter should therefore be interpreted in the light of the following general conditions pertaining to the social composition of Oxford as a whole and the three wards chosen for study between 1951 and 1971. First, the proportions of professional and skilled manual workers declined, the proportions of other non-manual and semi-skilled manual workers increased and the proportion of unskilled resident heads of private households remained the same for the city as a whole. Second, the proportion of professional groups declined in Cowley and Iffley and North wards but increased in South ward. Third, the proportion of skilled manual workers decreased in all wards. Fourth, the proportion of other non-manual workers increased in all wards. Fifth, the proportion of semi-skilled manual workers increased in Cowley and Iffley but remained roughly the same in the other two wards. Sixth, the proportion of unskilled manual workers increased in all wards. This means that the outcomes of property development during the study period effected increasing proportions of the lower social classes and decreasing proportions of skilled manual workers in all wards. They also effected increasing proportions of other non-manual groups in all wards and decreasing proportions of professional workers except in South ward.

The acquisition of new property rights

The majority of all property rights in land and development were established before the advent of effective town planning. Post-war planning acts froze those rights as they were in 1947 and brought the acquisition of future rights under state and, as a result, political control. The early development plans were therefore concerned with the political allocation of new or changed property rights at the margin. In studying such plans, one is looking at the operation of political power as it affected the acquisition of property rights in contemporary society following a long history of military, feudal and economic command of those rights.

The usefulness of examining post-war development planning and control is that the acquisition of new rights and development illustrates one of the output effects of the operation of power in contemporary society within the physical context left by previous societies. Cities therefore come to represent a horizontal archaeology of past societies. Examining today's cities is like looking at how living coral builds on dead.

Once the parameters of new property rights have been set in the development plan, the next stage, for those who wish to acquire some specific rights, is to approach the system of development control. This provides a relatively accurate documented channel through which most formal attempts to acquire new or changed property rights must pass. It is therefore a visible and formal focus of the way contemporary social groups engage in struggles and conflicts to acquire one of the outputs from state-regulated queues.

Before applications become visible and formal, however, a substantial degree of covert bargaining may be conducted between potential applicants and the planning authority. Some

Distribution and Consumption of New Development 231

of this is directed at the development control officers and some of it is directed at political levels which are not susceptible to empirical investigation. The eventual outputs of property rights illustrate the results of this bargaining; their nature and type illustrate the effectiveness and power of their protagonists.

Most of this kind of bargaining is centred on larger developments. Following Dobry (Department of the Environment, 1975a), these have been called 'B' types in the study of Oxford. They have been defined as applications for more than 1000 square feet of development or changes of use of this magnitude. Little bargaining takes place on applications for less than 1000 square feet, called 'A'. This is largely because nearly half of this type of application was permitted development. This is insignificant development which is not usually subject to formal planning control.

For the three wards chosen for study in Oxford, Table 6.3 shows the type of application made by different groups for all A and B type applications. Nearly all applications are made by existing property owners. This means that like the setting of development plan objectives only organisations or middle-class groups have much direct contact with or influence on planning objectives and outputs. Manual workers and poor groups must rely on indirect political pressure via the state to produce planning outputs relevant to their interests.

The five main groups of applicants who can be identified from development control records by this analysis are, first, feudal landowners such as the Duke of Marlborough, some colleges and the university; second, the state, which normally means a department of the local authority itself; third, industry and commerce; fourth, private individuals and, finally, voluntary associations such as the Oxford Preservation Trust. All these groups have different compositions from one another and also different relationships to the use of land.

Nearly half of all the Oxford applications were permitted development over which only nominal planning control is exercised. Most of these were submitted by private individuals wishing to build garages or extend their existing houses. Other groups submitting such applications were usually engaged in modifying minor details of buildings. Most permitted develop-

TABLE 6.3 *Type of application by type of applicant (A types multiplied by 10, plus B type applications)*

	Type of applicant					
Type of application	Feudal landowners (%)	State (%)	Industrial and commercial (%)	Private individuals (%)	Voluntary associations (%)	Total (%)
Permitted development	30	28	15	77	12	48
Outline	6	4	12	3	20	6
Full	61	63	72	20	67	45
Reserved matter	—	—	—	—	1	—
Permanent consent	1	2	—	—	—	—
Temporary approval	2	3	1	—	—	2
Total files = 100%	1226	508	1855	4595	193	9377
χ^2 20 = 3271.37 p < 0.1					No information	44

ments were A type applications. The other half of this type of development which actually required planning permission was usually concerned with such matters as shop fronts and advertising. Taken together they represented only small new distributions of property rights as a direct result of planning decisions. This was because they were either permitted development or matters of design. As long as they conformed with the aesthetic value judgements of development control officers and building regulations, their passage through planning was smooth and uninterrupted. Neither in their substance nor in the effects that planning had on them did they constitute a significant contribution to property rights. In total, therefore, their contribution to the distribution of significant amounts of property was neglibile.

It might even be argued that decisions about such applications could safely be left to building regulations. This would

Distribution and Consumption of New Development 233

have the merits of recognising what mostly *de facto* happens; speeding up the process of development control; and releasing more time for the consideration of major applications. This said, the following study will now focus on B type applications and developments because these are the ones which make a significant contribution to the distribution of property rights and buildings.

As far as B type applications are concerned, bargaining becomes formal when an application is submitted. Even then the submission of outline applications allows those seeking property rights to test the development control system without too much cost to themselves. Only 6 per cent of all applications were for outline planning permission. Among B types, however, one-third of all applications were for outline permission only.

Table 6.4 shows that a substantial proportion of all major applications, except those by the state itself, were for outline permission. State agencies, such as the Housing Department

TABLE 6.4 *Type of application by type of applicant (B type applications)*

Type of application	Type of applicant					
	Feudal land-owners (%)	State (%)	Industrial and commercial (%)	Private individuals (%)	Voluntary associations (%)	Total (%)
Change of use	21	13	16	3	21	15
Outline	20	13	31	41	29	28
Full	56	70	52	56	48	55
Reserved matter	1	—	—	1	2	1
Permanent consent	1	1	1	—	—	1
Temporary approval	1	3	—	—	—	—
Total files = 100%	276	158	765	205	63	1 469
χ^2 25 = 100.53 p < 0.1				No information		26

or the City Engineer's Department, have more opportunities to negotiate between departments and might be expected more readily to follow their own policy objectives. Accordingly, 70 per cent of state applications were for full planning permission. Feudal landowners, such as the colleges and university, were also more in tune with state objectives, having played a substantial part in setting them in the Development Plan. Some 56 per cent of their applications were for full permission. Commercial, industrial, private individuals and associations all submitted more than the average number of outline applications. This was due either to testing the regulations to see how far they could be adjusted in favour of applicants, or to degrees of uncertainty of what was acceptable development within the parameters of the Development Plan.

In these circumstances, refusal rates do not necessarily illustrate lack of power by either the state or applicants. Prior knowledge of the development plan influences the type of property rights sought. Power over development plan objectives brings a degree of acceptance of these objectives and therefore reduces the degree of subsequent probing. Feudal landowners and the state both had some power over development plan objectives and considerable acceptance of the eventual statutory document. Consequently, at 7 and 3 per cent respectively, they also had the lowest subsequent refusal rates for their applications. Table 6.5 also shows that those groups who sought to probe the limits of the planning system had higher than average refusal rates. Commercial and industrial applicants had a 25 per cent refusal rate. Those who both probed and had little part in the setting of objectives also had higher than average numbers of refusals. Private individuals had, for example, a 23 per cent failure rate.

On the other hand, only 38 per cent of all B-type applications actually received full approval. All the others had some conditions attached to them or were withdrawn or refused. In this way the political control of the acquisition of new property rights was quite strictly enforced. Even feudal landowners and the state only got full permission for just over half their total applications. Other groups acquired full permission for about one-third of their applications. Thus, despite all the covert and overt bargaining over property rights, the local

TABLE 6.5 *Local decision by applicant (B type applications)*

	Type of applicant					
Local decision	Feudal land-owners (%)	State (%)	Industrial and commercial (%)	Private individuals (%)	Voluntary associations (%)	Total (%)
Full approval	52	51	31	37	34	38
Conditional approval	18	17	20	14	19	18
Temporary approval	4	18	4	1	2	5
Refused	7	3	25	23	9	18
Refused under building regulations	—	—	1	1	—	1
Withdrawn	4	1	5	3	6	4
Permitted development	—	—	—	—	—	—
Deemed refused	—	1	1	1	—	1
Approved in principle only	15	9	13	20	30	16
Total files = 100%	280	162	780	207	64	1 493
χ^2 32 = 204.98 p < 0.1				No information		2

planning authority played a large and significant role in their allocation via the process of development control.

Most of these new property rights were allocated to existing freehold owners of land and developments. In this way the planning system allocates most to those who own most property in the first instance. Table 6.6 shows that the majority of all B type applications were submitted by freehold owners. They and lessors were the most successful in acquiring full planning permission, gaining around 40 per cent success. Non-owners, however, were a significant minority of 166 applications, 24 per cent of which gained full approval. Such applications came mainly from industrial and commercial groups. For most of the study period they could acquire such

TABLE 6.6 *Local decision by ownership (B type applications)*

	Ownership				
	Owner	Tenant	Non-owner	Lessor	Total
Full approval	39	—	24	45	38
Conditional approval	18	—	14	20	18
Temporary approval	55	—	3	9	5
Refused	17	—	31	14	18
Refused under building regulations	1	—	—	2	1
Withdrawn	5	—	5	2	4
Permitted development	—	—	—	—	—
Deemed refused	1	—	1	1	1
Approved in principle only	14	—	22	7	15
Total files = 100%	1152	10	166	157	1 485
χ^2 24 = 82.04 p < 0.1			No information		10

permission for land they did not own without a legal requirement to tell the actual owner what they were doing.

Table 6.7 shows what these and other applicants were trying to acquire in terms of new property rights. There were significant differences both within and between different groups. Among the organisations, commercial and industrial groups submitted most applications: indeed, they submitted more than half of all major applications. They were mainly concerned with housing, shops, industry, offices and storage in that order. In contrast, feudal landowners, the next largest applicants, were overwhelmingly concerned with university uses and, to a lesser extent, housing. The state, on the other hand, applied for housing, amenities, education and offices in that order.

Middle-class groups, as individuals, were almost exclusively concerned with housing. When combined in voluntary associations they sought a very wide variety of property rights, although some emphasis was placed on education, housing and amenities.

In total, the largest number of applications was for housing at 37 per cent; next was shops at 14 per cent; this was followed

TABLE 6.7 *Proposed main use by applicant (B type applications)*

Proposed main use	Type of applicant					
	Feudal land-owners (%)	State (%)	Industrial and commercial (%)	Private individuals (%)	Voluntary associations (%)	Total (%)
Housing	19	27	31	96	20	37
Retail	4	7	24	1	2	14
Office	4	10	11	1	5	8
Industry	1	3	16	—	2	9
Storage	1	7	9	—	2	6
Education	3	15	5	1	22	6
University	65	1	—	—	—	12
Amenities	1	22	1	—	14	4
Other	2	8	3	1	33	4
Total files = 100%	280	162	779	207	64	1 492

$\chi^2\ 32 = 1693.99\ p < 0.1$ No information   3

by university uses at 12 per cent. The number of applications, however, does not necessarily correspond with the amount and value of property rights actually sought or acquired. One industrial application can be as large in floorspace terms as many housing applications. The actual amount and value of property rights acquired will be examined later.

For the time being, it is necessary to examine not just the total applications by different groups for property rights but also which territories they are trying to locate them in.

Table 6.8 shows how different groups were trying to acquire different property rights in different areas. South, the poorest ward with residents in greatest need, was almost exclusively the preserve of the organisations as far as applications were concerned. Between them they sought the least housing and education of the three wards and the most shops and offices. In this ward even industry and commerce made more applications for housing than did the state, albeit for quite different potential users. Industry and commerce put in more applications in this ward than any other group, particularly for shops and offices. Even the state submitted as many applications for offices as it did for housing. Feudal landowners were mainly interested in acquiring university uses.

TABLE 6.8 *Proposed main use by applicant by ward (B type applications)*

	Applicant					
Proposed main use	Feudal land-owners (%)	State (%)	Industrial and commercial (%)	Private individuals (%)	Voluntary associations (%)	Total (%)
Cowley and Iffley						
Housing	—	35	33	96	(29)	46
Retail	—	9	21	1	—	15
Office	—	3	7	—	(4)	5
Industry	—	3	24	—	(4)	15
Storage	—	5	11	—	—	7
Education	—	23	1	—	(21)	5
University	—	—	1	—	—	1
Amenities	—	17	1	—	(25)	4
Other	—	5	1	3	(17)	2
Total files = 100%	12	106	439	138	24	719
χ^2 32 = 586.50 p < 0.1						
North						
Housing	18	—	37	93	(19)	31
Retail	4	—	22	2	(4)	10
Office	4	—	14	2	(4)	9
Industry	1	—	1	—	—	—
Storage	1	—	3	—	—	2
Education	3	—	20	2	(35)	10
University	69	—	—	—	—	33
Amenities	—	—	1	—	(8)	1
Other	—	—	2	1	(20)	4
Total files = 100%	219	13	157	43	26	458
χ^2 32 = 466.18 p < 0.1						

TABLE 6.8 (continued)

Proposed main use	Applicant					
	Feudal land-owners (%)	State (%)	Industrial and commercial (%)	Private individuals (%)	Voluntary associations (%)	Total (%)
South						
Housing	14	14	21	(100)	—	25
Retail	4	7	33	—	—	21
Office	4	14	19	—	—	14
Industry	2	2	9	—	—	6
Storage	4	9	12	—	—	9
Education	2	2	1	—	—	1
University	53	—	—	—	—	8
Amenities	8	37	1	—	—	7
Other	9	15	4	—	—	9
Total files = 100%	49	43	183	26	14	315
χ^2 32 = 403.98 p $<$ 0.1					No information	3

In North, the richest ward with residents in least need, the state made practically no applications. In contrast, feudal landowners made more applications than any other group, mostly for university uses. Commercial and industrial interests made fewer applications in this ward than any other. Those they did make were for the building of houses, shops and educational institutions such as commercial language schools. Individuals applied for permission to build private houses. In total, the two main groups of applications in North ward were for the university and housing.

Cowley and Iffley ward had the most applications, partly because it was a larger ward than the other two. Here feudal landowners were almost entirely absent and the largest number of applications came from the state, industry and commerce and private individuals for housing. In this manual working-class area, both public and private housing predominated among state and private applicants. This illustrates not only the relative availability of land there but also the political power and money incomes of organised and skilled labour in the motor car industry. Through their abilities to bring economic pressure to bear in the factories and political pressure via the Labour Party, their housing choices were maximised. Both types of power could be mobilised to gain access either to the public or private sector in housing. This is reflected indirectly via the rate of public and private applications to construct housing in the area.

The state also made higher than average numbers of applications for schools and amenities in Cowley and Iffley. Industry and commerce made higher than average numbers of applications for factories and shops. The area therefore illustrates the main changes at the margin over the post-war period in the progressive distribution of new property rights and services. In intention, at least, a disproportionate amount of new property rights was allocated indirectly to manual workers either because of their growing market power or because of their participation in organised political power via the Labour Party.

The intention was probably more progressive than the outcome. The submission of an application and its permission or refusal is not all there is to translating the formal search for property rights into actual development. A great deal of economic struggle and political bargaining intervenes before concrete developments are actually completed on site. The provisions and the objectives of the Development Plan are not as binding as they appear on paper. A number of groups pursue their interests irrespective of the intentions of development planning. The ability of some groups to acquire property rights in this way is illustrated next.

Illustrations of the informal acquisition of property rights

The economic and political struggles and bargains concerning the state development of such things as shopping centres and roads have already been detailed in Chapter 5. As a focus of such struggles the state is placed under more pressures from different quarters than any private group seeking property rights. Not surprisingly since, as it is pulled this way and that, the state develops contradictory aims and objectives often manifested as muddle and inefficiency. Many of its decisions must be taken in the context of this multilateral bargaining position.

Such considerations do not affect private interests who can enter an 'essentially bilateral bargaining situation' when it comes to the acquisition of property rights. Often this bilateral negotiating framework between them and the planning authority is maintained by secrecy. For most of the study period, both planning committee meetings and applications were conducted in secret. This was a critical weapon for the university, commercial and industrial interests when applying for planning permissions.

The approval for St Catherine's College, built on land considered part of a green belt, for example, was acquired almost without notice. In 1960, the Curators of the University Chest submitted an outline application for the new college. Permission was granted subject to the submission of detailed plans and without demur on the subject of the green belt. Full application and permission were submitted and granted in 1961. An entire college was then built in the green belt without much debate at the planning stage.

Even in controversial applications which actually ran counter to principles laid down in the Development Plan, university power could be critical in their success. Thus, although the Plan designated land in St Clement's for university expansion, some colleges preferred to develop in north Oxford. University College was one of the pioneers in this procedure.

Its development, carried out on the site shown in Map 6.1, 25 Staverton Road and numbers 100a, 102 and 104 Woodstock Road, was the first expansion by an Oxford college into the north Oxford Victorian suburb. As such, it provided a precedent for further encroachment by other colleges and departments of the university.

The Development Plan had zoned this part of north Oxford as residential. Prior to Ministerial approval of the Development Plan, local policy had already tried to maintain the residential character of north Oxford. The National Farmers' Union (NFU) had bought 104 Woodstock Road, and in 1952 applied to the

SOURCE   OS Map (1:1250) 5008SE Extract.

MAP 6.1   *Site of University College expansion in north Oxford*

city for a change of use from residential to offices and residential. Permission was refused, a decision which was upheld by the Minister of Housing and Local Government on appeal. Similar refusals were also given to the Diocesan Board of Finance (90 Banbury Road) and A. C. Neilson & Co. (302 Woodstock Road).

The NFU, on losing the appeal, sold 104 Woodstock Road to University College in 1953. Premises were eventually forthcoming for the NFU at 269 Banbury Road, just north of the

Summertown shopping centre. University College converted 104 into four flats in 1953. The rest of the site was acquired by the college in two stages: 25 Staverton Road in 1958, and 100a and 102 Woodstock Road in 1966 (100a was built in 1953).

In June 1967, the City Architect and Planning Officer received letters from two local residents and one of their ward councillors complaining of University College's use of two of the properties on the site as student accommodation (one of which did not have permission), and that it was rumoured new buildings were to be erected on the site.

These letters were the first the local authority had heard of University College's plans for the site, at least on an official basis. Contact was made with the College and an informal meeting was eventually held with representatives of the Planning Department, University College and their architects (Arup Associates) in October 1967.

Several problems were pointed out by the planning officers. The area was zoned as residential on the approved Town Map (1955 and 1967 in Amendment 1); an area in St Clement's had been designated for future university expansion; complaints had already been received from local residents concerning University College's use of two of the houses on the site as student accommodation - one of which was an illegal use; there were likely to be problems of traffic generation following a more intense use of the site. It was suggested that an outline application be submitted for the development of the site.

An application was submitted in December 1967 as an 'outline proposal for redevelopment to provide mixed residential and college use to include rooms for graduates and undergraduates, flats and dwelling houses for fellows, married graduates and staff'. In all, 120 units of accommodation were to be provided in two phases. Accompanying the application was an explanation by University College of the type of accommodation the college required and their reasons for selecting the Woodstock and Staverton Roads site.

The 'housing situation' for students and university members generally was deteriorating by this time. The college authorities had interpreted this to mean that they should provide accommodation for all those who required it, both outside the college as well as in.

Space and, therefore, expansion was limited on or near University College proper. Small-scale schemes were proposed in Merton Street and within the college, but these were not of sufficient size to satisfy the needs generated by growing student numbers. Two sites had been selected for college expansion: the Staverton Road site and the Old Parsonage, St Giles'. The latter would be altered and refurbished, the Staverton Road site would experience the greatest development.

With regard to the area designated for university expansion in St Clement's, University College had decided that it was not wholly suitable. Three main reasons were put forward. The densities envisaged for any development in St Clement's were higher than the college considered suitable for its members, particularly those with families. Even the St Clement's area was limited in size and, given the likely future expansion of the university and colleges, the area of land available would be insufficient for all the colleges' purposes, and University College would therefore be limited in its choices. Also, University College wanted to start work as soon as possible and St Clement's planning future was still undecided, mainly as a result of 'planning blight'.

University College also pointed out that there would not be great problems of traffic generation concerning the city centre from the Staverton Road site, since most graduates gravitated to the science area to the north of the city centre. The north Oxford site would be entirely residential, with collegiate activities remaining in the centre.

In the first instance, only two bodies were consulted on the college's proposals, the city's own consultants - Scott Wilson Kirkpatrick and Partners - who were preparing the report on the central area, and the North Oxford Residents' Association. Neither organisation had any objection in principle to the proposed development, their comments being limited to problems over access and car parking.

The local residents were complaining loudly and often about the development. One of their complaints concerned the lack of public consultation and the council's policy of only contacting the local 'Friends' or 'Association'. So that their voice might be more forceful, they formed the 'Staverton Road Residents' Group'. Sufficient pressure was brought to bear so that the application was referred to full council by Planning Committee in order that the local residents could be consulted.

The main argument against the college's proposals centred around the expansion of the university into a residential area, and the precedent likely to be caused by such a development. Planning Committee and council were satisfied that the proposal would not be detrimental to the area and were prepared to permit the development on the basis that the site was wholly residential, no 'college use' to be carried on. To fulfil this condition, a modified version of the application was submitted.

The local authority had the matter taken out of its hands as a result of the action of one of the local residents. On receipt of his letter asking for information about possible appeal procedures, the Minister for Housing and Local Government decided the application was sufficiently important to warrant a local inquiry, and duly called it in.

The inquiry was held in 1968. The Minister had cited four main aspects of the proposal as meriting inspection. First, its suitability and effects on its surroundings; second, its effect on the amenities enjoyed by the adjoining residents; third, the implications for traffic, safety and disturbance by noise; and fourth, the problem as to whether this was an isolated example of development for college and university residential needs in this part of north Oxford and, if not, whether there were any plans for dealing with future proposals.

The Inspector disagreed with the numerous objectors who had seen the development as forming a precedent for further university expansion in north Oxford. He saw it as an isolated case, and recommended approval subject to detailed plans being approved by the local authority. He said:

> The lack of any overall plans for dealing with future proposals for student accommodation does not justify rejection of this particular scheme, which is of a special kind to meet the special requirements of University College, and there is no evidence that any other college wants to carry out similar development or indeed, any kind of residential development in North Oxford. (Chase, 1968)

Various problems ensued, but these were design problems, mainly concerning the height of the new buildings. The development of the site has been carried out and University College achieved all it set out to do. The objectors achieved very little, the only positive outcome of their activities being a modification of the city's consultation procedures to take more notice of individuals rather than concentrate on local groups of Friends or Associations.

The Inspector's belief that no precedent would be set has proved wrong. Lady Margaret Hall has since had a major development involving a road closure in Benson Place; St Hugh's has expanded its site; St Anne's has developed its site more intensively; Jesus College has built a similar type of development to University College in Woodstock Road; various university departments have spread up the Banbury Road; the 'science triangle' at Keble Road has grown; the university has built a series of graduate flats at high density north of Summertown on Banbury Road.

Commercial and industrial concerns were equally successful in getting the property rights they required irrespective of provisions in the Development Plan and local residents. Marks & Spencer, for example, decided to expand their existing store in Cornmarket Street and Market Street. In 1958, they informed the City Engineer and the City Architect and Planning Officer that they intended to demolish numbers 13-16 Cornmarket Street and 15-19 Market Street and erect a new store.

The ground landlords, Christ Church College, had given their permission for the redevelopment to take place. They did require that at least one set of elevations be changed, but otherwise caused little hindrance to Marks & Spencer. The local authority was mainly concerned over access to the new building and stipulated that loading and unloading should be carried out off Market Street. In order to effect this, Marks & Spencer bought the Crown and Thistle public house, demolished it and used the extra space provided as a loading bay.

Bargaining was also carried out with Milward & Sons. This shoe shop moved from number 17 to a new shop unit constructed in the development next to W. H. Smith at the northern end of Marks & Spencer's premises.

Although the site is in the historic centre of Oxford, no

opposition was forthcoming to the demolition of the buildings. Furthermore, the Royal Fine Art Commission, when consulted about the elevations, only suggested minor modifications.

The negotiations over the redevelopment were kept secret. Both the *Oxford Mail* and the Oxford Preservation Trust asked to see the plans and elevations, but Marks & Spencer were reluctant to allow this, requesting that 'No information regarding the development proposals be given to the Preservation Trust until the approvals of Council and of Christ Church are given, when the drawings will be released to the *Oxford Times* for publication' (M & S to CAPO, 23 May 1960). Thus a major new store was built in Cornmarket without even the serious exercising of aesthetic judgements on the part of the planning authority.

Industrial interests also pursued the acquisition of property rights with little regard for the Development Plan or local residents. In 1955, for example, shortly after agreeing to limit its labour force, Morris Motors decided they required a new body-painting shop. They submitted an application relating to a 'body painting plant building, passenger tunnel and new car park (in principle)'. The site of the proposed paint plant is shown in Map 6.2, the land being used as a car park at that time. The new building was to be 237,600 square feet in area.

The Planning Committee had several reservations about the proposal. Included in these was the possibility of an increase in the number of workers at the plant at a time when the local authority wanted to limit the growth of employment. The old body-painting plant had also resulted in complaints from local residents on account of the noise and smells emitted.

The Board of Trade issued an industrial development certificate in October 1955 for 237,600 square feet for production and ancillary purposes. Morris Motors pointed out that they would be installing a catalytic process to cut down the emission of fumes into the atmosphere and thereby avoid the pollution accompanying the present operation of the old body-painting plant.

Morris Motors supplied 'satisfactory' answers to all the local authority's queries, but admitted that there would have to be a slight increase in the number of men employed in the plant to cover the period during which new operators were

248 *Planning, Production and Consumption in Oxford*

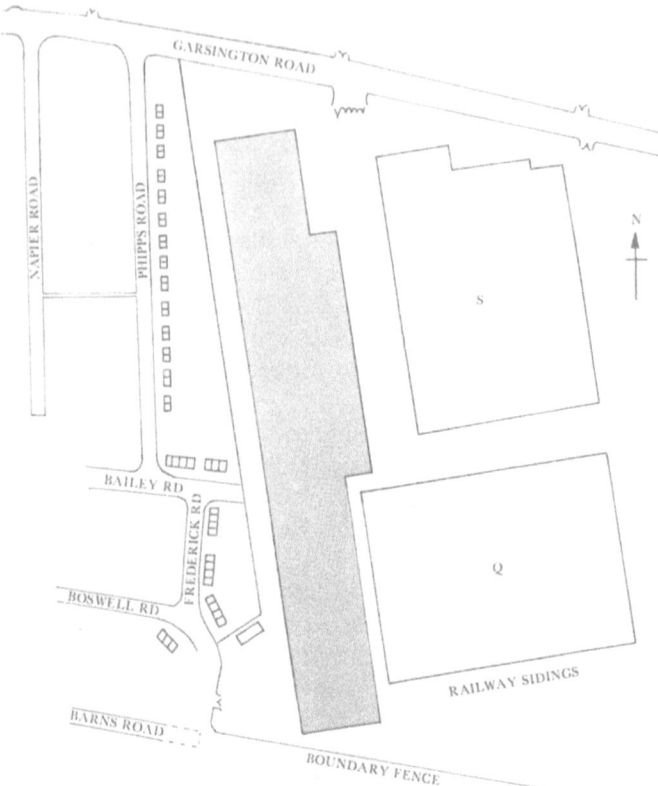

SOURCE Site Plan from application file A5182, April 1956, scale 1:2500.

MAP 6.2 *Morris Motors' body-painting plant*

trained for the new machinery. The Chief Sanitary Inspector was concerned that the catalytic process was inefficient and went to Port Talbot to see a similar piece of equipment in action.

Morris Motors did not wait for full permission before starting work, as was pointed out to the Planning Department by local residents. When the illegality of their actions was brought to the attention of Morris Motors they replied that although they were aware that 'full planning permission will have to be obtained when all details are available, certain preliminary works were put in hand in view of the urgency of the scheme' (MM to CAPO, 20 March 1956).

A full application was submitted in 1956. Planning Committee passed it subject to several conditions. The conditions related to the equipment to be installed - which was to be approved by the local authority; the discontinuation of the existing body-painting lines; the provision of a vehicular tunnel under Garsington Road should vehicle movements across the road exceed 150 vehicles an hour; no permanent increase in the number of workers. On the application form the floorspace to be built was put at 310,165 square feet - a large increase on the original figures and in excess of the Board of Trade's Industrial Development Certificate for 237,600.

Construction took place between 1957 and 1958, production beginning before completion of the building. As soon as production began the residents of Frederick's Road and Phipps Road complained of the noise and smells emanating from the new plant. On inspection it became apparent that Morris Motors had not installed the catalytic equipment they and the local authority had agreed upon. Several meetings were held with representatives of the local authority and Morris Motors to try and work out a compromise solution to the problems of noise and smell pollution without any enforcement action having to be taken.

Morris Motors increased the height of the extraction stacks, the local authority being unable to enforce the use of the special catalytic process equipment upon the firm. It is not known whether the numbers of workers employed for a 'temporary' period on the new plant were cut. Complaints about the noise and smell from the plant have continued up to the present day. Another of the objections voiced by local residents was the complete absence of any public consultation on the siting of the new plant - which is only 150 feet away from the houses in Phipps Road. Morris Motors had achieved all their objectives even with opposition from local residents and the local authority.

Again the common complaint of lack of consultation with local residents, secrecy and disregard of the Development Plan are illustrated. The power of such interests to do more or less as they liked was not confined to the few illustrations given here. Their ability to say one thing in public and do another in private is also illustrated. At the public inquiry into the Development Plan, Smith, the Vice-Chancellor, had said that there was strong support within the university and the Hebdomadal Council for the principle of a green fringe (*Oxford Times*, 4 December 1953, p. 5). Nevertheless, when it suited they built an entire new college in the green belt. In 1957, the university said it would confine future building development to areas scheduled for this purpose in the Development Plan (*Oxford Times*, 19 October 1957, p. 7). In 1968 it was developing in north Oxford. This was also despite complaints by Councillor Oliver Gibbs (Labour) that 'A great many of us feel in this Council that University Development should not mean planning approval for the University to go forward in any direction'. Alderman Fagg (Labour) also complained in the same debate that 'The University keep coming forward with bit after bit and no one knows where they are going' (*Oxford Times*, 7 January 1966, p. 13).

In 1953, both Morris Motors and the Pressed Steel Company agreed to place a limit on the numbers of people they would employ (*Oxford Times*, 13 March 1953, p. 8). Nevertheless, they introduced shift working and built new workshops which greatly increased the numbers of workers they employed there.

The illustrations show, therefore, that powerful interest groups acquire property rights via the development control process without undue modification whether or not they comply closely with the provisions of the Development Plan. These acquisitions were facilitated during the study period by covert bargaining, secrecy and lack of consultation with local residents. The abilities of powerful private interests to pursue their property right requirements single-mindedly is also an advantage when it comes to bargaining with the state which has to conduct simultaneous, multilateral bargaining. While involved in such negotiations it is also difficult for the state to exercise very specific control over development. This means that the planning system exercises rather less control over the acquisition of property rights, particularly of powerful groups, than might formally appear to be the case. Once constructed, the planning system has even less control over its use.

Who got what and where

The mere acquisition of property rights from the planning system does not ensure their translation into actual properties. A great deal of detailed planning, design and construction work is required to convert planning permissions into developments. Out of the estimated total applications in the three wards of Oxford, numbering 9421, 6 per cent were for outline permission only, 7 per cent were refused and 1 per cent were withdrawn. Thus, 14 per cent, 1319 applications, did not acquire property rights. Building regulation files, however, showing completions or starts before 1977, recorded 6168 for the sample. This leaves 1834 unstarted developments three years after the end of the study period. Out of the total sample, therefore, two-thirds were actually constructed and a fifth acquired permission but were not started by 1977.

This fifth was composed exclusively of A type applications, many of which would not have required building regulation permission anyway. Among B type applications the picture was somewhat different. Out of the 1495 applications, 28 per cent were for outline permission, 18 per cent were refused, 4 per cent were withdrawn and 1 per cent were deemed refusals. Thus 51 per cent did not acquire full planning permission. All the remaining 49 per cent or 728 developments were completed or started by 1977. Table 6.9 shows their distribution.

The largest amount of property was acquired by commerce and industry. They built 314 out of the total 728 completed or started applications. The smallest amounts of property went to private individuals and voluntary associations. Between these two extremes, feudal landowners completed 173 developments and the state 140.

In terms of numbers of developments, commerce and industry had the greatest shares of shops, offices, factories and storage. They thus acquired the greatest proportion of new productive floorspaces, as might be expected. The capital and revenue earning values of this type of floorspace is greater than any other. Not only did commerce and industry therefore acquire the greatest proportion of all new developments, but also the largest number of the most valuable new properties.

Feudal landowners, in this instance, were mainly concerned

TABLE 6.9 *Main use by applicant (B type completed or started before 1977)*

Main use	Feudal land-owners (%)	State (%)	Industrial and commercial (%)	Private individuals (%)	Voluntary associations (%)	Total (%)
Housing	17	24	18	96	(20)	27
Retail	2	7	22	1	–	12
Office	2	9	12	1	(4)	8
Industry	1	3	25	–	(4)	11
Storage	1	6	12	–	–	7
Education	2	16	7	1	(36)	8
University	70	1	1	–	–	17
Amenities	1	24	2	–	(12)	6
Other	4	10	1	1	(24)	4
Total files = 100%	173	140	314	76	25	728

$\chi^2\ 32 = 891.06\ p < 0.1$

with university uses. They also acquired a substantial proportion of new residential developments.

In contrast to other organisers, the state built a larger proportion of amenities and educational facilities, as might be expected. It also built a larger than average number of office developments and a substantial, although less than average, proportion of new housing developments.

Private individuals built housing. Voluntary associations completed only twenty-five developments over the entire twenty-one-year period.

As with aspirations for property rights, substantial differences emerged concerning who acquired what property in which territory. Table 6.10 shows that South, the poorer ward, acquired the lowest proportion of housing developments and the highest proportions of shops and offices. Most of the latter were acquired by commerce. The only other active developer in the area was the state. Instead of concentrating on housing, however, the state built mainly public amenities and offices. The latter were for its own use. The main distributions of new property in the poorer ward were therefore to commerce and

TABLE 6.10 *Main use by applicant by ward (B type completed or started before 1977)*

	Applicant					
Main use	Feudal land-owners (%)	State (%)	Industrial and commercial (%)	Private individuals (%)	Voluntary associations (%)	Total (%)
Cowley and Iffley						
Housing	—	33	20	98	—	36
Retail	—	9	16	2	—	11
Office	—	3	7	—	—	5
Industry	—	3	38	—	—	21
Storage	—	4	14	—	—	9
Education	—	23	2	—	—	9
University	—	—	2	—	—	2
Amenities	—	18	1	—	—	6
Other	—	7	—	—	—	1
Total files = 100%	6	94	179	51	11	341
χ^2 32 = 291.51 p < 0.1						
North						
Housing	16	—	26	—	—	23
Retail	3	—	24	—	—	9
Office	3	—	16	—	—	9
Industry	1	—	1	—	—	1
Storage	1	—	1	—	—	1
Education	2	—	24	—	—	11
University	13	—	—	—	—	42
Amenities	—	—	1	—	—	2
Other	1	—	7	—	—	2
Total files = 100%	140	9	70	16	11	246
χ^2 32 = 261.08 p < 0.1						

TABLE 6.10 *(continued)*

Main use	Applicant					
	Feudal land-owners (%)	State (%)	Industrial and commercial (%)	Private individuals (%)	Voluntary associations (%)	Total (%)
South						
Housing	(19)	8	5	–	–	14
Retail	–	5	39	–	–	19
Office	–	14	22	–	–	14
Industry	–	3	12	–	–	6
Storage	–	11	17	–	–	11
Education	–	3	2	–	–	1
University	(63)	–	–	–	–	12
Amenities	(7)	41	3	–	–	14
Other	(11)	15	–	–	–	9
Total files = 100%	27	37	65	9	3	141

χ^2 32 = 216.88 p < 0.1

the state, who built mainly shops and offices for their own use. Distributions to existing residents were minimal.

North, the richer ward, gained mainly university properties and private housing. Both were constructed almost exclusively by commerce, industry and feudal landowners. The former also constructed some shops and offices in the area, together with some educational institutions. A number of these were conversions or changes of use from, for example, large Victorian houses to private language schools. Local residents acquired some private housing.

Cowley and Iffley, the predominantly skilled manual working-class ward, in 1951 acquired mostly industry and housing developments. These were built mainly by commerce, industry, the state and private individuals. The first two concentrated on acquiring factories, shops and storage; the state built mainly council housing, schools and amenities; private individuals built private housing. Local residents therefore gained more

Distribution and Consumption of New Development 255

in the way of public and private housing in this ward than any other.

To summarise Table 6.10, it may be seen that most distributions of actual property developments do not go directly to local residents in any of the wards: most were distributed directly to private organisations. Most of these developments were for their own use and not for subsequent redistribution via the market to private individuals. In contrast, most of the state developments were for use by other individuals and were redistributed either via the queues for council housing, education or amenities, or via the market for commercial floorspaces.

As far as local residents were concerned, the process of planning has had the general effect of distributing new property and facilities in the manual working-class area and regressively redistributing property in the poor area. In terms of numbers of developments, therefore, the fruits of increases in property between 1953 and 1973 were distributed to private homeowners and some manual workers. Growth in the housing and public facility sectors was therefore used to strengthen the existing position of middle-class residents and improve the conditions of working-class groups represented by trade unions and the Labour Party.

In contrast, growth of commercial properties, in particular, distributed developments and profits to private, commercial organisers, and space for new jobs to middle-class service workers. This growth took place at the direct expense of existing semi- and unskilled working-class residents whose houses were demolished.

The growth of new property developments would appear, therefore, to have distributed regressively the largest number of developments to those with most in the first instance. It directly maintained the property rights of middle-class residents and indirectly increased the space available for service employment. It indirectly and progressively redistributed some housing and public facilities to some manual workers. The benefits to the best-off groups, however, were obtained at the direct expense of some of the worst-off residents.

Sometimes these physical distributions took place as a result of 'objective' locational decisions and sometimes they did not. The development of housing and other collective facilities in Cowley and Iffley was probably sensible in the light of the space available there and the location of the motor car works. The development of university facilities and housing in North ward was sometimes against the provisions of the Development Plan but may have saved some parts of St Clement's from demolition. The redevelopment of St Ebbe's had little to do with 'objective' land-use decisions. The commercial development could have taken place elsewhere at, for example, Gloucester Green, the bus station, and the demolition of the housing there was unnecessary, as shown by the subsequent attitudes taken in St Thomas and other similar areas.

Nevertheless, these findings for Oxford are typical of those found in the regions of Britain experiencing economic growth. Thomas (1969) found that the most striking failure of newtown policy was the lack of provision for the least favoured groups and in particular the poor and the aged. Glass (1970) found that in Camden the poor paid more for less housing. They paid three supplementary housing taxes on central area accommodation, on furnished property and on housing for newcomers. In this way they suffered most from existing planning and housing policies. Hall (1972, p. 267) said that 'After twenty-five years of effective town and country planning, nearly half of them under Labour, we find that the main distributive effect was to keep the poor, or a high proportion of them, poor'. In his major analysis of the effects of planning in urban England, he, and others, concluded that:

Those who have paid have been:
1. the aspirant rural or suburban dwellers,
2. those public housing tenants in the great cities, who have been housed in high-density, high-rise developments because of the shortage of building land,
3. lower-income families who live in privately-rented housing in the big cities. (Hall et al., 1973, p. 427)

This pattern is confirmed and substantiated in detail by the findings in Oxford.

Two unresolved questions arise from this work. The first is whether planning is more regressive in conditions of economic decline like those found in, for example, Glasgow and Belfast. The second is how economic growth could be combined with progressive redistribution to the poorest groups. Answers to these questions might be critical for the continued political viability of town planning in its present form in the future.

Returning to the detailed distribution of property in Oxford, numbers of developments are only an approximation of actual amounts of property. In addition, it is necessary to analyse the amounts of floorspace and numbers of housing units together with their value and subsequent effects on the social and economic structure of the city.

New productive floorspaces

Table 6.11 shows the distribution of gross new productive floorspaces by type of applicant by ward. Out of a total of 4,045,200 square feet, industry and commerce got 3,481,100. In other words, 86 per cent of the most valuable property went to private industrial and commercial interests. The only other significant institution to acquire much of this type of property was the state, which got 492,600 square feet or 12 per cent. Now, of course, in a largely private and market economy seeking the generally accepted goal of economic growth, this is not a surprising result. Indeed, any industrial economy with the same goal of economic growth might expect similar quantities of productive floorspaces. Ownership could be different but, state-owned or not, industrial and commercial economies require buildings and a large proportion of all built properties must be of this type.

What is again significant in distributional terms, however, is where these types of property were built with respect to the social characteristics of existing residents. Quite properly, the largest amounts of private industry and offices were built in Cowley and Iffley ward in the existing motor car complexes and new 'industrial' estate. Large amounts of retail floorspace were also built there in the Cowley Centre.

North ward had the smallest amount of new productive floorspace of the three wards. Much of it was for shops in the central area.

TABLE 6.11 *Gross new productive floorspaces by type of applicant by ward (B type completed or started before 1977)*

New floor-space x 000	Type of applicant					
	Feudal land-owners (sq.ft.)	State (sq.ft.)	Industrial and commercial (sq.ft.)	Private individuals (sq.ft.)	Voluntary associations (sq.ft.)	Total (sq.ft.)
Cowley and Iffley						
Industrial	–	152.6	1 653.3	–	1.9	1 807.8
Office	–	11.0	112.7	–	–	123.7
Retail	–	160.3	196.6	0.5	–	357.4
Storage	–	13.1	957.5	–	–	970.6
Sub-total	–	337.0	2 920.1	0.5	1.9	3 259.5
North						
Industrial	2.4	–	0.2	–	–	2.6
Office	17.1	11.2	30.5	2.0	–	60.8
Retail	40.4	–	83.5	–	–	123.9
Storage	5.2	2.2	50.0	–	–	57.4
Sub-total	65.1	13.4	164.2	2.0	–	244.7
South						
Industrial	–	0.2	19.3	–	–	19.5
Office	–	50.1	81.6	–	1.0	132.7
Retail	–	82.9	227.9	–	–	310.8
Storage	–	9.0	68.0	–	1.0	78.0
Sub-total	–	142.2	396.8	–	2.0	541.0
Grand total	65.1	492.6	3 481.1	2.5	3.9	4 045.2

South, on the other hand, got the largest amount of state office building and the largest amount of private shop construction. Some of this was in the existing central area. Some, on the other hand, as has been pointed out already, replaced existing working-class housing. This is the critical area where commercial and state properties have been acquired at the direct expense of existing residents. Their compensation, even when acquired, in terms of money or rehousing, in no way matched the property values created by their expulsion. Furthermore, the creation of commercial centres at Cowley and Westgate provided, particularly in the early years, a direct subsidy to commercial operators because some of them paid less than full market rents while the prices charged to their customers were fixed as though they were incurring full costs.

The first experience of planning and executing a mixed shopping, commercial and residential centre gained by the planning authority was the Cowley Centre. Plans for the Centre were incorporated in the Development Plan, in which land around Hockmore Street and Between Towns Road was designated for compulsory purchase. Under pressure from the Oxford branch of the National Council of Women, the Centre was eventually planned as a pedestrian precinct (*Oxford Times*, 4 December 1953, p. 5). It was designed principally as part of the authority's policy of reducing congestion in the centre of Oxford, partly by a process of decentralisation. It was also to serve as a district centre for the growing population of Cowley, as new council dwellings were constructed at Blackbird Leys and Littlemore.

In costs, execution and effects, Cowley Centre demonstrated a number of characteristics later duplicated at the Westgate. Construction began in the autumn of 1960; the first shop opened in 1962. The capital cost to the authority had been about £2.2million. Its part of the development had been built by the firm of John Laing.

The four main multiple stores, Woolworth's, Smith's, Sainsbury's and later the Oxford and District Co-operative Society, negotiated special and favourable terms for participation in the scheme. These terms included ninety-nine-year building leases at 'giveaway' ground rents. Table 6.12 shows the bargains they struck. Essentially, they acquired the land on which to build their own stores at minimal and unreviewed rents. The local authority bought the land, surrounded them with the necessary infrastructure and buildings of a completed centre and also prevented most of their competitors from entering the field. Similar stores in the same location had to rent ready-built premises on less favourable terms. Fine Fare,

TABLE 6.12 *Multiples' rents and leases in Cowley Centre*

Store	Size (sq. yards)	Lease (years)	Annual rent (£)
Sainsbury	1 133	99	600
Woolworth	746	99	433
W.H. Smith	405	99	266
Co-op	1 361	99	850

for example, acquired 1000 square yards on a sixty-three-year lease at £5500 per annum with reviews at ten and twenty-one years.

The standard shop lease for the Centre was fourteen or twenty-one years, with fixed increases of 6 or 7 per cent every seven years. These reviews have not kept pace with the rise in interest rates paid by the local authority on the loans raised to build the Centre. These have tripled from 5 per cent in 1958/9 to 15 or more per cent at the high point of 1977. This, together with the low rents charged to the multiples, has meant that the Centre has only once shown an operating surplus, as shown in Table 6.13.

Assuming that if they operated anywhere the shops and offices would pay normal rates, the operating deficit of the Cowley Centre represents a direct subsidy to those who live and work there. It was not the local authority's intention to provide such a subsidy when it appointed the London-based firm of Hillier, Parker, May and Rowland as sole letting agents for the scheme. In retrospect, this was a costly mistake which can only be remedied as the fourteen-year rent reviews fall due. It is impossible to put a precise figure on which users got how much subsidy but clearly the multiples with their low ground rents and favourable externality effects must have acquired a large share of it. In contrast, the residents of the council accommodation incorporated in the scheme had to pay higher than average rents. As a result, most of the accommodation had to be let on the open market. Hockmore Tower and Pound House made little contribution to shortening the queue for council housing.

The conversion of the type of development shown in Figure

Distribution and Consumption of New Development 261

TABLE 6.13 *Cowley Centre: expenditure and income*

Year	Capital expenditure (£000)	Debt charges (£000)	Total expenditure (£000)	Rent income (£000)	Rate income (£000)
1958/9	3.4	1.2	1.6	0.5	—
1959/60	42.7	1.9	5.7	0.9	—
1960/1	112.6	4.3	7.5	1.2	—
1961/2	245.1	15.7	20.9	0.6	—
1962/3	349.1	33.8	41.9	14.6	—
1963/4	652.4	60.6	69.3	39.3	16.0
1964/5	530.7	107.9	124.2	86.6	25.0
1965/6	43.1	132.2	150.2	118.2	47.2
1966/7	43.4	142.6	154.3	121.0	53.2
1967/8*	39.1	131.9	137.4	129.3	63.3
1968 9	20.9	121.6	127.6	132.6	65.6
1969/70	42.0	128.2	142.1	135.2	75.7
1970/1	38.0	132.4	145.8	140.8	88.7
1971/2	—	130.4	146.8	145.2	97.9
1972/3	—	139.2	157.9	172.6	97.9
1973/4	—	171.7	183.9	158.6	
Total	2 162.5	1 456.6	1 617.1	1 397.0	

*Cowley Centre passed from the Cowley Centre Committee to the Estates Committee in 1967.
SOURCE Abstracts of the Treasurer's Accounts, 1959-74 (inclusive).

6.1 probably had the effect of reducing some of the congestion in the city centre. This was achieved in the first fourteen years of its existence, at least, at the cost of a substantial direct subsidy to commercial operators in the Cowley complex. No doubt any subsequent increases in rents will be passed on to the community in its role as customers.

The opportunity costs of such a policy might be seen in terms of the willingness of some commercial operators, like Centramic, to build out-of-town shopping centres at no financial cost to the community. Having embarked on a policy of city-centre redevelopment and concentrated district centres, the local authority could not encourage such developments without incurring even greater losses in its own. It is also bound to be subject to pressure from existing local business interests

262 *Planning, Production and Consumption in Oxford*

FIGURE 6.1 *Hockmore Street and Cowley Centre*

who are firmly committed to the concept of a central business district.

This commitment is symbolised by the Westgate Centre, shown in Maps 6.3a and 6.3b. Work started in 1970 and was

Distribution and Consumption of New Development 263

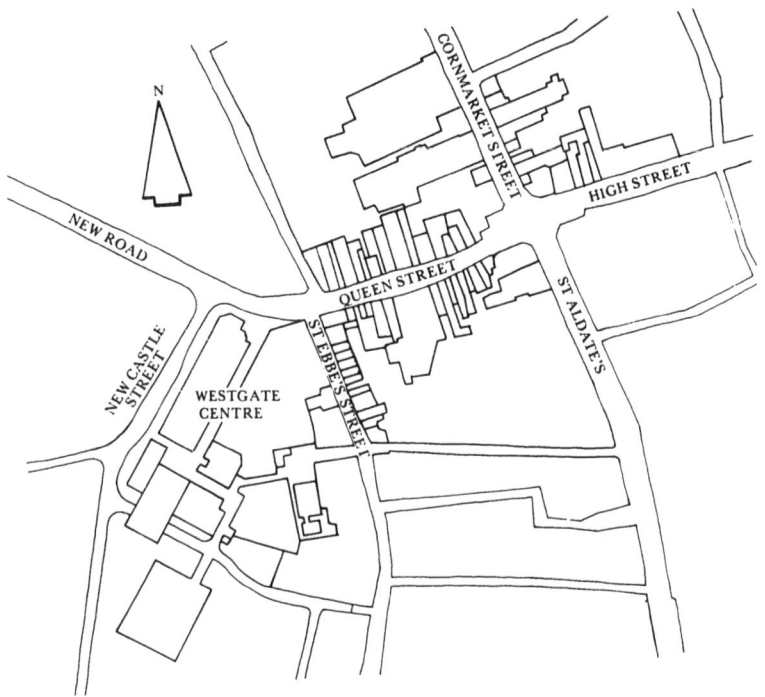

SOURCE   Oxford City Council pamphlet (n.d.).

MAP 6.3a   *Westgate Centre: location*

completed, largely by Taylor Woodrow Construction, in 1972 at a cost of £1.8million. It was designed to extend the central shopping area in a continuous fashion into St Ebbe's and to increase the rateable values there. The formal logic behind its construction was the necessity to maintain Oxford's regional shopping role.

In this development, it was Selfridges who negotiated highly favourable terms both in payments to the local authority before their store was opened and in the design of the centre. They were allowed to use the land acquired for them by the local authority at a peppercorn rent during the construction of their store. The centre was designed in such a way that

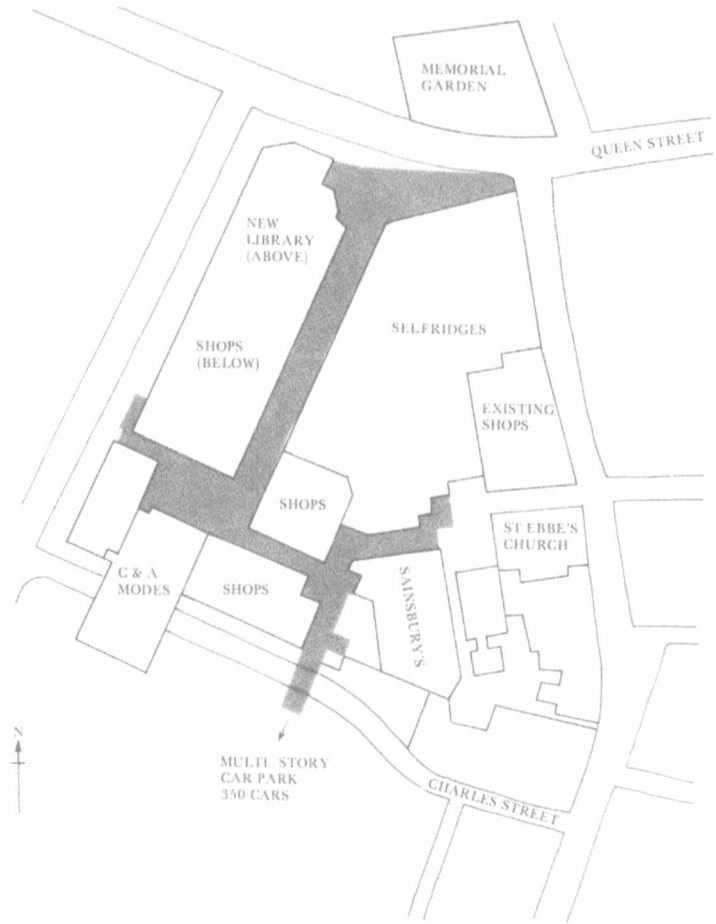

SOURCE   *Oxford Times* (4 October 1968) p. 32.

MAP 6.3b   *Westgate Centre: plan*

Selfridges also had the most floorspace, the best frontages and the site nearest to the existing shopping areas. In contrast, for example, to the bright entrances of Selfridges, the entrances to the rest of the centre are dark and satanic.

Assuming that all the users of Westgate would have to pay rates wherever they operated, Table 6.14 shows that the local authority was again subsidising total operating costs for users

TABLE 6.14 *Westgate Centre: expenditure and income*

Year	Capital expenditure (£000) [cumulative total]	Debt charges (£000)	Total expenditure (£000)	Income (rent + service charge) (£000)	Rate income (£000)
1969/70	122.0	–	–	–	–
1970/1	697.0	31.7	31.7	–	–
1971/2	1 280.0	28.8	28.8	–	–
1972/3	1 518.0	128.3	141.3	46.3	–
1973/4	1 562.0	175.8	221.6	272.8	–
1974/5	1 714.0	195.8	248.3	252.7	375.2
Total	1 714.0	560.4	671.7	571.8	375.2

A further £100,000 in capital expenditure is estimated to be required for Westgate, bringing total capital expenditure to £1,814,000.
SOURCE   Abstract of the Treasurer's Accounts, 1970–5 (inclusive).

of the Centre. In 1975, for example, capital expenditure by the authority had been £1.7 million. Its total annual expenditures were about £248,000, while its total income from rents and service charges was about £253,000. This represented a net surplus of £4372 to be precise. This was a net yield on capital expenditure of £1,714,000 or 0.26 per cent. The difference between this figure and that expected by any institutional investor in the private property market would represent the degree of subsidy by the local authority to the operators using Westgate. Marriott (1967) has shown that yields in the private sector for shops could be substantial.

The magnitude of the distributional effects of the acquisition of new productive floorspaces is greater than simple square footage and current yields. Such properties have capital and income values exceeding those of equivalent square footage of other types of property such as housing, schools, hospitals and so on in similar locations. Table 6.15 attempts to put monetary values on the income and capital values created by new property developments in the three studied wards of Oxford during the period 1953-73. Property valuation is more judgement than science and the figures should therefore be

TABLE 6.15 *Commercial property values* (B type completed or started before 1977)*

Valuation	Type of property			
	Industrial	Office	Retail	Storage
Gross floorspace (sq.ft)	1 829 900	317 200	792 100	1 106 000
Net floorspace (sq.ft)	1 647 000	240 000	713 000	996 000
Yield 1973	10%	6%	7%	11%
1977	12.5%	7.5%	8%	13%
Capitalisation 1973	10 YP	16.6 YP	14.3 YP	9.1 YP
1977	8 YP	13.3 YP	12.5 YP	7.7 YP
Rental per square foot 1973	60p	£1.75	£2.50	50p
Gross develop- 1973 ment values (adjusted)	£9 880 000	£7 379 000	£25 490 000	£3 172 000
1977	£9 882 000	£6 756 000	£35 650 000	£3 835 000

*Where net floorspace x capitalisation x rental = gross development value and capitalisation = 100 ÷ yield.

treated as careful approximations rather than absolutely accurate and firm data. Another reason for treating the figures with caution is that 1973 was an exceptional year for property values and prices. Accordingly, the figures for that year have been adjusted downwards by 10 per cent to provide a more 'average' valuation. The approximate 1977 figures are also given for the sake of comparison and because most of the approvals during the study period had been completed by that time. Only total figures have been used in order to minimise the effects of special or atypical developments.

Taken together, the figures show that by the end of the study period approximately £46 million worth of new productive floorspaces had been created or started. At the time of analysis, 1977, a further £10 million had been added to this total figure as a result of appreciation in property values. This £56 million worth of industrial and commercial property was distributed among 250 different and successful B type applicants. This represents an average distribution of approximately £224,000 worth of property per successful application by 1977. About 100 of these approvals were distributed to organisations or individuals submitting more than one application. Therefore, even within the small group of successful applicants, considerable differences in the distribution of property values arose. A minority acquired substantially more of both than did the 155 applicants who only secured a single development.

Substantial differences also arose between the sectors. The income from shopping spaces was, or should have been, consistently and substantially greater than from a square foot of any other use. This is reflected in the gross development value of the shopping developments.

In 1973 they were worth about £25 million and by 1977 this had risen to approximately £36 million. The yields from such property should have been 7 or 8 per cent. They have never reached these levels in the state-owned shopping centres. Thus, although the state has gained the notional capital values of these properties, the shortfall in yields represents one measure of part of the subsidy being distributed to the private operators of those shops. The other part of the subsidy would be composed of the costs avoided by the private operators as a result of state activities in compulsorily purchasing the land, servicing the sites and constructing the buildings. Savings in land acquisition costs alone would have been considerable. The distribution of this subsidy is all the more remarkable in the sense that the state does not acquire a normal yield even in the most profitable sector of the local property market.

The state also fails, of course, to make a yield on the offices it uses for its own purposes. The gross development value of office developments fell between 1973 and 1977. Even so, nearly £7 million worth of office developments received planning approval during the study period.

Some £10 million worth of gross development values were also created in the industrial sector and roughly £4 million worth of storage space was created. Bearing in mind the small number of organisations acquiring these types of property, each one gained a substantial amount. Pressed Steel, Fisher and Morris Motors, for example, between them gained eighty-one B type approvals for all productive floorspaces combined.

Not only were substantial gross development values dis-

268 *Planning, Production and Consumption in Oxford*

tributed to a relatively small number of organisations and individuals over the period, but also the opportunities for current and future income. The notional annual rental from the retail properties in 1977 was roughly £3 million. For offices, it was about £½ million. Thus, the distribution of the properties alone had considerable potential income effects for those who acquired them.

Housing

Turning from property concerned primarily with economic activity to other categories, the most important of these is housing. In this sector, a similar analysis to that conducted for production may be followed. Accordingly, the numbers and location of new housing can be shown. The activities of the local authority are illustrated. The capital values created and destroyed may be estimated, together with the notional income effects of development. First, an analysis is made of the numbers and location of new accommodation.

Table 6.16 shows the numbers and types of different accommodation units built by different applicants in the three study wards. Applicants are not necessarily the users of these units. In practice, apart from individuals building their own houses, most applicants are not the eventual users. This is in contrast to commercial developments, where a high proportion of applicants are also the eventual users.

Table 6.16 shows that most accommodation was built by the state or commercial building firms. The majority was built in the Cowley and Iffley ward, where the state built mainly terraced houses, flats or maisonettes while commercial builders concentrated mainly on the latter two types of accommodation. This reflects state provision of council housing for manual workers and private construction of accommodation for middle- and higher-income groups.

North, the richer ward, had virtually no council construction and a moderate amount of new private flats and houses. University accommodation has not been included in these figures because it does not constitute private residential dwellings and is excluded in census calculation of private resident populations.

TABLE 6.16 *New accommodation units by type of applicant by ward (B type completed or started by 1977)*

New accommodation units	Type of applicant					
	Feudal landowners	State	Industrial and commercial	Private individuals	Voluntary associations	Total
Cowley and Iffley						
Detached	—	11	31	28	—	70
Semi-detached	—	96	40	2	—	138
Terraced	—	243	41	—	—	284
Flats and maisonettes	—	418	243	9	—	670
Bungalows	—	9	1	18	—	28
Sub-total	—	777	356	57	—	1 190
North						
Detached	1	—	1	8	—	10
Semi-detached	—	—	—	—	—	—
Terraced	—	—	—	—	—	—
Flats and maisonettes	—	1	158	28	50	237
Bungalows	—	—	9	—	—	9
Sub-total	1	1	168	36	50	256
South						
Detached	1	—	—	5	—	6
Semi-detached	—	—	4	—	—	4
Terraced	—	7	—	—	—	7
Flats and maisonettes	—	125	10	2	—	137
Bungalows	1	—	—	—	—	1
Sub-total	2	132	14	7	—	155
Grand total	3	910	538	100	50	1 601

South, the poorest ward, gained a modest amount of new council flats and terraced houses. These, however, did not compensate for the numbers lost by demolition in St Ebbe's.

There, approximately 900 houses were demolished to be replaced by a total of 155 units in the whole of the South ward.

Taken together, the figures show that South acquired the smallest number of new housing units. Cowley and Iffley gained the largest amount of new housing from both the local authority and private enterprise. North, the richest ward, gained more new housing than South, the poorest, although its total was not as large as that for Cowley and Iffley.

The role played by the local authority in housing was a central one. The two reasons for this sprang from its planning function in allocating land in the Development Plan for different uses or changes of use and its executive function in the provision of public housing. In both cases, its performance leaves much to be desired.

The planning of public development in Oxford during the post-war years was characterised by two main factors. The first was a desire to redevelop existing areas comprehensively. This was partly a reflection of the tidiness syndrome both in development and administration. It was also a way of simplifying the complexity involved in redeveloping areas containing mixed uses and communication problems. On paper, it seemed much simpler to sweep all the old uses away and build up a new mixture on the cleared sites. The second characteristic which followed from the difficulties of adopting this technique in practice was delay. The gap between plan and action was usually large and, in some cases, mercifully infinite.

Delays in public development should have been no surprise. In seconding the adoption of the Sharp Report (1948) in council, Iliffe (Conservative), said that 'It will be at least 5000 years before there is the slightest possibility of any of these things being done' (*Oxford Times*, 26 March 1948, p. 8). Some years later, in debating the Donnington Bridge proposal, another councillor, Lower (Labour), characterised the web of planning as 'if you can't do anything right, don't do anything at all' (*Oxford Times*, 19 February 1954, p. 9). Even the local member of parliament, Turner, assured the annual dinner of the Insurance Institute of Oxford 'that none of these [road] schemes will ever take place' (*Oxford Times*, 27 January 1956, p. 10).

In practice, delays were substantial. The first shop opened

in Cowley Centre, for example, seven years after approval of the Centre in the Development Plan, 1955. Westgate Centre took even longer and did not open for business until 1972. The relatively uncontroversial bypasses mooted between the wars were not fully completed until the 1960s. Of the controversial inner relief roads proposed in the 1940s, only a small section running through St Ebbe's had been built by the 1970s. Even in 1969, the future of all homes in Jericho was not to be known for two or three years because the council, despite declaring them suitable subjects for redevelopment in the 1950s, had not surveyed them in detail (*Oxford Times*, 17 January 1969, pp. 21 and 30).

Despite these predicted and increasingly obvious administrative difficulties associated with comprehensive redevelopment, the planning authority remained committed to this technique until the 1970s. Once the principle had been established in the Development Plan, and the cumbersome administrative machinery involving compulsory purchases, public inquiries, rehousing, demolition and the sealing of development contracts had been set in motion, it tended to follow an autonomous bureaucratic logic. In 1957, Councillor Ingram (Labour, later Conservative) tried to persuade the Planning Committee that the redevelopment of St Ebbe's should take place little by little but the Committee asserted that piecemeal development would be a mistake (*Oxford Times*, 27 December 1957, p. 9). Instead, compulsory purchase orders were served on the residents. The same procedure was started for the Cowley Centre and parts of Jericho.

The effect of proposals for comprehensive redevelopment followed by delays was blight. In 1957, Councillor Ingram pointed out that 'It's all very well having development and redevelopment plans, but unless the way is clear for redevelopment work to go ahead, hardship, uncertainty and misery will follow. Today this is the position in St Ebbe's.' He also said 'that because of uncertainty over the future of St Ebbe's, landlords were not carrying out repairs' (*Oxford Times*, 8 February 1957, p. 11).

Among the worst of these landlords was the council itself. In 1958, Councillor Mrs O. Gibbs (Labour) described houses owned by the council in St Ebbe's and St Clement's.

The external painting was in an appalling condition. Most of the houses needed roof repairs and the chimneys repainting, and the guttering, in many cases, was in urgent need of repair. . . . If these properties were owned by a private landlord, he would be unable to raise the rents until the repairs were carried out. (*Oxford Times*, 24 January 1958, p. 11).

The deterioration in properties consequent upon designation for comprehensive development, followed by delays and exacerbated by the council as landlord, began to furnish a retrospective justification for the policy. If an area was not beyond repair before talk of redevelopment, it soon became so afterwards.

The proliferation of proposals for inner relief roads created more blight and decay. Eventually, in 1967, the Planning Committee called a halt to all major building projects in the path of possible relief roads in the city (*Oxford Times*, 5 May 1967, p. 32).

Blight and decay also developed in Jericho. Apart from the uncertainty about its future, the compensation paid on compulsory purchase of properties accelerated the general unwillingness to maintain the area. In 1967, a man who had paid £1700 for a house two years earlier was offered £25 site value by the council. Despite protests, the practice was still in operation in 1969 when a sixty-nine-year-old pensioner was offered £252 for his terraced house which would have been worth £1250 on the open market (*Oxford Times*, 17 January 1969, p. 13). The argument used to justify such compensation was that the sites were not large enough to build housing units which conformed with current building regulations. Meanwhile, the council also allowed its own properties in the area to deteriorate (Philips, *Oxford Times*, 3 May 1968, p. 15). In the event, however, Jericho survived in modified form. It owed its survival partly to delays which allowed residents to learn the lessons of St Ebbe's and partly because there was no thrust to establish commercial uses in the area.

The bulldozers ploughed through St Ebbe's. Luckily, what they destroyed was documented by Mogey (1956) in a classic comparison of life in a traditional working-class community

TABLE 6.17 *Length of residence in St Ebbe's since marriage*

Years	Percentage of total
0-4	21
5-9	10
10-14	33
20 and over	36
Total	100

SOURCE J.M. Mogey, *Family and Neighbourhood: two studies in Oxford* (Oxford University Press, 1956).

with that found in a new housing estate. The picture is one of a long-established community with only 21 per cent of the population having lived there for less than four years after marriage. Table 6.17 also shows that 36 per cent of the population had lived in the area for more than twenty years after marriage. Many of the 915 houses were of the type shown in Figures 6.2 and 6.3. The local economy was viable and varied as shown in Table 6.18. Many kinds of atypical and essential local services could be found down one little street or another in St Ebbe's.

Roaming the streets there was to discover continual surprises of sight and smell. Small alleyways, tributaries of the Thames, fascinating workshops and public houses with compelling unsavoury reputations were surrounded by neat or decrepit terraced housing; around each corner a new surprise awaited. It was to be replaced by the mostly public developments shown in Map 6.4.

Although some of the buildings remain unbuilt in 1977, the pattern has been established. North of Thames Street, car parks, shops, offices and the College of Further Education have replaced the old terraced houses. South of Thames Street, more car parks and some maisonettes may be seen.

Altogether some 900 houses were destroyed in St Ebbe's. The council built seventy terraced houses and 125 flats or maisonettes in the whole of South ward between 1953 and 1977. This represents a net loss of about 700 houses in St Ebbe's as a direct result of comprehensive redevelopment.

274 *Planning, Production and Consumption in Oxford*

1959

SOURCE   *Oxford Mail* and *Times*.

1973

SOURCE   Peacock.   FIGURE 6.2 *Friars Wharf*

Distribution and Consumption of New Development 275

1952

SOURCE   Sharp.

1976

SOURCE   Oxford City.

FIGURE 6.3 *Gas Street*

276 *Planning, Production and Consumption in Oxford*

TABLE 6.18 *Industries and shops in St Ebbe's*

Mainly neighbourhood shops		Mainly neighbourhood services		Other shops		Industrial buildings	
General stores	14	Pawnbrokers, second-hand clothes, furniture, junk	9	Wholesale agents	4	Boat-building	3
Public houses	16			Wireless	2	Cabinet-making	3
Cafes, fish and chips, hot suppers	7			Draper	2	Brewery	2
		Boot repairs	3	Jewellery	2	Dental repairs	1
Greengrocers	3	Hairdressers	3	Sports dealer	1	Power works	1
Butchers	2	Undertakers	3			Laundry	1
Dairy	1	Plumber and decorator	2	Motor repairs	1	Mineral waters	1
Confectioner	1	Total	20	Total	12		
Total	44					Motor engineers	1
						Printing	1
						Shirt-making	1
						Sign-writing	1
						Stone-carving	1
						Wheelwright	1
						Woodworking	1
						Total	19

SOURCE J. M. Mogey, *Family and Neighbourhood: two studies in Oxford* (Oxford U.P., 1956, p. 9).

Altogether, Table 6.19 shows that South, the poorest ward, lost an ignominious total of 681 private dwellings between 1951 and 1971 despite council and some private rebuilding in the area. The population living in private households also declined by 3682 over the period.

Distribution and Consumption of New Development 277

1 Fire Station	16 Shop Etc.	31 Chapels	46 Residence Etc.
2 Office	17 Shop	32 Hall	47 Residence
3 Commerce	18 Shop Etc.	33 Law Court	48 Mixed
4 Car Park	19 Commerce	34 Law Court	49 Mixed
5 Shop Etc.	20 College of Further Education	35 Office Etc.	50 Telephone Exchange
6 Shop Etc.	21 College of Further Education	36 Office Etc.	51 Telephone Exchange
7 Office	22 College of Further Education	37 Office Etc.	52 Residence Etc.
8 Club	23 Office	38 Road	53 Open
9 Residence Shop Etc.	24 Surface Car Park	39 Commerce	54 Hotel
10 Shop	25 M/S Car Park Shop	40 Open	55 Road
11 Shop Etc.	26 Market	41 Open	56 Residence
12 Office	27 Office Etc.	42 Open	57 Residence
13 Shop Library Etc.	28 Club	43 Road Reserve	58 Road
14 Shop Etc.	29 Office Etc.	44 Road Reserve	59 Lower School
15 Hall	30 Office Etc.	45 Recreation	60 Middle School

SOURCE Oxford City Central Area Redevelopment: Second Phase 1970–1980 (1970) p. 6.

MAP 6.4 *St Ebbe's redevelopment*

TABLE 6.19 *Private dwellings and population in private households*

Year	Area			
	Cowley and Iffley	North ward	South ward	Oxford
1951 population	23 564	6 894	8 716	91 629
dwellings	6 369	1 975	2 437	25 734
1961 population	26 337	6 873	6 531	94 005
dwellings	7 758	2 191	2 100	29 172
1971 population	22 710	6 079	5 034	95 425

SOURCE   Census 1951, 1961, 1971.

In contrast, North, the richest ward, gained 495 private dwellings. Its population living in private households also declined slightly. This ward had the best housing conditions of the three chosen for study at the beginning of the period and these were largely maintained, as shown in Figure 6.4.

Cowley and Iffley gained 1542 dwellings. Just over half of these were council accommodation. This again illustrates the main redistributive action of post-war planning and housebuilding, which was to allocate more housing of good basic quality to organised labour via the public sector than had previously been the case. This, together with a slight drop in population in the ward, reduced occupancy rates and improved the basic housing stock for residents.

These figures may be summarised. They show first a significant loss of housing and population in the poorest ward. Second, they indicate a redistribution of basic housing to organised labour in the disproportionately skilled manual ward. Third, they illustrate the maintenance and slight improvement of the best housing conditions in the richest ward. This again confirms the general picture of the maintenance of the property rights enjoyed by better-off residents, some redistribution to organised labour and the imposition of regressive costs on poorer members of the community.

The capital values created by new housing developments over the study period are estimated in Table 6.20. There the

Distribution and Consumption of New Development 279

SOURCE   Sharp (1948).

SOURCE   Sharp (1948).

FIGURE 6.4   *The university and north Oxford*

mean selling prices of different types of property in Oxford during 1964/75 are multiplied by the numbers constructed in the three study wards. The values of public housing are therefore calculated at prevailing market prices. Again the caveat should be observed that valuation is judgement and not science so the figures should be treated as careful estimates and not absolute values.

Table 6.20 shows, however, that according to 1974/5 prices, about £19 million worth of housing was constructed in the wards studied by 1977. This compares with approximately £46 million worth of new productive floorspaces at adjusted 1973 prices. In other words, total capital values created for production were more than twice those of accommodation. This illustrates the point that while economic growth can bring general benefits to the community and improvements in the conditions of people at successively lower levels in the social structure, this is not inconsistent with the greatest absolute and proportionate benefits still accruing to the organisers of production. The magnitude and proportion of these benefits may be decreased below what they might have been as a result of political action. Nevertheless, they remain substantial and disproportionate.

The activities of the local authority as the single largest constructor of accommodation in the study wards is reflected

TABLE 6.20 *Residential property values (B type completed or started before 1977)*

	Detached (£)	Semi-detached (£)	Terraced (£)	Flats and maisonettes (£)	Bungalows (£)
Jan.1974– June 1975	20 117	11 710	10 942	11 376	14 484
Numbers of units	86	142	291	1 044	38
Estimated value	1 730 062	1 662 820	3 184 122	11 876 544	550 892

SOURCE   P. J. Byrne and D. H. Mackmin, *The Residential Market in Oxfordshire and Parts of Berkshire* (University of Reading, 1976).

in the value of flats, maisonettes and, to a lesser extent, terraced houses. Most of this type of housing was built by the state. Out of a total of 1335 such units, the authority built 60 per cent of them. From a total of 1601 of all types, it constructed 57 per cent. If these figures were reflected in the allocation of property values to different social classes, then council tenants gained the use of about £11 million worth of housing while those in the private sector gained the ownership of about £8 million worth of accommodation. Insofar as there are strong relationships between housing tenure and social classes, then this represents a mildly progressive redistribution of the use of housing capital. On the other hand, using market prices to value council houses over-values them to the extent that within the housing sector the distribution of housing capital values was probably rather less progressive. In addition, the controlling rights of council tenants are less than those of property owners.

Public goods and services

Production and accommodation are not the only goods and services influenced by town planning. Table 6.9 showed that of all applications completed or started before 1977, 8 per cent were for educational services other than the university, 6 per cent were for amenities and 4 per cent were for other generally impure public goods. Production and accommodation were therefore the main functions of new properties, but just under a fifth were for other uses.

Most of these other uses were impure public goods like schools, community centres and open spaces provided by the state. They consisted essentially of goods and services for which no general market exists either because they could not be provided at a price everybody could afford or because their use would be very difficult to assess and charge for. Roads and parks would be prime examples of such facilities.

It is virtually impossible to assess the true capital value or income effects of such facilities. In theory, they are provided equally for everybody. Table 6.10, however, shows that they were provided unequally as between territories during the study period. The state, for example, provided more educational developments and amenities in Cowley and Iffley than it did in North, and more education but fewer amenities than it did in South. To some extent this reflected their satisfactory provision in North at the start of the period, the improved distribution to manual workers in Cowley and Iffley during the period, and the enforced population decline in South.

The quality of such amenities also varies by territory, but no objective data are available on, say, the quality of parks or schools. In general, their physical distribution over the study period tended to vary in the same direction as that for housing. In other words, the main reduction in their regressive distribution over the twenty-one years was to employed manual labour.

Conclusions

While the Development Plan system is primarily concerned with the allocation of land for the production of buildings, the development control process is primarily involved with the state regulation of the translation of those intentions into physical goods for consumption. In the wards studied in Oxford, 62 per cent of developments were primarily for individual or collective consumption. These included housing, education and amenities. The fairly substantial remainder were primarily associated with production, including offices, factories, storage and retail outlets.

The local state produced a mixture of developments for both collective consumption and private production. Its main concern was with the former, however, and three-quarters of all local authority developments consisted of housing, education and amenities. In contrast, nearly three-quarters of all industrial and commerical developments were to facilitate private production. The respective balances of these developments merely confirm the view that the state, in advanced industrial societies, tends to produce goods and services for consumption which are generally not forthcoming from the market at a price that most people can afford. In contrast, the private sector restricts its developments to those that are profitable.

The more important characteristic illustrated by development control is the level of corporate integration between private organisations and the state. In the case of the development of commercial precincts the level of integration was high. Commercial interests were insinuated into those of the local planning authority partly on the false premise that the relationships between the costs and rate revenue to the authority would be profitable. Taken together and compared with 'normal' market rates of return on such investments, this has not been the case. The distributional consequences of these circumstances have been regressive in that commercial organisations have received an effective subsidy, and the largest among them have received proportionately greater subsidies than the smaller concerns.

Even where the levels of corporate integration of objectives and personnel between the local planning authority and private organisations have not been high, the latter have been known to proceed with developments in the face of provisions contained in the Development Plan. Examples of this process have been given above. In general they show the larger organisations' freedom of manoeuvre despite formal claims by the state to regulate such things as land uses and developments.

The levels of corporate power and participation in the local planning authority's regulation of land and buildings is illustrated by the distribution of gains and losses accruing to different groups and organisations as a result of the authority's plans and decisions. The most noticeable characteristic of the distribution of property in Oxford was the lack of control by local residents of all social classes over the locational requirements of organisations when their interests were in conflict. Within these two main categories it was the weakest who had the least control and the most powerful who usually got what they wanted. The same phenomenon could be noticed within sectors within social classes.

St. Ebbe's was the outstanding example of both these phenomena. There the demands for central business district growth from commercial interests were brought into conflict with the housing requirements of working-class residents in the settled community of St Ebbe's, partly as a result of 'technical' decisions made in the name of planning. With the eventual removal of the gasworks and the possibility of providing commercial development in and around Gloucester Green there was no need for the destruction of St Ebbe's. Even with the implementation of the inner relief road plans of the Second Amendment, there was no need to destroy St Ebbe's on the grounds of access to the central buiness district. In view of the current rehabilitation of similar areas like Jericho and Osney Town, there was no need to demolish St Ebbe's on the grounds of housing conditions. Nevertheless, commercial interests were furthered and local residents were removed.

Within sectors it was the major commercial interests who gained more than their less powerful rivals, and organised middle-class groups who saved three old houses while poor, lower-class tenants received no compensation at all. Within the commercial sector, Selfridges acquired the best site in Westgate at less cost than it would have had to pay to buy and build on it in the open market. Lesser shops pay relatively higher costs. Besides this, the subsidy paid to the Centre in the form of normal market yields on investment foregone is greater for the larger stores than it is for the smaller shops.

Similarly, among local residents of St Ebbe's the poorest, who were normally private tenants, lost their accommodation without any compensatory gains. In contrast, a local architect and eventually the Oxford Preservation Trust managed to prevent the compulsory purchase and demolition of three houses in Charles Street. In both cases the most powerful acquired more property at relatively less cost than the least powerful. The local authority was an active agent in this process and did not make adequate efforts to explore the alternative ways of achieving roughly similar objectives.

In situations of comprehensive redevelopment like St Ebbe's, where the local authority acts as the agent of commercial interests and subsidises their activities by its powers of compulsory purchase, the provision of infrastructure, building and non-market rents, residents may have been better off under a free market system. At the very least, some owner-occupiers would have received substantially more for their properties as they have done in other parts of the city. Commercial operators would also have had to pay the full costs of their investments as do other stores outside the local authority developments.

To summarise, the distribution of output gains and losses via development control demonstrates the degrees of power held by a plurocracy of organisations and social groups in Oxford. The distribution of power is both structured and dynamic. The structure is complex: it is neither completely plural nor dominated by a single hegemonic class. It is, rather, a moving balance of forces between up to six social groups, although any single issue does not usually involve any more than half of them. Thus, while the planning of a city as a whole will involve landowners, state bureaucrats, industrialists, commercial interests, middle-class groups and labour, some issues will be of interest to perhaps only one of them while others will involve several. Where there is no clash of interests, some groups can appear relatively independent of the others. Where interests clash, various levels of conflict will arise and sometimes this will be institutionalised via the state. In both these political circumstances and in the market place, the most powerful groups will acquire more than the less powerful. The degree of difference will depend on the relative power of contending parties. As poor groups have little or no power, they normally acquire the least property or are brushed aside most easily.

Within these general structural parameters, some alternative courses of action are open to different social groups or individuals. It is not a totally determining or determined system. Viable alternatives are, however, limited and depend, among other things, on current ideologies or organising abilities. One of the most significant changes of this type during the study period was the change in attitudes on the part of local residents towards town planning. There was a general increase in the numbers of organised residents' associations and local community action. As the nature of power and planning was revealed to them so residents sought to develop their own local power bases by organising themselves and engaging in direct community action. In this way the power of individual consumers of planning was changed as increased resident power was added to the prevailing balance of forces.

The rise of resident power was reflected in central state legislation on participation in planning and greater openness and consultation at the local level. At first, much of this power was directed towards negative objectives and it remains to be seen whether it is sufficient to gain more positive results.

286 Planning, Production and Consumption in Oxford

Within the group of residents, greatest power is exercised by middle-class groups and least by the poor. This leaves unresolved the growing problem of all industrial societies concerning how those who are neither directly nor indirectly engaged in production can bring sufficient power to bear on the system of exchange to satisfy their material needs. It is also not possible in this study to give an example of the perceived needs of production being overridden by the perceived interests of consumers. The latter have increased their abilities to prevent corporate decisions destroying their homes. They have not yet demonstrated a positive ability to go much further than this.

Part V

Summary of Data and Relationships to Theory

Chapter 7

Summary and Conclusions

Introduction

This final chapter summarises the findings of the empirical analyses in Oxford and seeks to relate them to the more general theoretical propositions outlined in Parts I and II. To this end the historical, political, legislative and administrative context of planning in Oxford is reviewed briefly. The politics of development planning are outlined.

Next, the significance of these findings in terms of the theoretical propositions outlined earlier is assessed. The importance of power in determining favourable distributions is affirmed. The difficulties of conducting a convincing class analysis of these outcomes is also reiterated. Finally, the relevance of these findings for locating and interpreting the role of the state is discussed.

The general conclusions are reached that setting the rules of control at national and local levels are important ways in which powerful organisations and groups seek to gain distributional advantages in, for example, land uses and properties. The setting of these rules is seldom, if ever, the sole preserve of one social class or even a part of it. It is, instead, a matter of compromises effected between a limited number of powerful organisations.

The characteristics of large organisations are therefore important determinants of both the structure of power and the distribution of the outcomes of action. Normally, the more powerful organisations acquire more from the compromises included in laws and policies than the less powerful. This was the case in the study of land uses in Oxford.

Context

The analysis of Oxford City District Council, its committees, the structure of the local planning department, the logic employed to justify the content of its Development Plan and its development control procedures shows a complex and changing system. It is not a system which is or could be a particularly effective agency of class domination as some authors argue.

Instead, the planning system revealed in Oxford looks more like a relatively well-intentioned though imperfect and sometimes muddled attempt to regulate the distribution of land uses and property rights. Within the local state itself, this attempt has been based on architectural ideologies, pragmatism and a generally conservative form of administration.

This system was, however, established as a result of political decisions taken by central government and is also subject to political pressures at the local level. The whole system should therefore be seen in its political context. This context includes organised national political action and both formal and informal local pressures. The combinations of these different pressures make the local planning authority a complex focus of politics, power and control.

The main instruments used for exercising this control over land uses and property rights during the post-war period were development planning and control. Both were subject to influences and manipulation by organised power groups outside the local planning authority itself. Often these organisations acquired what they wanted but sometimes they did not. In the latter case, this could be because either there was important opposition to what one organisation wanted or because the local planning authority took a relatively autonomous view based on the value judgements of its senior members or some technical and professional code.

For most of the main study period, 1953-73, the Conservative Party held the largest single number of seats in Oxford City Council.

The balance between themselves and the Labour Party was, however, sometimes held by members elected from the university and the Liberal Party. In some senses, therefore, the local council, like the local parliamentary seat, was subject to changes in political composition. Like the local parliamentary candidate, some ward councillors held marginal seats. This type of possibility for political change was an important contextual factor in local politics because it probably made the council more sensitive to political pressures than councils permanently dominated by one or other of the main parties. This should be borne in mind when interpreting the range and distribution of the often contradictory and changing planning outcomes.

Internally, the political and administrative context of the study, as represented by the structure of the council, was characterised by declining numbers of committees and increasing numbers of administrative officers. While the numbers of elected council members remained constant throughout the study, the numbers of committees on which they sat to effect political control over departments was reduced by over a half. The emphasis in these reductions was on co-ordination and efficiency.

In contrast, the numbers employed within departments more than doubled during the study period. As the number of departments remained roughly constant, this represented a substantial increase in the size of individual departments. This trend represented an increase in the importance of the characteristics of large, hierarchically structured organisations as a feature of local government in Oxford.

The most salient feature of this trend, in terms of local power, was shifts in its location during the period of study. As far as it is possible to gauge such things, the nature of these changes can be summarised as movement towards the incorporation of major private organisations into local planning authority decision-making and the development of general and neighbourhood pressure groups seeking to exert power over the decisions in conditions characterised by the rise of corporations. Political control of the administrative apparatus of the local state therefore represented a changing context for conflicts, for example over land uses, during the post-war period.

This changing context was also represented at national

and local levels by changing legislation and development plans. At the national level there were very few years during the period studied which were not marked by some piece of legislation either directly or indirectly related to town and country planning. Throughout the period, political decisions were being taken which set up or dismantled, modified or rethought the legislative requirements or permissions concerning land uses and property rights. Thus, national political conflicts were translated into changing legislative and financial contexts for the working out of local pressures for the acquisition of favourable land uses.

The choice of relatively inflexible development plans to effect control of land uses at the local level meant that some of the central and many of the local predispositions for land uses were fixed and embodied in a plan produced in one era which was supposed to be operated in subsequent eras. In Oxford this resulted in a development plan embodying many of the value judgements and pragmatic responses of architect-planners concerned with land uses. This plan proved unsatisfactory in its outcomes for some groups and highly beneficial to others. On the whole, it proved unsatisfactory for some local residents and beneficial for some landowners, commercial and industrial organisations and some beneficiaries of local authority activities. After some of these sorts of outcomes had been experienced by local residents, pressures built up to modify the plan.

The plan was also subject to change through the continuing process of development control. This was essentially the activity which operated in eras subsequent to the production of the plan and effectively produced modifications on a daily, fragmented and individual basis. It was therefore an important process both in implementing the plan by controlling development in line with its provisions and in permitting individual changes in these provisions. It was also an important process in terms of the leeway afforded to officers to influence the nature and content of planning decisions. Development control officers could acquire a degree of independence in the recommendations they offered to the Planning Committee and therefore to council members.

In general, the political and administrative context represented by local state activity in the planning and control of land uses could be described as one of change. Central political decisions and legislation changed throughout the study period. The political composition of the council was also subject to change and marginality; its committee and departmental structure was altered. The Development Plan was formally amended twice but was continually modified by local pressure and development control decisions. The structure of power in planning did not remain the same throughout the decades studied.

There were limits to the degree of this change, but these limits were never clearly defined. They were supposed to be embodied in the Development Plan: this itself was changed and modified. They were also supposed to be embodied in the formal legislation, structure and procedures of the state: all these changed over time. Some could argue that these changes were not fast enough or sufficient to bring about as much change as they would require. There is a degree of truth in this, but it is not an absolute truth for considerable change did take place over the twenty-odd years studied and some of these changes brought improvements in the living conditions of those most in need. While the limits to change are not defined, it is possible in such a political system to organise and push towards them provided that adequate political strategies are devised.

Development planning

Within the changing context of central and local politics, power over development planning was exercised in different ways at different times by a limited number of different groups. The groups who exercised most power over development planning were those represented by formal organisations. Generally speaking, in order to exercise significant power over planning objectives, the main prerequisite was permanent, formal organisation together with command over resources and some incorporation into the decision-making processes of either local and/or central government. The main gains flowing from planning objectives consistently went to groups of this nature. Groups without these characteristics were not able to exert much influence over planning objectives and the gains accruing from them. Groups with none of these played little part in setting the objectives of development planning and sometimes suffered material and uncompensated losses as a result. In this respect, the study tends to confirm the hypothesis that the distribution of the outcomes of, for example, town and country planning is a strong indicator of the relative power of different organisations and groups.

In the case of Oxford, these distributions and therefore power were not equal at the time of the production of the Development Plan. Ancient landowners, industrial and commercial organisations and the state itself all owned more land and properties than other groups and therefore had potentially more power over land-use objectives than any other groups in the city. The main factors influencing changes in this structure were the election of a reforming Labour Government, the rise of an organised local Labour Party and the development of local pressure groups.

Frequently, those with the most power over Development Plan objectives were not actually residents in the territories in which they wished to acquire land uses and property rights. In this respect, some non-residents exercised more power over Development Plan objectives in particular areas than did the residents themselves. In some cases this meant that the objectives set did not serve the interests of local people but rather those of external organisations.

One of the critical indicators of the relative power of local residents was their ability, or lack of it, to veto proposals made for their areas by external bodies. In general, those residents with the most and highest-value properties were better able to resist such proposals than those with little rights over properties. This was not always the case, particularly where some phenomenon, like the Cutteslowe Walls, clearly infringed some general ideological principle such as equality or where residents could point to plainly disadvantageous results in other areas.

In practice, the cheapest way for external organisations to encroach into new territories was to exert their influence over the local state in order to formalise such encroachments in the Development Plan. Once this was achieved, the local state could enforce its powers of compulsory purchase and also provide the necessary infrastructure and buildings. This meant that territories like St Ebbe's could be taken over at much less cost both to private enterprise and the state than if a free market had been allowed to continue. In this way, the combined power of private organisations and the state could be employed to displace residents without having to pay even the levels of compensation that a free market in land and buildings would have required. This discrepancy was increased by the property blight which followed such proposals.

Many residents found the connections between these processes opaque or downright unintelligible. Unorganised groups, particularly the poorer working class, seldom understood the relationships between power and development planning. Only after the results of these relationships could be seen in one area did they begin to comprehend what might happen in others. Even so, organised labour via its trade unions and often the local Labour Party itself seldom attempted to mobilise effective political pressure on the general objectives of the Development Plan.

Not only were the larger organisations more effective at insinuating positively favourable objectives into the Development Plan, but also they were the most effective at vetoing or circumventing proposals which might have harmed their interests. Thus, while many of the plan's objectives were aimed at containing economic and population growth in the city, Oxford became the fourth largest employment centre in the south-east and the population of the county rose by roughly one-fifth per decade during the study period. This indicates continued economic expansion despite the restrictive provisions of the Development Plan.

The large organisations were also able to veto effectively other proposals which they regarded as disadvantageous to themselves. The university prevented the building of an inner relief road through Christ Church Meadow; the Cowley factories resisted being moved to another city.

In contrast, groups without permanent organisations, especially poorer, working-class groups, were often unable to veto or avoid the objectives of the plan. The restrictions on land availability imposed by the green belt, height restrictions and conservation increased the pressure for commercial expansion into areas of working-class housing. At first this pressure was not resisted. It resulted, however, in a declining amount of cheaper accommodation and, consequently, overcrowding. Shortages of accommodation and land led the state to take allotment land for housing purposes. Taken together, these represented incursions into some working-class interests which were not effectively resisted owing to a lack of a full appreciation of the connections between these various policies and lack of adequate power to resist them.

Again, like the local political and administrative context itself, these general characteristics were subject to exceptions and change. Some attempts by the large organisations to set Development Plan objectives were not successful. The gasworks, for example, was eventually persuaded to move, albeit too late for St Ebbe's and North Sea gas. Some of the more speculative expansions and developments required by landowners, commercial and industrial organisations, which were designed to test the limits of what might be permitted, were not included in Development Plans.

During the period of study, some areas of predominantly working-class housing which had been scheduled for redevelopment, such as Jericho, were reprieved. Plans for local authority housing and traffic management were changed. Many such changes were the outcome of changing balances of political forces at central and local levels. These were often influenced by the changing historical experiences of different groups and organisations.

The political history of development planning in Oxford since the Second World War could therefore be characterised as a moving balance of political forces within a context that was itself changing. In this relatively fluid set of conditions, planning objectives were seldom set solely as a result of the rational pursuit of private interests by dominant organisations. Although powerful organisations had a high probability of securing policy compromises which were predominantly in their favour, these policies were nonetheless compromises containing some elements of other groups' interests. The large organisations were also subject to occasional failures in their attempts to formalise their objectives on such political instruments as the Development Plan. In some respects, other groups became more adept at vetoing incursions into their territories as time went by and they gained political experience. In the 1970s, some of these local pressure groups have also been attempting to incorporate their own planning objectives into formal local authority policies. All this indicates slowly changing (but not unidirectional) balances of power at least over planning objectives during the post-war era.

Development control

Before the objectives of public and private groups and organisations can be translated into actual development, most of them have to pass through the process of development control. This process therefore provides a channel through which most plans must pass before land and property rights for new developments are confirmed. It therefore provides a relatively visible source of data showing the required and permitted new outcomes of physical developments in both town and country. Monitoring the development control process and the new developments which take place after its decisions is one way of measuring the immediate real outcomes of the political and administrative control of land uses and property rights.

These outcomes were not distributed equally between different groups and organisations in Oxford. The main differences occurred between different groups and organisations in different locations and, more surprisingly, between similar groups in different sectors. Thus, while larger organisations generally acquired more of the most valuable properties in working-class residential areas, there were important differences between organisations and their acquisition of commerical developments and between members of the working classes and their acquisition of local authority housing.

In theory, these differences in distribution to different groups and organisations should have been entrained by the formal provisions of the Development Plan. In practice, a further indication of relative power was the ability of some organisations to circumvent these provisions. The use of power to secure favourable inclusions in the objectives of the plan was not the only way in which some organisations secured actual land uses and property rights. Some colleges, commercial and industrial organisations acquired uses of properties which did not entirely conform either with the provisions of Development Plans or with strict development control conditions.

The groups who acquired most over the study period were commercial and industrial organisations. They gained the largest quantities of the most valuable types of property. Sometimes they also acquired these properties with the assistance of, and effective subsidies from, the local state.

The local authority itself was the next most successful organisation in acquiring property. Much more of this development was then passed on to other users than was transferred, at market prices, by commercial and industrial organisations. Local authority property transferred in this way included such impure public goods as housing and schools. On the other hand, various parts of the local state also retained properties, especially offices, for their own uses, particularly in the central area.

A third group also acquired considerable new property during the study period. Ancient landowners, particularly some of the colleges, actually completed more individual development schemes than the local state. While a majority of these were for educational purposes, an important minority consisted of commercial development and housing.

Taken together, feudal landowners, the state, commercial and industrial organisations completed the majority of all significant developments. The eventual users of these properties were not necessarily those who were responsible for their construction. About one fifth of those built by commercial and industrial organisations, a third of those commissioned by feudal landowners and 90 per cent of state developments were eventually used by other groups. Sometimes this simply meant transferring use between members of these groups. In the case of the state, however, a large proportion of the properties it constructed was used by groups such as local authority housing tenants and schoolchildren.

Private individuals were responsible for one-seventh of all B type developments. Most of these were housing for their own use.

Summary and Conclusions 299

Private or public authority housing, schools and other amenities were the main gains made in terms of direct use by middle- and working-class residents. They also acquired some benefits in terms of jobs and therefore incomes from the construction of industrial and commercial premises. In some important instances, however, the community at large were forced to carry some of the costs of commercial development and, more recently, of continued industrial activity as well. In general, the capital values of the properties acquired and used by commercial and industrial organisations were substantially greater than those acquired by all other groups.

Such distributions are not untypical of those in any advanced industrial society at similar stages of economic development. The trend, at least in Britain and as exemplified by Oxford, is to control land uses and produce buildings collectively rather than individually. A large proportion of all the land and buildings in central Oxford is now owned by various state agencies. A large part of the total economy is directly or indirectly supported or controlled by state agencies. It would not therefore be accurate to describe a large part of the physical and economic development of the city as owned or dominated by a social class or any part of a social class primarily composed of the private owners of capital. Such groups, along with ancient landowners, remain an important element in the balance of forces, as illustrated by development planning and control. Newer groups, such as organised labour, have played a part in this balance of forces and have acquired some gains in terms of property rights. If such effects can be wrought by some new organisations, there is no reason to suppose that other new organisations could not enter the bargaining processes and, if they developed appropriate strategies and resources, could produce favourable outcomes for themselves.

The history of planning in Oxford would tend to confirm this view. In the early post-war years, an important characteristic of the political distribution of property was the lack of power of local residents of all social classes over the locational requirements of both private and public organisations when their interests were in conflict.

Central business district expansion into St Ebbe's was the

prime example illustrating this phenomenon. There, the demands from commercial organisations came into conflict with the housing needs of local residents with the outcome that local residents were displaced. Later, when similar redevelopment proposals were brought forward for other essentially working-class residential areas, residents' associations were formed and the proposals resisted. This change, together with the wider effects of such state provisions as housing and education, illustrate the changing and complex nature of the power structure, at least in Oxford, as exemplified by the incidence of the distributional outcomes of post-war land-use planning.

The long-term changing nature of the local power structure was already evident after the Second World War. Its essential characteristic consisted of the slow addition and incorporation of new organisations whose power stemmed from different sources. At first, there had been those organisations and individuals whose power rested on the ownership of land. These included the colleges and the aristocracy, some of whose landholdings were defined in the Domesday Book and many of whose contemporary landholdings had been in the same hands since the sixteenth and eighteenth centuries respectively. Second, there were the local commercial and industrial concerns whose power rested on the private ownership of capital. Collectively, these were probably not as important as the feudal landowners until the coming of the motor-car industry in the twentieth century. Third, there was the local state, which saw its most rapid period of growth after the rise to central electoral power of the Labour Party. The legislative provisions of the post-war Labour Government, which placed statutory responsibilities into the hands of local authorities like Oxford, instigated a doubling of its administrative staff.

At the time of the production of the Development Plan, these were the main groups and organisations with effective power over its contents. This power, however, was set within the context of national political power and its outcomes in terms of central government policies. As a result, the plan contained provisions that served the interests of the major local organisations and some of those groups represented by the Labour Government in Whitehall. The most important divisions in the power structure at this time were thus between the major local organisations, the central Labour administration and different groups of local residents. On the whole, the latter groups had the least effects on development planning.

A further set of divisions in the power structure which influenced planning and were reflected in development outcomes were those within particular groups of organisations. Thus, some ancient landowners were more influential than others, some industrial and commercial concerns were more powerful than others and some sections of both the local and central state had more control over development planning than others. As a reflection of this, the incidence of the distributional outcomes of development were not equal either between major groupings or within them. There were differences in both vertical and horizontal distributions.

Social classes as such did not exert influence on development planning. Partly as a result of the differences between major groups of organisations and partly because of the divisions between organisations of the same type, even where organisations might be seen as primarily representing the interests of a particular social class, such mobilisation did not ensure uniform influence or distributional outcomes. At their most significant, the effects of organisations which could be said to represent particular class interests were fragmented and partial.

The power structure which existed during the production of the post-war Development Plan in Oxford therefore consisted of a limited number of internally fragmented groups and organisations. These were mostly physically located at the local level but some operated at national and international levels. Some external organisations at these levels also influenced the objectives contained in plans. This was essentially a corporatist type of power structure in which a small number of organisations with different bases for their power exercised influence or manipulation over major planning objectives. The same organisations did not exercise uniform power over all objectives nor did the same interests always confront each other. With the passage of time, the most significant groups to challenge this structure were those formed by local residents and voluntary associations. It remains to be seen how significant they will prove in the long run.

This complex structure of power was reflected in the complicated incidence of the costs and benefits of the outcomes of development control over the study period. These were not uniform either between major divisions or within them. Some long-term landowners were able to avoid the perceived costs of inner relief roads and to gain developments, in some cases for commercial uses, which they required. In general, the ability of the landowners with the largest landholdings to achieve such a favourable balance of results was greater than those with fewer endowments.

The same could be said of commercial and industrial concerns. The former were able to foster central business district expansion with the aid of the local authority, which minimised their costs and maximised their revenues in the prevailing circumstances. The larger among them acquired the most favourable terms for their activities. Although most of them were able to avoid planning costs in terms of forced redevelopment for inner relief roads, some smaller businesses in the market section of the local economy were displaced both in St Ebbe's and in Cowley.

A similar pattern emerged in the gains made by industrial concerns. In the areas chosen for study it was the largest industrial enterprises which acquired the largest quantity of developments and eventually also the largest state subsidies. In contrast, smaller industrial concerns were sometimes displaced and normally allowed to disappear if they ran into financial difficulties.

The incidence of the distribution of the outcomes resulting from the land uses and properties completed by the local state is more difficult to trace. Some of the buildings, such as schools, could be used by any children normally resident in their catchment areas. Relative residential segregation means in effect, however, that different schools are used by children with different mixtures of social backgrounds. Insofar as the state completed most of its educational developments in Cowley and Iffley ward, only three in South and none in North, most of these new developments were located in an area with a predominantly skilled manual-worker composition at the start of the study period. Cowley and Iffley ward increasingly housed semi- and unskilled manual workers over the period of the study and so the availability of local educational opportunities for these groups increased over the years.

A similar picture emerges in the distribution of local authority housing. Most of the local authority developments were built in Cowley and Iffley ward. This again indicates an increasing distribution first to skilled manual workers and secondly to semi- and unskilled manual workers.

In contrast, most of the local state's industrial and commercial developments were constructed in South and Cowley and Iffley wards. This indicates that most of the residential displacement incurred as a result of these developments was probably experienced by manual workers and in particular the poorer groups among them. Thus the local state, under multilateral pressures, produced the somewhat contradictory physical outcomes that, on the one hand, it was building facilities like schools and houses for manual workers while, on the other, it was dismantling some of these very same facilities used by similar groups of people. At the same time, it was providing commercial organisations with sites, infrastructure and buildings at direct cost to some of Oxford's poorest inhabitants and at less than full market costs to the largest commercial organisations. The local state was therefore a powerful but contradictory and sometimes regressive source of physical developments.

Privately individuals mostly gained housing in North and Cowley and Iffley wards. In this respect, private housing, as might be expected, was acquired by better-off non-manual residents and some skilled manual workers rather than other groups. In general, these groups were more adept at avoiding the costs of physical incursions into their residential territories than less well-off members of the community. This was not always the case, as was shown by college developments and the Cutterslowe Walls in north Oxford. Better-off groups therefore exercised more power over planning outcomes than less affluent groups, but not as much as formal organisations.

A similar pattern emerged with respect to voluntary associations. Their small number of developments took place mostly in North and Cowley and Iffley wards. They were composed mostly of housing, educational and other amenities.

Their use was acquired mainly by non-manual and skilled workers. Judged in terms of their number and value of developments, such associations were not particularly powerful in the development of Oxford. The influence of some of them, such as the masonic lodges, rotary, round table and social clubs behind the scenes, though impossible to measure empirically, was probably quite considerable. Many of the individual members of local commercial, industrial and state bureaucracies were members of such associations. In practice, most of these individuals would be connected with the upper echelons of these organisations. In this way a relatively powerful and informal set of networks existed. At critical times, such as the production of the Development Plan and when contentious private developments were required, this set of networks could be employed to influence favourable outcomes for their protagonists.

Theoretical conclusions

The evidence summarised above illustrates the development of corporatist power structures focused on the planning of land uses. It shows the importance of major landowning, industrial and commercial organisations in the setting of Development Plan objectives and in the organisation of beneficial property rights and buildings. It also shows their success in minimising the costs of such acquisitions. In addition, the evidence also illustrates the significance of major organisations like trade unions and the Labour Party in securing improvements in housing, educational and amenity facilities, particulary for skilled manual workers. Conversely, the data shows some of the regressive costs which may be borne by unorganised groups who do not have organisations representing their interests in the corporatist power structure.

In sociological terms, the main bases of the divisions between these groups are the division of labour, the use of organisations to co-ordinate this divided labour, the hierarchical structuring of these organisations, the differential possession or use of goods, services and knowledge, economic and political action. The combinations and degree of relative importance of these bases for social division change over time.

Summary and Conclusions 305

The history of these changes in industrial societies, like Britain, is marked by a declining importance of those divisions based on the conditions of free markets and a rising importance of those divisions based on organisations, planning and queues. Economic units like the firm and social collectives like trade unions grow and organise. Both seek to control the markets for their products and services by monopolies and closed shops. These are conditions of imperfect competition. In such conditions, the most important form of social division is the formal organisation.

Social classes formed under the short-lived conditions of free markets continue to exist as do other forms of social division. In most cases they form relatively passive distributive groupings. Their relative ability to compete in markets or queues depends on the power of the organisations to which they belong or on their relative ability to generate alternative organisations with the relevant skills and resources.

Thus, at least in Oxford, the main active divisions between groups with different power bases were those between groups of organisations. These groups were developed and added to over time. Historically, more types of organisation exercised power over urban development in the twentieth than in previous centuries. The trend has therefore been towards the development of formal state control of land uses, the incorporation of major landowning, industrial and commercial organisations into this decision-making process, and the proliferation of pressure groups. Thus, state bureaucracies have increased their scope and size. More recently, residents' organisations have also joined the struggles over land uses and property rights in their areas. The results have been that the main divisions evident in Oxford over the study period were organisations representing ancient landowners, industry, commerce, the state, voluntary associations and a highly fragmented collection of private individuals.

Varying levels of conflict between and sometimes within these divisions were endemic. The main reason for this was that they had different values and aspirations which could not be mutually satisfied to everybody's benefit. Although the total amount of property was increasing throughout the period, the quantities in some sectors, like housing, were insufficient to meet the needs of all groups, and some organisations acquired a disproportionate share of what was constructed anyway.

The ubiquity of this conflict provided one stimulus to the growth of state activities. While conflicts could be settled within organisations, no third party was required. Where different organisations competed for a scarce resource like land and, in particular, where different groups wished to use the same location for different purposes, some formal resolution of these conflicts was required. The co-ordinated state planning of land uses was one institutionalised way of doing this. The local state itself, however, also had an interest in land for its own use.

The analysis illustrates a primarily corporatist power structure in the making of land-use planning decisions and in the subsequent implementation of those decisions. In those decisions concerned with land used for production purposes, the power structure was based on economic conditions of imperfect competition. In those decisions concerned primarily with the provision of goods and services, the power structure illustrated somewhat similar political conditions which were labelled imperfect pluralism.

Because power was associated with organisation, and organisation requires the combination of skills and resources, the relative difficulty in acquiring these attributes debarred some groups from exercising effective power over land-use planning. The establishment of a permanent organisation was therefore an important barrier which usually had to be overcome before new groups could bring much power to bear on the objectives and outcomes of planning. This differential access to organisational resources means that only a limited number of such organisations are able to compete in power struggles, that social classes as such are not effective in determining political outcomes and that there are also important differences in power even among those who can muster formal organisations to serve their interests.

There were two main ways of exercising power. One way was to create the general value framework within which decisions were taken by being incorporated into the higher echelons of the decision-making processes. This was almost exclusively the preserve of the larger organisations. The university, for example, was effective in creating an emphasis on the preservation of its interests in the development of the city as opposed to the majority of its non-university working-class residents. Large industrial organisations established a framework of relative non-intervention in their affairs. Commercial groups asserted the principle of central business district expansion. The local planning authority gave prominence to aesthetic and architectural values.

The other main way of exercising power was in the confrontation that took place within the confines of these general frameworks. Here, again, the larger organisations also held the advantage. The university prevented the construction of an inner relief road through its territory. Morris Motors built a paint shop which did not conform with its industrial development certificate. The large multiple stores negotiated very favourable terms for entering the new shopping precincts. The local state took allotment land for housing. In contrast, local working-class residents were removed from St Ebbe's, and middle-class residents had neighbouring houses converted into college uses despite their protests.

The outcomes of these activities generally reflected the degrees of power held by the relevant organisations. Thus, the quantity and capital value of the properties acquired by industrial, commercial, landowning and state organisations were much greater than those acquired by any local residential groups. Among the former, the largest industrial and commercial concerns gained the most. Among the latter, organised and skilled labour experienced the greatest relative improvement in its housing, educational and other collective amenities.

These improvements were wrought largely as a result of the working out of political forces at the level of the national state. These were then experienced at the local level as mandatory and statutory obligations placed upon the local authority to provide such facilities as housing and schools. In this way the activities of the local state were not wholly determined by the interplay of local political forces.

The net results of all these activities in terms of land-use outcomes were unequal distributions of scarce commodities among individual members of society based on their functional roles in, or relations with, collective organisations. Those who belonged to organisations which were incorporated in central or local state decision-making, like trade unions, political parties and oligopolies, acquired more in terms of property rights than unorganised and unincorporated individuals. The poorer members of society without roles in the economy or formal organisations acquired few property rights during the study period and sometimes had the few they possessed taken away from them with less than full market rates of compensation.

These results illustrate a fairly clear relationship between the power of incorporated, producing oligopolies and major political organisations in collective decisions over the use of land and the acquisition of benefits accruing from those uses. They also show that those smaller production units in the market sector of the economy and pluralistic interest groups in the polity, who are generally not incorporated into the internal decision-making centres of the state, have less opportunity to influence significantly planning decisions or outcomes. Unorganised individuals, particularly the poorer members of the local community, have little influence and gain few benefits from land-use planning.

These findings have some important implications for the debate which was outlined in Chapter 1, about where power resides and how it is exercised in local communities. In conditions of corporatism there is no suggestion that power is possessed primarily by individual electors. They are usually not the initiators of intercorporate negotiations nor are they asked to vote on which organisations should be party to important decisions, which should be accorded representative status and which should be excluded from such negotiations. The electorate, therefore, exert little power over who should be party to major state decisions and who should not. Conversely, major oligopolies and monopsonies can usually force themselves into strategic bargaining positions in state decisions affecting their interests. In addition, the formal state bureaucracies, public corporations and quasi-autonomous non-governmental organisations are all either generally staffed by individuals drawn from the incorporated establishment and/or not directly subject to electoral accountability.

Appendix 1

Members of the Planning, Central Area Redevelopment and Housing Committees and their known connections, 1950/1 to 1973/4

Conservative members

Andrews; Mrs	Plg 52; Hsg 50-1
	Hon. Freeman of the City; various women's and community organisations
Blagrove	Plg 67-9; Hsg 71-4
	British Leyland
Blake, Lord	Plg 60-3; Hsg 72-4
	Provost of Queen's College; lawyer
Bowdery	Plg 70, 72; Hsg 64-74
	Kinkin & Frewin, builders – still on council
Bryan-Brown, Mrs	Hsg 50-1
	University connections via husband
Burton	Hsg 61-3
	Burton's Dairies
Cantwell	CAR 70-1
	Still on council
Chaplin	Hsg 50-9, 60-3; Chn 54-8
	Retired hairdresser
Couling	Hsg 50-1
	Oxford United FC
Day, Miss	Hsg 55-6

310 *Appendix 1*

Dickins	Hsg 63-4
	South Oxford Conservative Club - Chairman
Ellis, Mrs	Hsg 67-71
	Ran a private nursing home
Fell	Plg 56-7; Hsg 55-8
	Diploma Correspondence College and Oxford English Centre
Gee, Mrs	Hsg 68-72
Good, Miss	Hsg 64-6
Goulton-Constable, Mrs(d.)	Plg 55-60; Hsg 52-9
	Housewife
Gowers	Plg 52-5
	Solicitor, Oxford Regional Hospital Board, Morris Motors
Green	Plg 57-8
Green, Mrs	Hsg 69-72
Gunby	Hsg 50-3
	British Leyland
Halstead	Plg 69-71
	St Anne's College
Hamilton-Edwards	Plg 67-71; CAR 67-9
	Author
Hands, Miss	Hsg 68-71
Harold, Mrs	Plg 65-9; CAR 65-70
	Oxford graduate, worked at Harwell
Harrison	CAR 69-71
	ex-Lord Mayor, hairdresser on Westgate site
Ingram (see labour)	Plg 60-6; CAR 63-6; Hsg 60-74
	Legal executive, crossed from Labour, still on council
Jackson	Plg 70; Hsg 69-71
	All Souls College
Jones	Plg 67-8; Hsg 67-9
King	Plg 52-3

Appendix 1 311

Minns	Plg 52-6
	Builder, nephew of Lord Nuffield.
Mould	Hsg 59-62
Organ	Hsg 51-4
	Builder
Overall	Hsg 66-8
Packford, Mrs	Hsg 50-4
Pinto-Duschinsky	Plg 68-72; CAR 67-71
	Pembroke College
Pratley	Plg 57
	Hairdresser
Rome	Plg 60-1; Hsg 59-62
	Ex-RAF squadron leader
Simpson	Plg 64-72; CC 60-2, 64-6; Hsg 60-3
	Cowley Conservative Club, Regional Hospital Board, magistrate. Still on council
Somerville, Mrs	Plg 54
Spokes (d.)	Plg 52-72 (ch'n 53-7, 64); CAR 63-71 (ch'n 63, 66-7); CC 58, 60-1; Hsg 51-6
	Jeweller, university connections, Preservation Trust - assisted Ministry on drawing up Listed Buildings list
Spokes, Miss A.	CAR 63
	Daughter of the above, Age Concern
Stevenson, Mrs	Hsg 50-2
	Main interest mental health
Teal, Mrs	CC 58
Todd, Mrs J.	Plg 68-71; CAR 67-71; CC 66; Hsg 67-9
	Failed parliamentary candidate
Townsend, Lady	CAR 63-6; Hsg 50-9
	Mayor three times

312 *Appendix 1*

Tribe, Mrs	CC 62-3; Hsg 61-4, 65-8
Walker	Hsg 50-2
	Car business
Walker, W. C. (d.)	Plg 53-7, 61-2; CC 58
	Director Benfield & Loxley, Mayor, Southfield Golf Club
White	Hsg 69-71
White, Mrs (d.)	Plg 52-5
	Mayor
Wood, Mrs	CAR 66-8
	Women's organisations
Young, Lady J.	Plg 60-71 (ch'n 67-8); CAR 63-71 (ch'n 68-71); CC 64-6
	Daughter of Baker (Jesus) – husband also at Jesus, leader of Conservative group, Oxford graduate

Labour members

Blundell	Plg 70-2
	University
Bowerman, Mrs	Hsg 50-1
	Chairman of Oxford Co-operate Society
Briscoe	Plg 62-7; CAR 63-7; CC 63-6
	Corpus Christi College
Bromley	Plg 54-9, 68-72 (ch'n 58-9); CC 58-66
	Typesetter, TWA, wife a magistrate
Brooks	CC 58-61
Buxton	Hsg 66-9
	Exeter College
Carr, Mrs	CAR 64; Hsg 59-65
Church	Hsg 52-5
	Chairman Oxford and District Trades Council
Cone	Hsg 58-61
Conners	Hsg 54-61

Constable	Plg 59-67; Hsg 63- Retired schoolmaster, Oxford Utd - director
Cooper	Plg 72; Hsg 72
Dent	Hsg 51-4 Technician in Univ. Labs., JP, still in politics
Dudman	Plg 64-6; CAR 71 Chartered accountant
Fagg	CAR 63-5; Hsg 56-74 British Leyland, Oxford Utd
Foot	Plg 56-7; Hsg 54-7 University connections - war historian
Fowler	CC 62-3; Hsg 61-4 Don, became MP
Gibbs	CC 58-62 Chartered accountant, Southern Sports Council, Oxford Utd
Gibbs, Mrs O.	Plg 58-67, 71; CAR 63-5, 70 Wife of the above
Gunn	Plg 72; CAR 71
Haydock	Plg 54-5
Ingram (see Conservative)	Plg 57-60; Hsg 56-60
Ireland	CC 63-5
Liddle	Hsg 71-4
Lihou (d.)	Plg 58-60; CC 63-5; Hsg 64-6 British Leyland
Loughran	Hsg 64-7
Lower, Mrs	Plg 61-4, 66-9; CAR 63-6; CC 66 Husband on council at same time, secretary of WEA
Luard	Hsg 59-61 MP for Oxford
McCarthy, Mrs	Hsg 71-4
McKay	Plg 65; CAR 66-8; CC 66; Hsg 65-9

314 *Appendix 1*

Macintosh	CC 58-9
Magee	Plg 59; Hsg 58-60, 64-7
Nimmo	CC 58-66 (ch'n 66)
	Civil servant, later sat on Planning Committee
Oakeshott	Hsg 72-4
	Oxford graduate, PPS in Labour Government, later on Planning
Owen	Plg 56
Parker	Hsg 63-8
	British Leyland, attempt at shop in Headington
Pickstock	Plg 52-6, 58-9; CAR 63-71; CC 58-66 (ch'n 58-65); Hsg 53-7
	Mayor, University Extra Mural Studies. His initiative got Cowley Centre off the drawing board
Ramsay	Plg 71-2
	Architect
Roberts	Plg 53; CC 58-62
	Oxford & District Co-op.
Sharpe	Plg 72
	Nuffield College
Thomas	Plg 72
	Oxford Polytechnic
Town	Hsg 72-4
Warrell	Plg 58
	Pub landlord
Williamson	Hsg 61-7, 70-4 (ch'n 64-7, 72-4)
	Ordained as priest - works at British Leyland

Liberal member

Davies	Plg 63
	Wolsey Hall, Parliamentary candidate for Oxford

University members

Baker, Jesus College	Plg 52-63, 65-6 (chairman 60-2, 65-6); CAR 63-6; CC 58-63, 66 Oxford Citizens Housing Association
Brown, A. B., Worcester	Plg 52-64 (chairman 52); CC 58
Chester, Sir N., Nuffield	Hsg 52-60
Cooke, Magdalen	Plg 52-3
Garrard, St John's	Hsg 57-8
Griffiths	Hsg 68-72 CAR 68-71
Griffiths, Miss	Hsg 72-4
Hart, Mrs	Hsg 62-4
Keith-Lucas, Nuffield	Hsg 50-65 (chairman 62-3) Specialist in local government administration
Maclagan, Trinity	Plg 52-72; CAR 64-71; CC 58-66 On board of B. H. Blackwell; Royal Herald; St Catherine's Society; now chairman of Linton Road Residents' Association
Thompson, Mrs, St John's	Hsg 57-61; CAR 63; CC 58-65
Wheare, Exeter	Plg 52 Professor of Public Administration; one of the Park Town Trustees
Yardley, St Edmund Hall	CAR 67-71 Professor of Law; member of the Rent Tribunal

Appendix 2

First amendment to the Development Plan

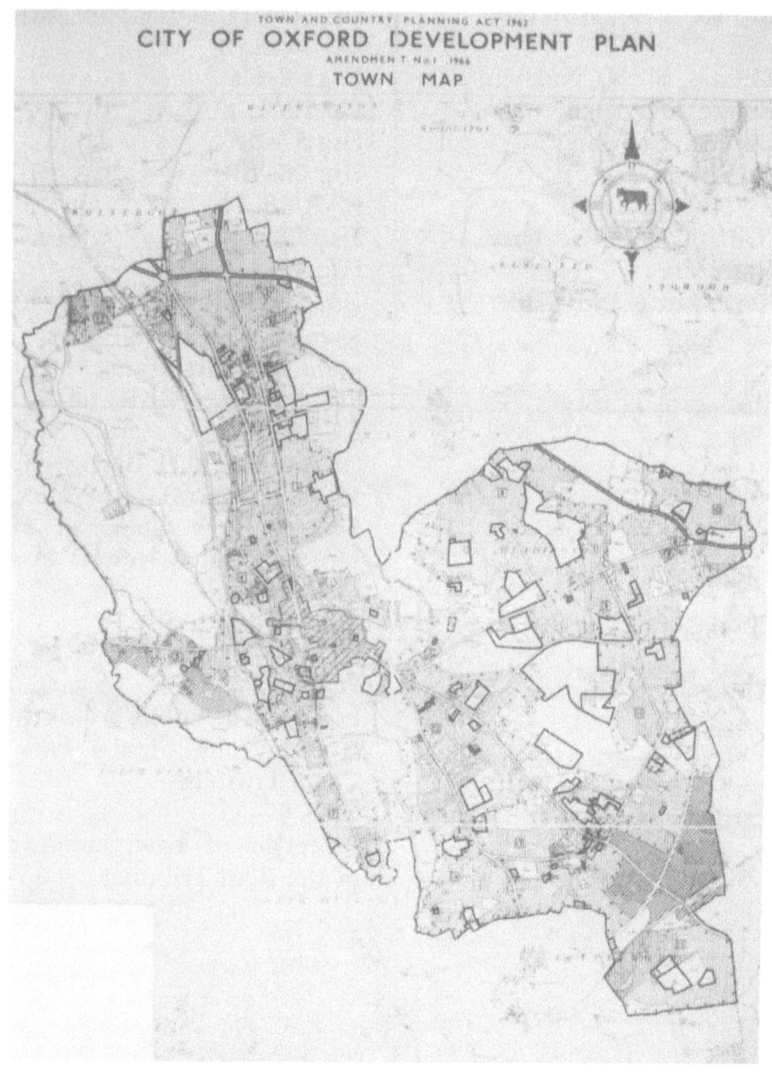

Appendix 3

Second amendment to the Development Plan

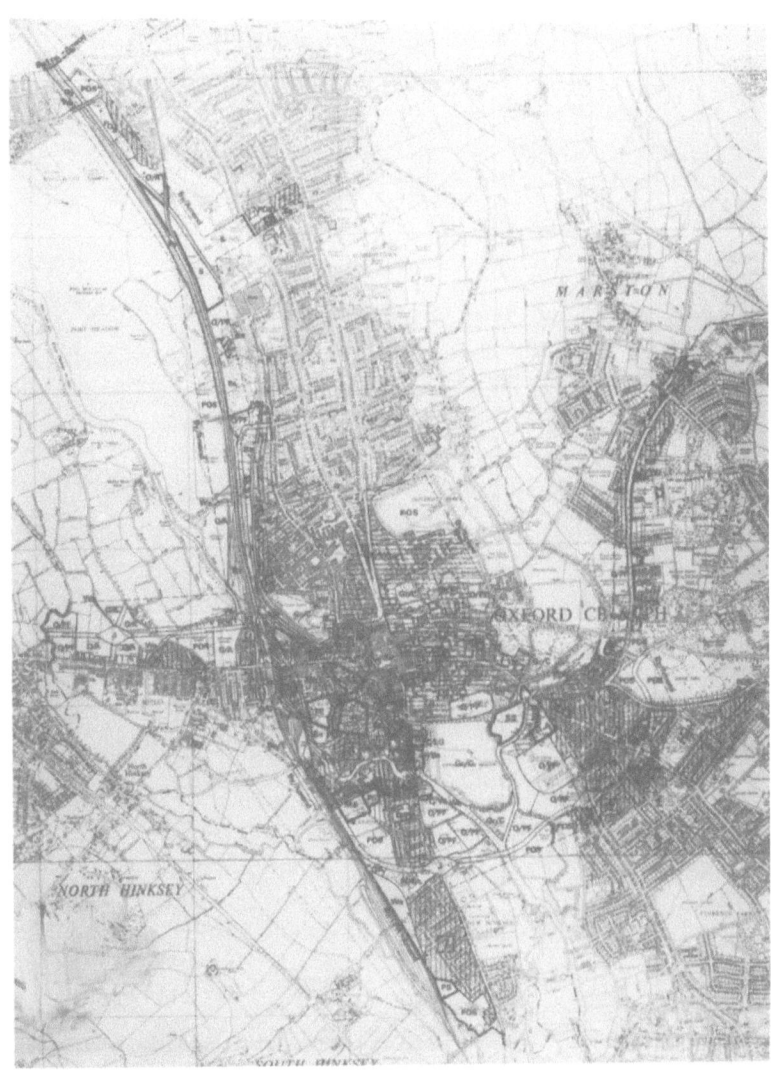

Appendix 4

Latest plan for St Ebbe's (now substantially completed)

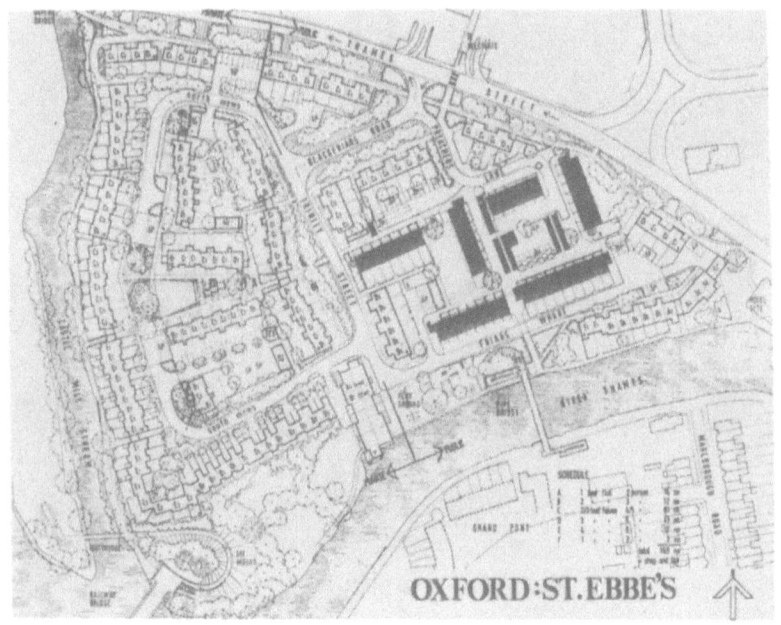

Appendix 4 319

Latest plan for St Ebbe's (now substantially completed)

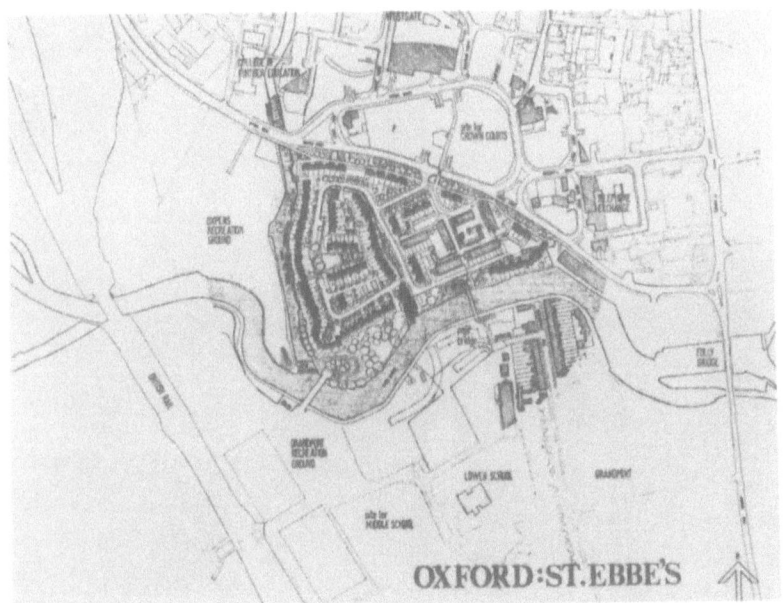

Bibliography

AARONOVITCH, L. (1961) *The Ruling Class: a study of British finance capital* (London: Lawrence & Wishart).
AGGER, L. (1956) 'Power Attributions in the Local Community. Theoretical and Research Considerations', *Social Forces*, 34, May, pp. 322-31.
AGGER, R. E. et al. (1964) *The Rulers and the Ruled: political power and impotence in American communities* (New York: Wiley).
AIKEN, M. and ALFORD, R. (1970a) 'Community Structure and Innovations: the case of public housing', *American Political Science Review*, **64**.
   (1970b) 'Community Structure and Innovation: the case of urban renewal', *American Sociological Review*, 35.
ALDOWS, T. (1972) *Battle for the Environment* (London: Fontana).
ALMOND, G. A. and COLEMAN, J. S. (eds) (1960) *Politics of the Developing Areas* (Princeton U.P.).
ALMOND, G. A. and VERBA, S. (1963) *The Civic Culture: political attitudes and democracy in five nations* (Princeton U.P.).
ALT, J. E. (1971) 'Some Social and Political Correlates of County Borough Expenditures', *British Journal of Political Science*, vol. 1, part 1, pp. 49-62.
ALTHUSSER, L. (1969) *For Marx*, trans. Ben Brewster (London: Allen Lane The Penguin Press).
ALTHUSSER, L. and BALIBAR, E. (1970) *Reading 'Capital'*, trans. Ben Brewster (London: New Left Books).
ALTSHULER, A. A. (1970) *Community Control* (New York: Pegasus).
AMBROSE, P. and COLENUTT, R. (1975) *The Property Machine* (Harmondsworth: Penguin Books).
ANDERSON, W. (ed.) (1970) *Politics and Environment: a reader in ecological crisis* (Hemel Hempstead: Goodyear).
APTER, D. E. (1966) *Politics of Modernisation* (University of Chicago Press).
ARNSTEIN, S. R. (1971) 'A Ladder of Citizen Participation in the USA', *Journal of the Town Planning Institute*, 57, pp. 176-82.
ARON, R. (1967a) *18 Lectures on Industrial Society* (London: Weidenfeld & Nicolson).
   (1967b) *Industrial Society* (London: Weidenfeld & Nicolson).
ARROW, K. (1951) *Social Choice and Individual Values* (New York: Wiley).

322 Bibliography

ARUP ASSOCIATIONS (May 1967) *An Appraisal for St. John's College Development Area* (London: Arup).

AXELROD, R. (1970) *Conflict of Interest* (Chicago: Markham).

BACHRACH, P. and BARATZ, M. S. (1962a) 'Two Faces of Power', *American Political Science Review*, 56, May, pp. 947-52.

(1962b) 'Decisions and Non-decisions: an analytical framework', *American Political Science Review*, LVII, September.

(1970) *Power and Poverty: theory and practice* (New York: Oxford University Press).

BACON, R. and ELTIS, W. (1976) *Britain's Economic Problem: too few producers* (London: Macmillan).

BAILEY, R. (1973) *The Squatters* (Harmondsworth: Penguin Books).

(1977) *The Homeless and the Empty Houses* (Harmondsworth: Penguin Books).

BALBUS, I. (1971) 'The Concept of Interest in Pluralist and Marxian Analysis', *Politics and Society*, 1, pp. 151-79.

BANFIELD, E. C. (1961) *Political Influence* (New York: Free Press of Glencoe).

BANFIELD, E. C. and WILSON, J. Q. (1963) *City Politics* (Cambridge, Mass.: Harvard U.P.).

BARAN, P. A. and SWEEZY, P. M. (1966) *Monopoly Capital: an essay on the American economic and social orders* (New York: Monthly Review Press).

BARKIN, D. and HETTICH, W. (April 1968) *The Elementary and Secondary Education Act: a distribution analysis*. Working Paper EDA8. (Washington University, St Louis: Institute of Urban and Regional Studies) MP. 63130.

BARKIN, D. and LEGLER, J. (April 1968) *Alternative Measures of Fiscal Redistribution: gross vs. net aid*. Working Paper EDA9. (Washington University, St Louis: Institute of Urban and Regional Studies) MO. 63130.

BARLOW REPORT (1940) *Report of the Royal Commission on the Distribution of the Industrial Population*, Cmnd 6153 (London: HMSO).

BARRET, R. R. and TOPHAM, N. (1977) 'Evaluating the Distribution of Local Outputs in a Decentralised Structure of Government', *Policy and Politics*, 6.

BARRY, B. (1965) *Political Argument* (London: Routledge & Kegan Paul).

BEALEY, F. et al. (1966) *Constituency Politics* (New York: Free Press).

BEER, S. (1965) *Modern British Politics* (London: Faber).

BELL, D. (1961) *The End of Ideology: on the exhaustion of political ideas in the fifties* (London: Collier).

(1973) (1976) *The Coming of Post-industrial Society: a venture in social forecasting* (Harmondsworth: Penguin Books).

BELL, G. D. (ed.) (1967) *Organisations and Human Behaviour: a book of readings* (Englewood Cliffs, N.J.: Prentice-Hall).

BELLUSH, J. and HAUSKNECHT, M. (1967) *Urban Renewal: people, politics and planning* (New York: Anchor Books).

BENDIX, R. (1966) *Max Weber: an intellectual portrait* (London: Methuen).

BENDIX, R. and LIPSET, S. M. (1957) 'Political Sociology', *Current Sociology*, vol. VI, no. 2.
(1966) *Class, Status, Power* (London: Routledge & Kegan Paul).
BENSMAN, J. and VIDICH, A. (1964) 'Power Cliques in Bureaucratic Society', *Social Research*, 29, Winter, pp. 467-74.
BENSON, C. S. and LUND, P. M. (1969) *Neighbourhood Distribution of Local Public Services* (University of California, Berkeley: Institute of Governmental Studies).
BERLE, A. A. and MEANS, G. C. (1932) *The Modern Corporation and Private Property* (New York: Harcourt Brace).
BERLE, A. A. (1960) *Power without Property* (London: Sidgwick).
BERNSTEIN, E. (1961) *Evolutionary Socialism* (New York: Schocken Books).
BEST, M. and CONNOLLY, W. E. (1976) *The Politicised Economy* (Lexington, Mass.: Heath).
BETTLEHEIM, C. (1976) *Economic Calculation and Forms of Property* (London: Routledge & Kegan Paul).
BIRCH, A. H. (1959) *Small Town Politics* (London: Oxford U.P.).
(1964) *Representative and Responsible Government* (London: Allen & Unwin).
BIRD, R. (1968) 'The Relationship of Economic and Physical Planning', *Report of the Town and Country Summer School* (London: RTPI).
BLAU, P. M. (1964) *Exchange and Power* (New York: Wiley).
BLAU, P. M. and SCOTT, W. R. (1964) *Formal Organisations* (London: Routledge & Kegan Paul).
BOADEN, N. and ALFORD, R. R. (1969) 'Sources of diversity in English local government decisions', *Public Administration*, vol. 47, Summer, pp. 203-23.
BOADEN, N. (1971) *Urban Policy Making* (London: Cambridge U.P.).
BOLLENS, J. C. (ed.) (1961) *Exploring the Metropolis* (Berkeley: University of California Press).
BOLLENS, J. C. and SCHMANDT, H. J. (1970) *The Metropolis: its people, politics and economic life* (New York: Harper & Row).
BONJEAN, C. M. and LINEBERRY, R. L. (1971) *Community Politics: a behavioural approach* (London: Collier-Macmillan).
BOOKER, C. (1977) 'Physical Planning: another illusion shattered', *National Westminster Bank Quarterly Review*.
BOOTH, C. (1906) *Life and Labour of the People of London*, 17 vols (London: Macmillan).
(1974) 'Andre Gunder Frank: An Introduction and Appreciation', in Oxaal, I. et al., *Beyond the Sociology of Development: economy and society in Africa and Latin America* (London: Routledge & Kegan Paul).
BOTTOMORE, T. B. (1964) *Elites and Society* (Harmondsworth: Penguin).
BOUDON, R. (1971) *The Uses of Structuralism* (London: Heinemann).
BRAND, J. (1974) *Local Government Reform in England 1888-1974* (London: Croom Helm).
BRAYBROOKE, D. and LINDBLOM, C. E. (1963) *A Strategy of Decision: policy evaluation as a social process* (New York: Macmillan).

BRAYBROOKE, D. (1974) *Traffic Congestion Goes Through the Issue Machine* (London: Routledge & Kegan Paul).
BRIER, A. P. (1970) 'The Decision Process in Local Government', *Public Administration*, 48.
BROWN, T., VILE, M. J. C. and WHITMORE, M. F. (1972) 'Community Studies and Decision Taking', *British Journal of Political Science*, 2, pp. 133-53.
BRYCE, J. (1888) *American Commonwealth* (New York: AMS Press).
BRZEZINSKI, Z. K. and HUNTINGTON, S. (1964) *Political Power USA/ USSR* (London: Chatto & Windus).
BUCHANAN, C. D. (1963) *Traffic in Towns* (Harmondsworth: Penguin Books).
BUKHARIN, N. I. (1926) *Historical Materialism: a system of sociology* (trans. from 3rd Russian edition) (London: Allen & Unwin).
BUKHARIN, N. I. and PREOBRAZHENSKY, E. (1927) *The ABC of Communism* (originally published 1921) (London: CPGB).
BULPITT, J. G. (1967) *Party Politics in English Local Government* (London: Longmans).
BURGESS, E. W. and BOGUE, D. J. (1964) *Urban Sociology* (Chicago and London: Phoenix Books).
BURKE, E. M. (1968) 'Citizen Participation Strategies', *Journal of the American Institute of Planners*, September, pp. 287-94.
BURNHAM, J. (1941) *The Managerial Revolution* (New York: John Day).
CANT, D. H. (1976) *Squatting and Private Property Rights* (Bartlett School of Architecture and Planning, University College London).
CARCHEDI, G. (1975) 'On the Economic Identification of the New Middle Class', *Economy and Society*, 4, February, no. 1.
CARTER, I. (1974) 'The Highlands of Scotland as an Underdeveloped Region', in Kadt, E. de, and Williams, G., *Sociology and Development* (London: Tavistock).
CASSON, CONDER & PARTNERS, *Keble College*: 1967 *Plan* (London).
CASTELLS, M. (1972) (1977) *The Urban Question* (London: Edward Arnold).
    (1973) (1975) *Luttes Urbaines et Pouvoir Politique* (Paris: Maspero) (see B. Lynne Lord (1973) for a mimeographical translation).
    (1978) *City, Class and Power* (London: Macmillan).
CAWSON, A. (1977) *Environmental Planning and the Politics of Corporatism*, Working Paper 7, Urban and Regional Studies, University of Sussex.
    (1978) 'Pluralism, Corporatism and the Role of the State, *Government and Opposition*, vol. 13, pp. 178-98.
CHAMBERLAIN, E. H. (1933) *The Theory of Monopolistic Competition* (Cambridge, Mass.: Harvard U.P.).
CHANG CHUN-CHIAO (1975) 'On Exercising All-round Dictatorship over the Bourgeoisie', *Peking Review*, no. 14.
CHANG PENG-YA (1966) 'Soviet Revisionist Leading Clique Restores Capitalism', *Peking Review*, no. 48.
CHAPMAN, L. (ed) (1971) *The History of Working Class Housing* (Totoya, N. J.: Rowman & Littlefield).

CHASE REPORT (1968) Inspector's Report on inquiry into University College developments: North Oxford.
CHIBGALL, S. and SAUNDERS, P. (1977) 'Worlds Apart: notes on the social reality of corruption', *British Journal of Sociology*, 28.
CHISHOLM, M. and MANNERS, G. (1971) *Spatial Policy Problems of the British Economy* (Cambridge U.P.).
CHILDHOOD AND GOVERNMENT PROJECT, *Annual Report 1973-74.* Childhood and Government Project of the Earl Warren Legal Institute, University of California, Berkeley, 1 October 1974.
CLARK, C. (1940) (1951) *The Conditions of Economic Progress* (London: Macmillan).
CLARK, T. N. (1967) 'Power and Community Structure: who governs, where and when?', *Sociological Quarterly*, 8, Summer, pp. 291-316.
 (ed.) (1968) *Community Structure, Power and Decision-Making: a comparative analysis* (Chicago: Science Research Associates).
 (1973a) 'Community Social Indicators from Analytical Models to Policy Applications', *Urban Affairs Quarterly*, vol. 9, September, pp. 3-36.
 (1973b) *Community Power and Policy Outputs* (London: Sage).
CLEMENTS, P. V. (1969) *Local Notables and the City Council* (London: Macmillan).
CLIFF, T. (1964) *Russia: A Marxist Analysis* (London: Socialist Review Publishing Co.).
COCKBURN, C. (1977) *The Local State* (London: Pluto).
COLEMAN, J. S. (1957) *Community Conflict* (Glencoe, Ill.: The Free Press).
COLLETTI, L. (1972) *From Rousseau to Lenin: studies in ideology and society* (London: New Left Books).
COLLISON, P. and MOGEY, J. (1959) 'Residence and Social Class in Oxford', *American Journal of Sociology*.
COLLISON, P. (1963) *The Cutteslowe Walls* (London: Faber).
CONN, P. H. (1971) *Conflict: an introduction to political science* (New York: Harper & Row).
CONNOLLY, W. E. (1969) *The Bias of Pluralism* (Chicago: Atherton).
 (1972) 'On Interests in Politics', *Politics and Society*, 2, pp. 459-79.
COOLEY, C. (1894) 'The Theory of Transportation', *Publications of the American Economic Association*, vol. IX, May, no. 3.
COTGROVE, S. (1974) 'Technology, Rationality and Domination', University of Bath, mimeo.
COULANGES, F. de (1956) *The Ancient City* (New York: Doubleday Anchor).
COUSINS, J. et al. (1974) 'Aspects of Contradiction: regional policy: the case of north-east England', *Regional Studies*, 2.
COUSIN, P. F. (1973) 'Voluntary Organisations as Pressure Groups', *London Review of Public Administration*, nos. 3 and 4.
CRENSON, M. A. (1971) *The Unpolitics of Air Pollution* (Baltimore: Johns Hopkins U.P.).

CROSLAND, C. A. R. (1964) *The Future of Socialism* (London: Cape).
CROUCH, C. (1977) *British Political Sociology Yearbook*, vol. 3: *Participation in Politics* (London: Croom Helm).
CURL, J. S. (1977) *The Erosion of Oxford* (Oxford Illustrated Press).
DAHL, R. A. (1956) *A Preface to Democratic Theory* (University of Chicago Press).
    (1957) 'The Concept of Power', *Behavioural Science*, 2, July, pp. 201-14.
    (1958) 'A Critique of the Ruling Elite Model', *American Political Science Review*, 52, pp. 463-9.
    (1961) *Who Governs?* (New Haven: Yale U.P.).
    (1967) *Pluralist Democracy in the United States: conflict and consensus* (Chicago: Rand McNally).
DAHRENDORF, R. (1957) (1972) *Class and Class Conflict in Industrial Society* (London: Routledge & Kegan Paul).
DALE, L. (1944) *Towards a Plan for Oxford City* (London: Faber).
DAMER, S. and HAGUE, G. (1971) 'Public Participation in Planning: a review', *Town Planning Review*, 42, pp. 217-32.
DANIELSON, M. N. (ed.) (1966) *Metropolitan Politics: a reader* (Boston, Mass.: Little, Brown & Co.).
DAVIDSON, D. et al. (1956) *Decision Making* (Stanford U.P.).
DAVIES, B. (1968) *Social Needs and Resources in Local Services: a study of variations in standards of provision of personal social services between local authority areas* (London: Joseph).
DAVIES, J. G. (1972a) *The Evangelistic Bureaucrat: a study of a planning exercise in Newcastle upon Tyne* (London: Tavistock).
    (1972b) 'The Local Councillor's Dilemma', *Official Architecture and Planning*, pp. 112-14.
DEARLOVE, J. (1973) *The Politics of Policy in Local Government* (London: Cambridge U.P.).
DENNIS, N. (1970) *People and Planning* (London: Faber).
    (1972) *Public Participation and Planners' Blight* (London: Faber).
DEPARTMENT OF THE ENVIRONMENT (1972) *Circular on Public Participation* (London).
    (1975a) *Review of the Development Control System (Dobry Report)* (London: HMSO).
    (1975b) *Gradual Renewal: article and comment reprinted from the Architects' Journal*, Area Improvement Occasional Paper 2-75 (London).
DICKSON, D. (1974) *Alternative Technology and the Politics of Technical Change* (London: Fontana).
DITCHLEY FOUNDATION (1969) *Public Participation in Urban Planning* (Ditchley Paper no. 21) (Enstone, Oxfordshire: Ditchley Foundation).
DJILAS, M. (1957) (1976) *The New Class: an analysis of the Communist system* (New York: Praeger).
DOMHOFF, G. W. (1967) *Who Rules America?* (Englewood Cliffs, N. J.: Prentice-Hall).
DOWNS, A. (1957) *An Economic Theory of Democracy* (New York: Harper).

DRAIN, G. (1966) *Organisation and Practice of Local Government* (London: Heinemann).
DREWRY, G. (1977) 'Corruption: the Salmon Report', *Political Quarterly*, vol. 48, pp. 87-91.
DUNCAN, O. D. and DUNCAN, B. (1955) 'A Methodological Analysis of Segregation Indexes', *American Sociological Review*, vol. 20, pp. 210-17.
DUNLEAVY, P. J. (1976) 'An Issue Centred Approach to the Study of Power', *Political Studies*, 26, pp. 423-34.
(1977) 'Protest and Quiescence in Urban Politics: a critique of some pluralist and structuralist myths', *International Journal of Urban and Regional Research*, 1, pp. 193-218.
DUNNING, E. G. and HOPPER, E. I. (1966) 'Industrialisation and the Problem of Convergence: a critical note', *Sociological Review*, no. 14, pp. 163-86.
DURKHEIM, E. (1893) (1933) *On the Division of Labour in Society* (Chicago: Free Press).
DYCKMAN, J. (1961) 'Planning and Decision Theory', *Journal of the American Institute of Planners*, 27, pp. 335-45.
EASTON, D. (1965) *A Systems Analysis of Political Life* (New York: Wiley).
ECKSTEIN, H. (1960) *Pressure Group Politics* (London: Allen & Unwin).
ECONOMIC DEVELOPMENT COMMITTEE FOR THE DISTRIBUTIVE TRADES (NATIONAL ECONOMIC DEVELOPMENT OFFICE) (1968) *The Cowley Shopping Centre* (London: HMSO).
EDGAR, R. (1971) *Urban Power and Social Welfare* (London: Sage).
ELKINS, S. L. (1974) *Politics and Land Use Planning: the London experience* (London: Cambridge U.P.).
ELLUL, J. (1965) *The Technological Society* (London: Cape).
ENGELS, F. (1845) (1973) *The Condition of the Working Class in England in 1844* (Moscow: Progress Publishers).
(1872) (1970) *The Housing Question* (Moscow: Progress Publishers).
ETZIONI, A. (1968) *The Active Society* (New York: Free Press).
EVERSLEY, D. (1972) 'Rising Costs and Static Incomes: some economic consequences of regional planning in London', *Urban Studies*, October.
FELDMAN, A. S. and MOORE, W. E. (1962) 'Industrialisation and Industrialism, Convergence and Differentiation', *Transactions of Fifth World Congress of Sociology* (Washington, D.C.).
FEUER, L. S. (ed.) (1972) *Marx and Engels: Basic Writings on Politics and Philosophy* (London: Fontana).
FINER, S. E. (1958a) 'Transport Interests and the Road Lobby', *Political Quarterly*, 1.
(1958b) *Private Industry and Political Power* (London: Pall Mall).
(1958c) 'Interest groups and the political process in Great Britain', in Ehrmann, H. W., *Interest Groups on Four Continents* (University of Pittsburgh Press).
(1965) *Anonymous Empire* (London: Pall Mall).
(1976) 'The Year of Corruption', *New Society*, 26 February.

FISHER, S. (1964) 'Community Power Studies: a critique', *Social Research*, 29, Winter, pp. 449-66.
FLORENCE, P. S. (1961) *The Ownership, Control and Success of Large Companies* (London: Sweet & Maxwell).
FORD, J. (1975) 'The Role of the Building Society Manager in the Urban Stratification System: autonomy versus constraint', *Urban Studies*, 12, pp. 295-302.
FOSTER, C. D. (1966) 'Social Welfare Functions in Cost-benefit Analysis', in Lawrence, J. R. (ed.), *Operational Research and the Social Sciences*, (London: Tavistock) pp. 305-18.
FRANK, A. G. (1967) *Capitalism and Underdevelopment in Latin America* London: Monthly Review Press).
FRANKLIN, B. (ed.) (1973) *The Essential Stalin: major theoretical writings 1905-1952* (London: Croom Helm).
FREEDMAN, L. (1969) *Public Housing: the politics of poverty* (New York: Holt, Rinehart & Winston).
FRIEDLAND, R. (1976) 'Class Power and Social Control: the war on poverty', *Politics and Society*, 6, no. 4, pp. 459-89.
FRIEDRICH, C. J. (1972) 'In Defence of a Concept', in Schapiro, L. (ed.), *Political Opposition in One-party States* (London: Macmillan).
FRIEDRICH, C. J. and BRZEZINSKI, Z. K. (1965) *Totalitarian Dictatorship and Autocracy* (New York: Praeger).
FRIEND, J. K. and JESSOP, W. N. (1969) *Local Government and Strategic Choice* (London: Tavistock).
FROMAN, L. A. (1967) 'An Analysis of Public Policies in Cities', *Journal of Politics*, 27, pp. 94-108.
GALBRAITH, J. K. (1956) *American Capitalism: The Concept of Countervailing Power* (New York: Houghton Mifflin).
(1962) *The Affluent Society* (Harmondsworth: Penguin Books).
(1967) *The New Industrial State* (New York: Signet).
(1974) (1975) *Economics and the Public Purpose* (London: Pelican).
GAMBLE, A. and WALTON, P. (1976) *Capitalism and Crisis* (London: Macmillan).
GARNIER, F. (1973) 'A propos de "la question urbaine"', *Espaces et Sociétés*, 8, February, pp. 123-9.
GARRARD, J. (1977) 'The History of Local Political Power', *Political Studies*, 25.
GEDDES, P. (1915) *Cities in Evolution* (London: Benn).
GERAS, N. (1972) 'Althusser's Marxism: an account and assessment', *New Left Review*, 71, p. 66.
GERSHUNY, J. I. (1976) *After Industrial Society?* (Science Policy Research Unit, University of Sussex).
GERTH, H. H. and MILLS, C. W. (eds) (1967) *From Max Weber* (London: Routledge & Kegan Paul).
GIDDENS, A. (1973) *The Class Structure of Advanced Societies* (London: Hutchinson).
GILBERT, C. (1972) *Community Power Structure: propositional inventory, tests and theory* (Gainsville: University of Florida Press).

GINZBERG, E. (ed) (1964) *Technology and Social Change* (New York: Columbia U.P.).
GLADDEN, E. N. (1972) *Local, Corporational and International Administration* (London: Staples Press).
GLASS, R. (1955) 'Urban Sociology in Great Britain: a trend report', *Current Sociology*, IV, no. 4, pp. 5-19.
    (1959) 'The Evaluation of Planning: Some Sociological Considerations', *International Social Science Journal*, II, 3, pp. 393-402.
    (1966) 'Conflict in Cities', in Ciba Foundation, de Reuck, A. and Knight J. (eds), *Conflict in Society* (London: Churchill).
    (1970) 'Housing in Camden', *Town Planning Review*, vol. 41.
GLOTZ, G. (1930) *The Greek City* (New York: Knopf).
GLUCKSMAN, A. (1972) 'A Ventriloquist Structuralism', *New Left Review*, 72, March-April.
GLUCKSMANN, M. (1971) 'Review Article on Structuralism', *British Journal of Sociology*, vol. 22, no. 2, June.
    (1974) *Structuralist Analysis in Contemporary Social Theory* (London: Routledge & Kegan Paul).
GLYN, A. and SUTCLIFFE, B. (1972) *British Capitalism, Workers and the Profits Squeeze* (Harmondsworth: Penguin Books).
GOLDTHORPE, J. (1968) 'Social Stratification in Industrial Society', in Bendix, R. and Lipset, S. M. (eds), *Class, Status and Power* (London: Routledge & Kegan Paul).
GOODMAN, R. (1972) *After the Planners* (Harmondsworth: Penguin Books).
GORDON, D. M. (1971) *Problems in Political Economy: an urban perspective* (London: Heath).
GOUGH, I. (1975) 'State Expenditure in Advanced Capitalism', *New Left Review*, 92, pp. 53-92.
GOULDNER, A. (1967) *Enter Plato* (London: Routledge & Kegan Paul).
GRAMSCI, A., Letters, articles, letters from prison and the prison notebooks, 1910-1935. 'Works' published as *Opere* in 7 vols, 1948-53 by Eihaudi, Turin. See especially vol. 5 (1949), *Note sul Machiavelli, sulla Politica e sullo Stato Moderno*.
    (1971) *Selections from Prison Notebooks* (London: Lawrence & Wishart).
GRAMSON, W. A. (1968) *Power and Discontent* (Homewood: Dorsey).
GRANT, W. (1977) 'Corporatism and Pressure Groups', in Kavanagh, D. and Rose, R., *New Trends in British Politics* (London: Sage).
GRANT, W. P. (1977) *Independent Local Politics in England and Wales* (Farnborough: Saxon House).
GREEN, P. and LEVINSON, S. (eds) (1970) *Power and Community* (New York: Pantheon).
GREER, S. A. (1962) *Governing the Metropolis* (New York: Wiley).
GRIFFITH, J. A. G. (1966) *Central Departments and Local Authorities* (London: Allen & Unwin).
GROVE, J. L. and PROCTOR, S. C. (1966) 'Citizen Participation in Planning', *Journal of the Town Planning Institute*, December, pp. 414-16.

GUTTSMAN, W. L. (1963) *The British Political Elite* (London: MacGibbon & Kee).
GYFORD, J. (1976) *Local Politics in Britain* (London: Croom Helm).
HABERMAS, J. (1971) *Towards a Rational Society* (London: Heinemann).
(1976) *Legitimation Crisis* (London: Heinemann).
HADDON, R. F. (1970) 'A Minority in a Welfare State Society: the location of West Indians in the London housing market', *New Atlantis*, 2 (i), pp. 80–133.
HALL, P. (1972) 'Planning and the Environment', in Townsend, P. and Bosanquet, N. (eds), *Labour and Inequality* (London: Fabian Society).
HALL, P. et al. (1973) *The Containment of Urban England*, vol. 2: *The Planning System – objectives, operations, impacts*, (London: Allen & Unwin).
HAMPTON, W. (1970) *Democracy and Community* (London: Oxford U.P.).
HARE, R. (1948) *Oxford's Traffic: a practical remedy* (Buckingham: Hillier).
HARLOE, M. (ed.) (1977) *Captive Cities* (London: Wiley).
HARRIS, N. (1974) 'Urban England: review articles', *Economy and Society* vol. 3, no. 3.
HARRISON, M. (1975) 'British Town Planning Ideology and the Welfare State', *Journal of Social Policy*, 4, pp. 259–74.
HARVEY, D. (1971) 'Social Processes, Spatial Form and the Redistribution of Real Income in an Urban System', in Chisholm, M., et al., *Regional Forecasting* (London: Butterworth) pp. 270–300.
(1973) *Social Justice and the City* (London: Arnold).
(1974) 'Class Monopoly Rent, Finance, Capital, and the Urban Revolution', *Regional Studies*, November.
HAWLEY, W. D. and WIRT, F. M. (1974) *The Search for Community Power* (Englewood Cliffs, N.J.: Prentice-Hall).
HAWLEY, W. D. et al. (1976) *Theoretical Perspectives on Urban Politics* (Englewood Cliffs, N.J.: Prentice-Hall).
HIGHTOWER, H. C. (1969) 'Planning Theory in Contemporary Professional Education', *JAIP*, 35, pp. 326–9.
HILL. D. M. (1970) *Participating in Local Affairs* (Harmondsworth: Penguin).
(1974) *Democratic Theory and Local Goverment* (London: Allen & Unwin).
HILL, R. (1977) 'Two Divergent Theories of the State', *International Journal of Urban and Regional Research*, vol. 1, pp. 37–44.
HINDESS, B. (1971) *The Decline of Working Class Politics* (London: MacGibbon & Kee).
HOFFMAN, G. W. and NEAL, F. W. (1962) *Yugoslavia and the New Communism* (New York: Twentieth Century Fund).
HOGBEN, L. et al. (1938) *Political arithmetic* (London: Allen & Unwin).
HOLFORD, SIR W. (1963) *Future Requirements of the Science Departments*, Supplement (4) to *Oxford University Gazette*, no. 3157, 23 May, pp. 1253–66.

HOOPER, A. (1974) 'On the New Urban Analysis: social justice and city', *Policy and Politics*, vol. 3, no. 1.
    (forthcoming) *The Neo-Marxist View of Urban Sociology* (London: Macmillan).
HOROWITZ, I. L. (ed.) (1963) *Mills, C. Wright, Power, People and Politics* (London: Oxford University Press).
HUNT, R. N. (1975) *The Political Ideas of Marx and Engels* (London: Macmillan).
HUNTER, F. (1953) *Community Power Structure: a study of decision makers* (Chapel Hill: UNCP).
    (1959) *Top Leadership, U.S.A.* (London: Oxford U.P.).
ILLICH, I. (1973) *Tools for Conviviality* (London: Calder & Boyars).
INKELES, A. and BAUER, R. A. (1959) *The Soviet Citizen* (Cambridge, Mass.: Harvard U.P.).
IONESCU, G. (1967) *The Politics of the European Communist States* (London: Weidenfeld & Nicolson).
    (1972) *Comparative Communist Politics* (London: Macmillan).
ISSS (1959) *Programme of the League of Yugoslav Communists* (International Society for Socialist Studies).
JACOB, P. E. (ed.) (1971) *Values and the Active Community: a cross-national study of the influence of local leadership* (London: Collier-Macmillan).
JACOBS, J. (1965) *The Death and Life of Great American Cities* (Harmondsworth: Penguin Books).
JANOWITZ, M. (1961) *Community Political Systems* (Glencoe, Ill.: Free Press).
    (1962) 'Community Power Structure and Policy Science Research', *Public Opinion Quarterly*, 20, Fall, pp. 398–410.
JEFFREY, N. and CALDWELL, M. (eds) (1975) *Planning and Urbanism in China* (Oxford: Pergamon Press).
JENKINS, S. (1973) 'The Politics of London's Motorways', *Political Quarterly*, 44.
JEVONS, W. S. (1871) *Theory of Political Economy* (London: Macmillan).
JOHNSON, T. J. (1972) *Professions and Power* (London: Macmillan).
    (1971) *Urban Residential Patterns* (London: Bell).
JONES, G. N. (1969) *Planned Organisational Change: a study in change dynamics* (London: Routledge & Kegan Paul).
JONES, G. W. (1969) *Borough Politics* (London: Macmillan).
JONES, R. E. (1967) *The Functional Analysis of Politics* (London: Routledge & Kegan Paul).
KADT, E. DE and WILLIAMS, G. (1974) *Sociology and Development* (London: Tavistock).
KAHN, R. L. and BOULDING, E. (eds) (1964) *Power and Conflict in Organisations* (New York: Basic Books).
KAHN, S. I. (1970) *How People Get Power: organising oppressed communities for action* (New York: McGraw-Hill).
KANTOR, P. (1974) 'The Governable City: islands of power and political parties in London', *Polity*, 7.

(1976) 'Elites, Pluralism and Policy Areas in London', *British Journal of Political Science*, 6, pp. 311-34.

KAPLAN, H. (1963) *Urban Renewal Politics: slum clearance in Newark* (Columbia U.P.).

KAUTSKY, J. (1968) *Communism and the Politics of Development* (London: Wiley).

KAVANAGH, D. and ROSE, R. (1977) *New Trends in British Politics* (London: Sage).

KELLER, S. (1963) *Beyond the Ruling Class* (New York: Random House).

KERR, C. D., HARBISON, F. H. and MAYERS, C. A. (1962) *Industrialism and Industrial Man: the problems of labour and management in economic growth* (London: Heinemann).

KEYNES, J. M. (1936) *General Theory of Employment, Interest and Money* (London: Macmillan).

KLEIN, J. (1965) *Samples from English Cultures* (London: Routledge & Kegan Paul).

KLEINBERG, B. S. (1973) *American Society in the Post-industrial Age* (Columbus, Ohio: Merrill).

KOLAJA, J. (1965) *Workers' Councils: the Yugoslav experience* (London: Tavistock).

KORNHAUSER, W. (1959) *Politics of Mass Society* (New York: Free Press).

KUHN, T. S. (1962) *The Structure of Scientific Revolutions* (University of Chicago Press).

LACLAU, A. (1975) 'The Specificity of the Political: of the political in the Poulantzas and Miliband debate', *Economy and Society*, 4, February, no. 1.

LACLAU, E. (1971) 'Feudalism and Capitalism in Latin America', *New Left Review*, 67, pp. 19-38.

LANE, D. (1976) *The Socialist Industrial State: towards a political sociology of state socialism* (London: Allen & Unwin).

LANE, R. E. (1959) *Political Life: why people get involved in politics* (Glencoe, Ill.: Free Press).

LARNER, R. J. (1966) 'Ownership and Control in the 200 Largest, Non-financial Corporates, 1929 and 1963', *American Economic Review*, vol. 56, no. 4 part 1, September, p. 777.

LASSWELL, H. D. (1958) *Politics: who gets what, when, how?* (New York: World Publishing Co.).

LATAKOS, I. and MUSGRAVE, S. (eds) (1920) *Criticism and Growth of Knowledge* (London: Cambridge U.P.).

LEE, E. G. (1960) *The Politics of Non-partisanship: a study of California city elections* (Berkeley: University of California Press).

LEE, J. M. (1963) *Social Leaders and Public Persons* (Oxford: Clarendon Press).

LEFEBVRE, H. (1969) *Dialectical Materialism* (London: Cape).

LENIN, V. I. (1933) *What Is To Be done? Burning questions of our movement* (originally published March 1902) (London: Martin Lawrence).

(1913) *The Teachings of Karl Marx*, article for the Russian Encyclopaedia 1914.
(1916) (1934) *Imperialism – the highest stage of capitalism* (New York: International Publishers).
(August–September 1917) (1919) *The State and Revolution, Marxist Teaching on the State and the Tasks of the Proletariat in the Revolution* (London: Allen & Unwin).
(1919) (1972) *The State and Revolution* (Moscow: Progress).
LEVY, F. S., MELTSNER, A. J. and WILDAVSKY, A. (1974) *Urban Outcomes: schools, streets and libraries* (Berkeley: University of California Press).
LICHFIELD, N. (1971) 'Cost Benefit Analysis in Planning: A Critique of the Roskill Commission', *Regional Studies*, vol. 5, pp. 157-83.
LINDBERG. L. (ed.) (1975) *Patterns of Advanced Societies* (Council for European Studies).
LINDBLOM, C. E. (1965) *The Intelligence of Democracy* (New York: Free Press and London: Collier-Macmillan).
(1968) *The Policy Making Process* (Englewood Cliffs, N.J.: Prentice-Hall).
LINEBERRY, R. L. (1977) *Equality and Urban Policy: the distribution of municipal public services* (London: Sage).
LIPSET, S. M. (1963) *Political Man* (London: Mercury).
LIPSET, S. M. and BENDIX, R. (1951) 'Social Status and Social Structure', *British Journal of Sociology*, vol. 11.
LIPSET, S. M. and DABSON, R. B. (1973) 'Social Stratification and Sociology in the Soviet Union', *Survey*, vol. 19, Summer.
LIPSKY, M. (1970) *Protest in City Politics: rent strikes, housing and the power of the poor* (Chicago: Rand McNally).
LOCKWOOD, D. (1958) *The Blackcoated Worker* (London: Allen & Unwin).
LOJKINE, J. (1977) *Le Marxisme, L'Etat et la Question urbaine* (Paris: Presses Universitaires de France).
LOMAS, G. (1975) *The Inner City* (London Council of Social Service).
LUCE, R. D. and RAIFFA, H. (1957) *Games and Decisions* (New York: Wiley).
LUKACS, G. (1922) (1971) *History and Class Consciousness* (London: Merlin Press).
LUKES, S. (1974) *Power, a Radical View* (London: Macmillan).
LUXEMBURG, R. (1951) *The Accumulation of Capital* (originally published in 2 vols – 1913 and 1919) (London: Routledge & Kegan Paul).
(1922) *The Russian Revolution: an appreciative criticism* (Ann Arbor, Mich.: University of Michigan Press; Dreadnought Publications).
(1937) *Reform or Revolution?* (New York: Three Arrows Press). Originally published in German in 1899.
LYND, R. S. and LYND, H.M. (1929) *Middletown* (New York: Harcourt, Brace).
(1937) *Middletown in Transition* (New York: Harcourt, Brace).
McCONNELL, D. (1973) 'Groups and Planning: a case study of East

Oxford', unpublished thesis (Department of Town Planning, Oxford Polytechnic).
McCONNELL, G. (1966) *Private Power and American Democracy* (New York: Knopf).
McFARLAND, A. S. (1969) *Power and Leadership in Pluralist Systems* (Stanford University Press).
McKENZIE, R. T. (1964) 'Some Problems of Democratic Government in Britain', in Ehrmann, H. W. (1964), *Democracy in a Changing Society* (London: Pall Mall Press).
MACPHERSON, C. B. (1978) 'Do We Need a Theory of the State?', *European Journal of Sociology*, XVIII.
McLELLAN, D. (1975) *Marx* (London: Fontana).
McLOUGHLIN, J. B. (1973) *Control and Urban Planning* (London: Faber).
MABBOTT, J. D. (1958) *The State and the Citizen* (London: Arrow Books).
MAHN, M. (ed) (1972) *People and Politics in Urban Society* (London: Sage).
MAINE, H. S. (1894) *Ancient Law* (London: Murray).
MANDEL, E (1968) *An Introduction to Marxist Economy Theory* (London: Merlin Press).
    (1969) *The Inconsistencies of State Capitalism*, International Marxist Group Pamphlet.
    (1974) *Marxist Economic Theory* (London: Merlin Press).
MANN, P. H. (1965) *An Approach to Urban Sociology* (London: Routledge & Kegan Paul).
MANNHEIM, K. (1951) in Gerth, H. H. and Bramsted, E. K. (eds), *Freedom, Power and Democratic Planning* (London: Routledge & Kegan Paul).
    (1952) *Essays on the Sociology of Knowledge* (London: Routledge & Kegan Paul).
MARCH, J. G. and SIMON, H. A. (1958) *Organisations* (London: Wiley).
    (1967) 'Dysfunctions in Organisations', in Bell, G. D. (ed.), *Organisations and Human Behaviour: a book of readings* (Englewood Cliffs, N.J.: Prentice-Hall).
MARCUSE, H. (1958) *Societ Marxism: a critical analysis* (London: Routledge & Kegan Paul).
    (1964) (1968) *One-Dimensional Man* (London: Sphere Books).
MARRIOTT, O. (1967) *The Property Boom* (London: Hamilton).
MARRIS, P. and REIN, M. (1967) *Dilemmas of Social Reform* (London: Routledge & Kegan Paul).
MARSH, O. and GRANT, W. (1977) 'Tripartism: reality or myth?', *Government and Opposition*, vol. 12, no. 2, Summer.
MARSHALL, A. (1890) *Principles of Economics* (London: Macmillan).
MARTIN, A. F. and STEEL, R. W. (1954) *The Oxford Region* (Oxford University Press).
MARTIN, R. (1977) *The Sociology of Power* (London: Routledge & Kegan Paul).
MARTINDALE, D. (1968), see introduction to WEBER, M. (1968), below.
MARX, K. and ENGELS, F. (1846) (1974) in Arthur, C. (ed.), *The German*

Ideology, Part 1 (London: Lawrence & Wishart).
   (1848) (1975) *The Communist Manifesto* (London: Penguin).
   (1973) *Marx and Engels Selected Works* (London: Lawrence & Wishart).
MARX, K. (1852) (1973) *The Eighteenth Brumaire of Louis Bonaparte*, see Marx and Engels, *Selected Works* (London: Lawrence & Wishart).
   (1857) (1973) in McLellan, D. (ed.), *Grundrisse* (St. Albans: Paladin).
   (1859) (1971) *A Contribution to the Critique of Political Economy* (London: Lawrence & Wishart).
   (1867) in Strachey, J. (ed.), *Capital*, vol. 1 (London: Nelson) (undated).
MASSAM, B. (1975) *Location and Space in Social Administration* (London: Edward Arnold).
MAUD COMMITTEE (1967) *Report of the Committee on the Management of Local Authorities* (London: HMSO).
MEDRICH, E. A (December 1974) 'Patterns of Consumption in the Public Sector: a framework for investigating the impact of local government services on client groups', in *Childhood and Government Project* (Berkeley: University of California).
MELLOR, R. (1975) 'Urban Sociology in an Urbanised Society', *British Journal of Sociology*, XXVI, no. 3, pp. 276-93.
   (1977) *Urban Sociology in an Urbanised Society* (London: Routledge & Kegan Paul).
MERELMAN, R. (1968) 'On the Neo-Elitist Critique of Community Power', *American Political Science Review*, 62.
MERRINGTON, J. (1975) 'Town and Country in the Transition to Capitalism', *New Left Review*, 93, pp. 71-92.
MESTHENE, E. G. (1970) *Technological Change: its impact on man and society* (Cambridge, Mass.: Harvard U.P.).
MESYAROS, I. (1971) 'Alienation and the Necessity of Social Control', *Socialist Register*.
MEYERSON, M. and BANFIELD, E. C. (1955) *Politics, Planning and the Public Interest* (New York: Free Press).
MILIBAND, R. (1969) *The State in Capitalist Society* (London: Weidenfeld & Nicolson).
MILL, J. S. (1848) *Principles of Political Economy; with some of their applications to social philosophy* (London: Routledge & Kegan Paul).
MILLER, D. C. (1958) 'Industry and Community Power Structure: a comparative study of an American and English city', *American Sociological Review*, 23, February, pp. 9-15.
   (1970) *International Community Power Structure* (Bloomington: Indiana U.P.).
MILLS, C. W. (1959) *The Power Elite* (New York: Oxford U.P.).
MINETT, M. J. (1974) 'A Positive Approach to Development Control', in *Development Control and Plan Implementation*. Proceedings of a seminar at the University of Warwick, 1974 (London: PTRC).
MINISTRY OF HOUSING AND LOCAL GOVERNMENT (1969) *People and Planning* (Skeffington Report) (London: HMSO).

MINISTRY OF TOWN AND COUNTRY PLANNING (1950) *Report of the Committee on Qualifications of Planners*. Prepared by a committee under the chairmanship of Sir George Schuster (London: HMSO) Cmnd 8059.

MOGEY, J. M. (1956) *Family and Neighbourhood: two studies in Oxford* (Oxford U.P.).

MOLLENKOPF, J. H. (1975) 'The Post-War Politics of Urban Development', *Politics and Society*, 5, pp. 245-7.

MOREHOUSE, H. F. and CHAMBERLAIN, C. (1974) 'Lower-Class Attitudes to Property', *Sociology*, 8.

MORRIS, D. S. and NEWTON, K. (1971) 'The Social Composition of a City Council, 1925-66', *Social and Economic Administration*, 5.

MORRIS, P. (1972) 'Power in New Haven: a reassessment of "Who Governs?"', *British Journal of political Science*, 2.

MORRIS, R. W. (1968) *Urban Sociology* (London: Routledge & Kegan Paul).

MORRIS, R. N. and MOGEY, J. (1965) *The Sociology of Housing: studies at Berinsfield* (London: Routledge & Kegan Paul).

MOSER, C. A. and SCOTT, W. (1961) *British Towns: a statistical study of their social and economic differences* (London: Oliver & Boyd).

MOYNIHAN, D. P. (1969) *Maximum Feasible Misunderstanding* (New York: Free Press).

MUCHNICK, D. (1970) *Urban Renewal in Liverpool* (London: Bell).

MUMFORD, L. (1938) *The Culture of Cities* (New York: Secker & Warburg).

MUNROE, W. B. (1926) *The Government of American Cities* (New York: Macmillan).

MUSIL, J. (1971) 'Town Planning as a Social Process', *The New Atlantis*, vol. 2, no. 2.

NADEL, M. V. (1975) 'The Hidden Dimension of Public Policy: private governments and the policy-making process', *Journal of Politics*, 37, pp. 2-35.

NETZER, D. (1970) *Economic Theory and Urban Problems* (London: Basic Books).

NEWTON, K. (1973) 'Links Between Leaders and Citizens in a Local Political System', *Policy and Politics*, 1.

(1976) *Second City Politics* (London: Oxford U.P.).

NISBET, R. (1964) *Power and Community* (Oxford: Galaxy Books).

O'CONNOR, J. (1973) *The Fiscal Crisis of the State* (New York: St Martin's Press).

OFFE, C. (1972) 'Advanced Capitalism and the Welfare State', *Politics and Society*, vol. 2, pp. 479-88.

(1974) 'Structural Problems of the Capitalist State', in Beyme, K., *German Political Studies*, vol. 1 (London: Sage).

(1975) 'The Theory of the Capitalist State and the Problems of Policy-formation', in Lindberg, L., Alford, R. and Grouch, C., *Stress and Contradiction in Modern Capitalism* (Lexington, Mass.: Lexington Books).

Bibliography 337

(1976) 'Political Authority and Class Structures', in Coniston, P., *Critical Sociology* (Harmondsworth: Penguin Books).
OLSON, M. (1965) *The Logic of Collective Action* (Cambridge, Mass.: Harvard U.P.).
OPEN UNIVERSITY, THE (1973) *The System of Control: social sciences - a second-level course - Urban Development Units 19-21* (Milton Keynes: Open University Press).
ORTEGA Y GASSET, J. (1951) *Revolt of the Masses* (London: Allen & Unwin).
OSSOWSKI, S. (1957) (1973) *Class Structure in the Social Consciousness* (London: Routledge & Kegan Paul).
OXFORD CENSUS TRACT COMMITTEE (1957) *Census 1951 - Oxford Area: selected population and housing characteristics by census tracts* (Oxford U.P.).

(1957) (corrected 1959) *Census 1951 - Oxford Area: selected population and housing characteristics by census tracts. Index* (Oxford: John Mogey).
OXFORD CHAMBER OF TRADE (1949) *A Plan for the Development of the City of Oxford* (Oxford: Alden).
OXFORD CITY (1932) *1932 Town and Country Planning Act Draft Scheme* (Oxford).

(1944) *How Oxford is Run: a description of the activities of the corporation departments* (Oxford: Holywell Press). (Originally a series of articles in the *Oxford Mail*.)

(1953) *Development Plan - written analysis* (Oxford).

(1955) *Development Plan - written statement* (Oxford).

(December 1960) *Proceedings of an Inquiry at Large into the Proposals for the Provision of Relief Roads for Oxford*, 4 vols (CAPO).

(1962) (1975) *High Buildings in Oxford: report of the city Planning Officer* (Oxford).

(1963) *Shopping Habits in a New Suburban Precinct* (CAPO).

(1964a) *Development Plan - written analysis: review 1964-81* (Oxford).

(1964b) *Survey of Shopping at Cowley Centre* (CAPO).

(January-February 1965a) *Development Plan Review 1964-81: proceedings of a public inquiry into proposals for alterations or additions to the Development Plan for the City of Oxford*, 4 vols (CAPO).

(1965b) *City of Oxford Development Project: Cowley Centre* (Oxford).

(1966a) *Original Jericho Statement* (Oxford).

(1966b) *Development Plan - written analysis: review 1966-81* (Oxford).

(1967a) *Development Plan - amendment no. 1 written statement* (Oxford).

(1967b) *City of Oxford - local shopping centres* (Oxford).

(1968a) *North Oxford Conservation Area* (Oxford).

(1968b) *Oxford Central Area Study* (Consultant's report) (Oxford).

(1969) *Iffley Conservation Area* (Oxford).

338 *Bibliography*

(1970a) *Development Plan - amendment no. 2 written statement* (Oxford).
(1970b) *Local Shopping Centres* (Oxford).
(1971a) *Headington Quarry Conservation Area* (Oxford).
(1971b) *Old Headington Conservation Area* (Oxford).
(1971c) *Central Conservation Area* (Oxford).
(1971d) *Proof of Evidence - Centramic Properties Ltd to develop shopping centre at Gosford and Water Eaton* (Oxford).
(1971e) *Schools for Foreign Students* (Oxford).
(1971f) *Oxford Roads* (Oxford).
(1972a) *Statutory Sites under the National Parks and Access to the Countryside Act 1949* (Oxford).
(1972b) *Development Plan Amendment - Oxford Roads* (Oxford).
(1972c) *Development of Churchill/Warneford Hospitals* (Oxford).
(1972d)*Local Plans No. 1 - East Oxford* (Oxford).
(1972e) *Employment Policy - manufacturing service industry and office development* (Oxford).
(1972f) *Relocation of Badly Sited Concerns* (Oxford).
(1972g) *Central Area Redevelopment: second phase 1973-80* (Oxford).
(1972h) *Houses in Multiple Occupation* (Oxford).
(1973a) *Redevelopment of Large Residential Properties* (Oxford).
(1973b) *Headington Hill - statement of policy* (Oxford).
(1973c) *Balanced Transport Policy (report to council)* (Oxford).
(1973d) *Residential Development in Iffley Road* (Oxford).
(1973e) *City of Oxford Conservation Areas* (Oxford).
(1973f) *Land Availability for Housing* (Oxford).
(1973g) *Houses in Multiple Occupation* (Oxford).
(1973h) *Non-conforming Uses - relocation priorities* (Oxford).
(1973i) *Rawlinson Road Conservation Area* (Oxford).
(June 1973j) *South Oxford Local Plan: first report* (Oxford).
(1973k) *Shotover* (Oxford).
(1973l) *Oxford United* (Oxford).
(1973m) *East Oxford Preliminary Local Plan Policies* (Oxford).
(1973n) *Proposed Car Park - Walton Crescent/Richmond Road* (Oxford).
(1973o) *Beauchamp Lane Conservation Area* (Oxford).
(March 1974a) *St Ebbe's Action Area Plan: discussion paper digest* (Oxford).
(1974b) *Iffley: public comment and modifications to planning committee's interim policy statement, July 1974.* Report of CAPO to Committees (Oxford).
(July 1974c) *Iffley: a Report by planning committee on the local plan prepared for the Donnington Hospital Trust by Development Planning Partnership* (Oxford).
(1975) *Oxford Central Area: St Thomas's discussion paper summary* (Oxford).
(March 1976) *Central Area Local Plan: St Ebbe's Interim statement* (Oxford).

Bibliography 339

(various years 1947-75) *Abstract of the Treasurer's Accounts for the Year Ended 31st March* . . . (Oxford).
OXFORD PRESERVATION TRUST (1942) *Report of the Committee on Planning and Reconstruction* (Oxford U.P.).
OXFORDSHIRE COUNTY COUNCIL (1975) *Oxfordshire Tomorrow* (Oxford).
OXFORD UNIVERSITY GAZETTE (8 March 1966) *Development Plan for the County Borough of Oxford* - a supplement to no. 3268.
PAHL, R. E. (ed.) (1968) *Readings in Urban Sociology* (Oxford: Pergamon Press).
PAHL, R. E. and WINKLER, J. T. (1974) 'The Coming Corporatism', *New Society*, 10 October, pp. 72–6
PAHL, R. E. (1968) (1976) *Whose City?* (Harmondsworth: Penguin Books).
  (1977) 'Stratification, the Relation between States and Urban and Regional Development', *International Journal of Urban and Regional Research*, vol. 1, pp. 6-17.
PARENTI, M. (1972) 'Power and Pluralism: a view from the bottom', *Journal of Politics*, 32, pp. 501-30.
PARK, R. E., BURGESS, E. W. and McKENZIE, R. D. (eds) (1925) *The City* (Chicago U.P.).
PARSONS, T. (1954) 'The Professions and Social Structure', in Parsons, T., *Essays in Sociological Theory* (Glencoe, Ill. Free Press).
  (1960) 'Characteristics of Industrial Societies', in *Structure and Process in Modern Societies* (Glencoe, Ill. Free Press).
PATEMAN, C. (1970) *Participation and Democratic Theory* (Cambridge U.P).
PEATTIE, L. R. (1968) 'Reflections on Advocacy Planning', *Journal of the American Institute of Planners*, March, pp. 80-8.
PETERSON, P. E. (1971) 'British Interest Group Theory Re-Examined', *Comparative Politics*, 3.
PFAUTZ, H. W. (ed.) (1906) (1967) *Charles Booth on the City: physical pattern and social structure* (London: Chicago U.P.).
PIAGET, J. *Structuralism* (London: Routledge & Kegan Paul).
PICKVANCE, C. G. (1974) 'On a Materialist Critique of Urban Sociology', *Sociological Review*, 22 (2), May.
  (ed.) (1976) *Urban Sociology: Critical Essays* (London: Tavistock).
  (1977) 'Marxist Approaches to the Study of Urban Politics: divergences among some recent French studies', *International Journal of Urban and Regional Research*, I, pp. 219-55.
PINTO-DUSCHINSKY, M. (1977) 'Corruption in Britain', *Political Studies*, 25.
PIRENNE, H. (1946) *Medieval Cities* (Princeton U.P.).
PIZZORNO, A. (ed.) (1971) *Political Sociology* (Harmondsworth: Penguin Books).
PLAMENATZ, J. (1954) 'Interests', *Political Studies*, 2.
PLOWDEN, S. (1972) *Towns against Traffic*, particularly chap. 4, 'Oxford' (London: André Deutsch).
POLSBY, N. W. (1963) *Community Power and Political Theory* (New Haven: Yale U.P.).

POLTER, A. (1961) *Organised Groups in British National Politics* (London: Faber).
POULANTZAS, N. (1973a) 'On Social Classes', *New Left Review*, 78, April.
  (1973b) *Political Power and Social Classes*, translation of 1968 French edition; ed. O'Hagan, T. (London: New Left Books).
  (1974) 'Internationalisation of Capitalist Relations and the Nation-State', *Economy and Society*, vol. 3, pp. 145-79.
  (1975) *Classess in Contemporary Capitalism* (London: New Left Books).
  (1976) 'The Capitalist State: a reply to Miliband and Laclau', *New Left Review*, no. 95, January-February, pp. 63-83.
PRETECEILLE, E. (1973) *La Production des Grands Ensembles* (Paris: Mouton).
  (1977) 'Equipment collectifs et Consummation sociale', *International Journal of Urban and Regional Research*, I, pp. 101-24.
PREWITT, K. and STONE, A. (1973) *The Ruling Elites: élite theory, power and American democracy* (New York: Harper & Row).
QUINN, J. A. (1950) *Human Ecology* (New York: Prentice-Hall).
RABINOWITZ, F. F. (1969) *City Politics and Planning* (New York: Atherton Press).
RAWLS, J. (1962) 'Justice as Fairness', in Laslet, P. and Runciman, W. G. (eds), *Philosophy, Politics and Society*, II (Oxford: Blackwell).
RAYSON, T. (1946) *The King is in his Counting House: a prospect of Oxford* (Oxford: Alden).
REDFIELD, R. (1955) *The Little Community* (Chicago U.P.).
REX, J. (1961) *Key Problems of Sociological Theory* (London: Routledge & Kegan Paul).
  (1972) *Race, Colonialism and the City* (London: Routledge & Kegan Paul).
  (1974) *Approaches to Sociology* (London: Routledge & Kegan Paul).
REX, J. and MOORE, K. (1967) *Race, Community and Conflict* (Oxford U.P.).
RICARDO, D. (1817) *Principles of Political Economy and Taxation* (London: Dent).
RICCI, D. (1971) *Community Power and Democratic Theory* (New York: Random House).
RICHARDSON, J. J. (1969) *The Policy-making Process* (London: Routledge & Kegan Paul).
RICHARDSON, N. H. (1970) 'Participatory Democracy and Planning - the Canadian experience', *Journal of the Town Planning Institute*, 56, pp. 52-5.
RIKER, W. H. and ORDSHOOK, P. C. (1973) *An Introduction to Positive Political Theory* (Englewood Cliffs, N.J.: Prentice-Hall).
ROBINSON, J. (1933) *The Economics of Imperfect Competition* (London: Macmillan).
ROBSON, W. A. and REGAN, D. E. (eds) (1971) *Great Cities of the World: their government, politics and planning*, 2 vols (3rd edn)

(London: Allen & Unwin).
ROSE, A. M. (1967) *The Power Structure: political process in American society* (New York: Oxford U.P.).
ROSSI, P. H. (1960) 'Power and Community Structure', *Midwest Journal of Political Science*, 4, November, pp. 390-401.
ROSSI, P. H. and DENTLER, R. A. (1961) *The Politics of Urban Renewal* (Glencoe, Ill.: Free Press).
ROSTOW, W. W. (1960) *The Stages of Economic Growth: a non-communist manifesto* (Cambridge U.P.).
ROWNTREE, B. S. (1901) *Poverty: a study of town life* (London: Macmillan).
RUSH, M. and ALTHOFF, P. (1971) *An Introduction to Political Sociology* (London: Nelson).
RUSSON, H. (1972) 'Oxford Replanned and Replanned and . . .', unpublished thesis, Department of Town Planning, Oxford Polytechnic.
ST SIMON, C. H. COMTE DE, 'L'Industrie' (1817); 'L'organisateur' (1819); 'Du Systeme Industriel' (1821); 'Catechisme des Industriels' (1823).
    (1976), in Ionescu, G. (ed.), *The Political Thought of Saint-Simon* (Oxford U.P.).
SALISBURY, R. H. (1970) *Interest Group Politics in America* (New York: Harper & Row).
SARTORI, G. (1962) *Democratic Theory* (Detroit: Wayne U.P.).
SAUNDERS, P. (1974) 'Who Runs Croydon? Power and politics in a London borough'. Ph.D. thesis, London University.
    (1979) *Urban Politics: a sociological interpretation* (London: Hutchinson).
SAY, J. B. (1803) *Traite d'Economie politique* (Paris: Guillaumin).
SAYRE, W. S. and KAUFMAN, H. (1965) *Governing New York City* (New York: Norton).
SCARROW, H. A. (1971) 'Policy Pressures by British Local Government: the case of regulations in the "public interest"', *Comparative Politics*, 4, pp. 113-34.
    (1972) 'The Impact of British Domestic Air Pollution Legislation', *British Journal of Political Science*, 2.
SCASE, R. (ed.) (1977) *Industrial Society: class, cleavage and control* (London: Allen & Unwin).
SCHATTSCHNEIDER, E. E. (1960) *The Semi-Sovereign People: a realist's view of democracy in America* (New York: Holt, Rinehart & Winston).
SCHMITTER, P. C. (1974) 'Still the Century of Corporatism, *Review of Politics*, 36, pp. 93-4.
SCHOEFLER, S. (1954) 'Towards a General Definition of Rational Action', *Kyklos*, vol. 8, pp. 245-71.
SCHON, D. A. (1967) *Technology and Change* (New York: Seymour Lawrence Books).
SCHUBERT, G. A. (1960) *The Public Interest* (Glencoe, Ill.: Free Press).
SCHUMACHER, E. F. (1976) *Small is Beautiful* (London: Abacus).
SCHUMPETER, J. A. (1976) *Capitalism, Socialism and Democracy* (London: Allen & Unwin).

SHARANSKY, I. (ed.) (1970) *Policy Analysis in Political Science* (Chicago: Markham).
SCOTT REPORT (1942) *Report of the Committee on Land Utilisation in Rural Areas*, Cmnd 6378 (London: HMSO).
SCOTT WILSON KIRKPATRICK and PARTNERS, HUGH WILSON and LEWIS WOMERSLEY (December 1968) *Oxford Central Area Study* (London).
SENNETT, R. (1970) *The Uses of Disorder* (New York: Knopf).
SHARP, T. (1948) *Oxford Replanned* (London: Architectural Press).
SHARP, L. J. (1962) *A Metropolis Votes* (Greater London Papers no. 8) (London School of Economics).
    (ed.) (1967) *Voting in Cities* (London: Macmillan).
    (1975) 'Innovation and Change in British Lane Use Planning', in Hayward, J. and Watson, M. (eds), *Planning, Politics and Public Policy* (London: Cambridge U.P.).
SHONFIELD, A. (1968) *Modern Capitalism: a changing balance of public and private power* (Oxford U.P.).
SIMON, H. A., SMITHBERG, D. W. and THOMPSON, V. A. (1968) *Public Administration* (New York: Knopf).
SIMMEL, G. (1903, 1936) *The Metropolis and Mental Life* (Chicago U.P.).
SIMMIE, J. M. (1974) *Citizens in Conflict* (London: Hutchinson).
SLATER, P. (1977) *Origin and Significance of the Frankfurt School* (London: Routledge & Kegan Paul).
SMALLWOOD, F. (1965) *Greater London: the politics of metropolitan reform* (Indianapolis, Ind.: Bobbs-Merrill).
SMITH, A. (1776; new ed. 1950) *An Inquiry into the Nature and Causes of the Wealth of Nations* (London: Methuen).
SMITH, A. H. (1959) *Collected Papers on the Planning of Oxford*.
SMITH, C. G. and SCARGILL, D. (1975) *Oxford and Its Region* (Oxford U.P.).
SMITH, P. J. (ed.) (1975) *The Politics of Physical Resources* (Harmondsworth: Penguin Books).
SOROKIN, P. (1964) *The Basic Trends of Our Times* (New York: Conn.: College and University Press).
SPENGLER, O. (1928) *The Decline of the West* (New York: Knopf).
STACEY, M., BATSONE, E., BELL, C. and MUNOTT, A. (1975) *Power, Persistence and Change: a second study of Banbury* (London: Routledge & Kegan Paul).
STEDMAN-JONES, G. (1971) *Outcast London: a study in the relationship between classes in Victorian Society* (Oxford: Clarendon Press).
STEEPMAN, M. (1972) *Housing Investment in the Inner City: the dynamics of decline* (Cambridge, Mass.: MIT).
STEWART, J. D. (1958) *British Pressure Groups* (Oxford: Clarendon Press).
    (1974) *The Responsive Local Authority* (London: Charles Knight).
STRACHEY, J. (1925) *Revolution by Reason: an account of the financial proposals submitted to the Labour movement by Mr Oswald Mosley*

(London: Leonard Parsons).
— (1934) 'Liberty and the Modern State', in *Aristotelian Society Supplementary*, vol. 13, pp. 31-41.
— (1935) *The Nature of Capitalist Crisis* (New York: Covici Friede).
— (1956) *Contemporary Capitalism* (New York: Random House).
SWEEZY, P. M. and BETTELHEIM, C. (1971) *On the Transition to Socialism* (New York: Monthly Review).
SZELENYI, I. (1975) *Regional Management and Social Class* (London: Centre for Environmental Studies).
THOMAS, R. (April 1969) *London's New Towns: a study of self-contained and balanced communities.* Political and Economic Planning Broadsheet 510 (London).
THOMPSON, J. G. (1927) *Urbanisation: its effects on government and society* (New York: E. P. Dutton).
TOFFLER, A. (1970) *Future Shock* (London: Bodley Head).
TOULMIN, H. A. (1915) *The City Manager* (New York: Arno).
TOURAINE, A. (1974) *The Post-Industrial Society* (London: Wildwood House).
TRISTAM, R. (1975) 'Ontology and theory: a comment on Marx's analysis of some of the problems', in *Sociological Review* (N.S.), 23, no. 4, pp. 764-5.
TROTSKY, L. (1918) *Our Revolution: essays on working-class and international revolution 1904-17*, collected and translated with biographical and explanatory notes by M. J. Olgin (New York: Holt & Co.).
— (1926) *Towards Socialism or Capitalism?* . . . trans. by R. S. Townsend and Z. Vergerova (London: Methuen).
— (written 1929) (1931) *The Permanent Revolution* (New York: Pioneer Publications).
— (1935) (1973) *The Class Nature of the Soviet State* (London: New Park Publications).
— (written 1936) (1973) *The Revolution Betrayed: where is the Soviet Union and where is it going?* (London: Faber & Faber).
— (1938) *The Death Agony of Capitalism and the Tasks of the Fourth International* (Special Issue of Workers' International News).
ULMER, S. S. (ed.) (1970) *Political Decision-making* (London: Van Nostrand Reinhold).
URRY, J. and WAKEFORD, J. (eds) (1973) *Power in Britain* (London: Heinemann).
UTHWATT REPORT (1942) *Final Report of the Expert Committee on Compensation and Betterment*, Cmnd 6386 (London: HMSO).
VIDICH, A. J. and BENSMAN, J. (1968) *Small Town in Mass Society* (Princeton U.P.).
WALLACE, W. (1972) 'Blueprint and Planning Process: a case study', unpublished thesis, Department of Town Planning, Oxford Polytechnic.
WALLIA, C. S. (ed.) (1970) *Toward century 21: technology, society and human values* (New York: Basic Books).
WALTON, J. (1966) 'Discipline, Method and Community Power: a note on the sociology of knowledge', *American Sociological Review*, 31,

October, pp. 684-9.
WARNER, W. L. (1963) *Yankee City* (New Haven: Yale U.P.).
WARREN, B. (April 1972) 'Capitalist Planning and the State', *New Left Review*, No. 72.
WARREN, R. L. (ed.) (1969) *Politics and the Ghettos* (New York: Atherton Press).
WAXMAN, C. L. (ed.) (1968) *Poverty, Power and Politics* (New York: Grossett & Dunlap).
WEBBER, M. M. (October 1968 and January 1969) 'Planning in an Environment of Change', *Town Planning Review*, vol. 39, nos 3 and 4, pp. 179-95 and pp. 227-95.
WEBBER, A. F. (1899) *The Growth of Cities in the Nineteenth Century* (New York: Macmillan).
WEBER, M. (1968) *The City* (London: Collier-Macmillan).
—— (1964) *The Theory of Social and Economic Organisation* (New York: Free Press of Glencoe).
WESTERGAARD, J. H. (1964) 'Land Use Planning since 1951', *Town Planning Review*, no. 3, October, pp. 219-37.
WESTERGAARD, J. (1973) *The Class Structure of Contemporary Britain* (London: Heinemann).
WESTERGAARD, J. and RESLER, H. (1976) *Class in a Capitalist Society* (London: Pelican).
WHITAKER, B. (1968) *Participation and Poverty* (London: Fabian Society).
WILCOX, D. (1904) *The American City: a problem in democracy* (London: Macmillan).
WILENSKY, A. (1964) 'The Professionalisation of Everyone?', *American Journal of Sociology*, 70, pp. 137-58.
WILLIAMS, O. P. (1971a) *Metropolitan Political Analysis* (New York: Free Press).
—— (1971b) *Metropolitan Political Analysis: a social access approach* (London: Collier-Macmillan).
WILSON, J. Q. (1963) 'Planning and Politics: citizen participation in urban renewal', *Journal of the American Institute of Planners*, November, pp. 242-9.
—— (1968) *City Politics and Public Policy* (New York: Wiley).
WINKLER, J. (1974), see PAHL and WINKLER, above.
—— (1976) 'Corporatism', *European Journal of Sociology*, vol. 17, pp. 100-36.
—— (1977) 'The Corporate Economy: theory and administration', in Sease, R., *Industrial Society: class, cleavage and control* (London: Allen & Unwin).
WIRTH, L. (1938) 'Urbanism as a Way of Life', *American Journal of Sociology*, XLIV (i), July, pp. 1-24.
—— (1964) *On Cities and Social Life* (Chicago: Phoenix Books).
WOLFINGER, R. E. (1960) 'Reputation and Reality in the Study of Community Power', *American Sociological Review*, 25, October, pp. 636-44.
—— (1971) 'Non-Decisions and the Study of Local Politics', *American*

Political Science Review, 65.
WOOTTON, G. (1970) *Interest Groups* (London: Prentice-Hall).
YAFFE, D. (1973) 'The Crisis of Profitability: a critique of the Glyn-Sutcliffe thesis', *New Left Review*, 80, August.
YOUNG, K. (ed.) (1975) *Essays in the Study of Urban Politics* (London: Macmillan).

Name Index

Aaronovitch, L. 70
Abercrombie, P. 180
Armer, F. 180
Aron, R. 48, 50
Arrow, K. 42

Bacharach, P. 8, 9, 10, 12, 21
Banfield, E. C. 19
Baran, P. A. 67, 71, 72
Baratz, M. S. 8, 9, 10, 12, 21
Beer, S. 19
Bell, D. 35, 39, 160, 161
Bell, G. D. 161
Bendix, R. 35, 36
Benson, C. S. 23
Betjeman, J. 198
Beveridge, Lord 178
Blake, R. 175
Buchanan, C. 185
Bücher, K. 50
Burgess, E. W. 51, 225
Burnham, J. 95, 115

Castells, M. 11, 12, 15, 16, 19, 20
Cawson, A. 100, 110, 111
Clark, T. N. 138
Chase Report 245
Collison, P. 141, 142, 207
Crenson, M. A. 20, 21
Crossman, R. 185
Curl, J. S. 168

Dahl, R. A. 9, 12, 18
Dahrendorf, R. 36, 39, 45, 95
Dale, L. 171, 172
Davies, B. 27, 29
Davies, J. G. 116
Dennis, N. 116
Department of the Environment 143, 222, 223, 231

Djilas, M. 40, 47, 48, 95, 123
Dobry, G. 143, 222, 223, 231
Dunleavy, P. 11

Engels, F. 4, 37, 66, 72, 74, 75, 78, 86, 87, 89, 94

Fisher, S. 11, 18
Ford, J. 116
Friedland, R. 27, 28

Galbraith, J. K. 40, 47, 48, 117
Gamble, A. 68
Giddens, A. 41, 45, 46
Glass, R. 256
Glucksmann, M. 13, 87
Glyn, A. 78
Goldthorpe, J. 46
Gouldner, A. 161
Gramsci, A. 72, 80, 85, 86, 89, 95, 98, 121
Grant, W. 102, 104

Hall, P. 256
Harvey, D. 19, 22
Hill, C. 184

Jellicoe, Lord 183

Kaysen, C. 12

Lane, D. 40, 47, 49
Laswell, H. D. 15
Lenin, V. I. 72, 73, 76, 79, 85, 86, 88, 89, 94, 123
Levy, F. S. 23
Lineberry, R. L. 23, 24, 25
Lipsett, S. M. 35, 36
Lucas, Lord 184
Lund, P. M. 23

Name Index

Lynd, R. S. and Lynd, H. M. 17

McKenzie, R. D. 51, 225
McLoughlin, J. B. 221
Mandel, E. 68, 69
Mannheim, K. 18
Marcuse, H. 40, 115
Marriott, O. 265
Marsh, O. 102, 104
Martin, R. 9
Martindale, D. 52
Marx, K. 4, 35, 36, 37, 38, 40, 45, 49, 62, 63, 65, 66, 72, 74, 75, 78, 79, 80, 82, 86, 87, 88, 89, 94, 98, 121, 122, 123, 125
Meltsner, A. J. 23
Merton, R. 161
Miliband, R. 68, 85, 86, 91, 92, 123
Miller, D. C. 18, 19, 29
Mills, C. W. 12, 19
Ministry of Housing and Local Government 152, 193
Minns, F. J. 172, 189
Mogey, J. 141, 142, 272, 273, 276
Moore, K. 116
Mosca, G. 35
Moser, C. A. 133, 134, 135, 136, 137
Mumford, L. 185
Musil, J. 54

Oxford City Council 167, 169, 174, 187, 189, 194, 195, 197, 198, 200, 201, 203, 204, 205, 206, 207, 212, 214: *see also in Subject Index*
Oxford Mail and Oxford Times 155, 171, 173, 174, 175, 176, 177, 184, 185, 187, 189, 190, 191, 193, 194, 195, 198, 199, 204, 206, 210, 211, 213, 221, 250, 259, 270, 271, 272
Oxfordshire County Council 227

Pahl, R. E. 101, 104, 116, 117
Pareto, V. 35
Park, R. E. 51, 225
Parsons, T. 13
Pickvance, C. 11, 16
Pizzorno, A. 12, 19, 20
Poulantzas, N. 35, 67, 68, 69, 72, 73, 77, 80, 81, 82, 83, 84, 85, 86, 87, 89, 90, 93, 95, 96, 97, 98, 123

Resler, H. 76, 92, 93
Rex, J. 13, 14, 116
Rossi, P. 15

St Simon 50
Sandys, D. 174, 176, 177, 178, 180
Saunders, P. 29
Schattschneider, E. E. 15
Schmitter, P. C. 101, 102
Schumpeter, J. A. 18, 95
Scott, W. 133, 134, 135, 136, 137
Selznick, P. 161
Sharp, T. 165, 169, 171, 173, 188, 197, 203, 204, 210
Simmel, G. 52
Simmie, J. M. 101
Skeffington, H. 152, 193
Sutcliffe, B. 78
Sweezy, P. M. 67, 71, 72, 78

Thomas, M. 201
Thomas, R. 256
Titmuss, R. 22
Touraine, A. 12
Trotsky, L. 71, 72, 75, 76, 77, 80, 94, 95, 98, 123

Urry, J. 70

Wakeford, J. 70
Walker, P. 187
Walton, P. 68
Weber, M. 18, 35, 39, 45, 50, 64, 101, 160, 161
Westergaard, J. 12, 13, 14, 76, 92, 93
Wildavsky, A. 23
Winkler, J. 98, 101, 102, 103, 104, 107, 108, 114, 115, 116, 117, 118, 119, 120

Subject Index

aesthetics 167
authority 8

Bonapartism 86, 98, 121
British National Government 1931 86
bureaucracy 40, 64, 93, 160-1: autonomy 161, 165, 217, 221-2; growth 291; knowledge 94; political domination 117

Caesarism 86, 98, 121
capital: competitive 68, 72; finance 70-1; imperialist theory 49; monopoly 68-9, 70, 73, 90; profit maximisation 100; state monopoly 71-3
capitalism 45, 50
central government, secrecy of 176
Christ Church Meadow 171, 174-5, 183, 185, 188
cities as political units 53-4
collective facilities 202-9
commercial property: distribution 257-8; values 266-8
Communist Party of the Soviet Union 47
communist revolutions 94-5
community action 152, 154: working-class 193
Condorcet paradox 42-3
'conjuncture' 89
corporate state, empirical limits of 114
corporations 46: secrecy 250
corporatism 98: business-interest representation 216; definition 105-6; economics 101-2, 104; free markets 105; interest representation 101-2, 104; nationalism 114-15; order 114-15; success 114-15; unity 114-15
corporatist administration 118-20

corporatist power structures: distributional outcomes 307-8; planning 304-7
corporatist state, definition of 122
Cowley Community Association 193
Cowley Shopping Centre 259-62
Cutteslowe Walls 207-9

development, definition of 219
development control 132: application types 143, 220-1, 231-2; bargaining 233-4; change 292; distribution 133; outcomes 225; property rights 224, 297; reform 222-4; tenure type 235-6
development plans 132, 198: change 293; Oxford 166; power 293-7; value judgements 292
distributive groupings 33, 256
division of labour 41, 78, 100: organisations 43-4

ecological fallacy 141
electoral control 48
externalities 53-4, 214-15

factors of production 131

General Development Order 219
German jurists 121
green belt in Oxford 206
guild socialists 106, 109, 118

housing: comprehensive redevelopment 198-9; council housing location 202; council objectives 200-1; types and location 268-79; values in Oxford 280-1; working-class 198, 201-2
Housing, Town Planning, etc., Act 1909 131

350 Subject Index

'imperfect pluralism' 89
income 22
incorporation 113
industrial society 39, 45-6, 50-1, 55, 66-7, 93
interests 14, 15: functional representation 112-13; incorporation 291; representation 64, 98, 109-11
international economy 74

land: corporatism 131; social conflict 305; user groups 141, 231, 300-4
Liberal pluralists 121

managerialism 115-16
Marks & Spencer Ltd 246
Morris Motors 201, 247-50, 267

National Economic Development Organisation 107

oligopoly 108: the market 99
organisations 55: distributive outcomes 289
Oxford: gasworks 214-15; distribution of planning applications in wards 237-40; social characteristics of wards 139, 141-3, 226-9; social-class composition 225-6
Oxford City Council: committees 154; composition 149-51; departments 157-9; secrecy 155-6; transport policy 187
See also in Name Index
Oxford Preservation Trust 174, 182, 195
Oxford University 171-3, 175, 177-8, 182, 184-5: power of 241-6

planning: ideology 165-6; interest groups 166; legislation and national pressure 292; political control in Oxford 152; power 290; profitability 210-14; social-class domination 290
planning applications, types of 220
political change in marginal constituencies 291
political pluralism 110
political systems 19
politics, definitions of 8, 16
power: bureaucracy 95-6; cities 132-3; community studies 17-18;

core assumptions 92-3; definitions 7-16; distribution of public funds 28; distributional outcomes 55; functional groups 101; land uses 132; organisations 19-21, 40; outcomes 21-7, 112; private corporations 103; social class 89
preservation 167-8
Pressed Steel Company 250, 267
principal component analysis 133-5: Oxford 136-7
proletariat 74, 87: classless society 80
property distribution 252-7 (see also land)
property rights: distribution 225, 251-81, 297-9; post-war planning 230
public corporations 118
public interest 100

Rhodesia 108
roads: bypasses 169-70; inner relief 171-88; intermediate relief 170-1; traffic survey 178, 184; transport policy 187
ruling class 63, 91

St Catherine's College 241
St Ebbe's 171, 174-5, 177, 185, 188-97, 299: Charles Street 195; commercial expansion 189, 191; council buildings 197; housing 272-7; industry 276; participation 193-4; planning objectives 189-90; rehousing 190; traffic 190-1
St. Thomas' 200
social class 67, 81: distribution 56, 76-7; interests 54-5; power 83, 96-7; social structure 34, 36-40, 43; Soviet Union 48; the state 65; urban conflicts 56
social conflict and the growth of the state 306
social democracy 90
social strata 82
social stratification in cities 51
social structuration 41-2, 49, 55
social structure in organisations 305
societal corporatism 104
sovereignty and the rule of law 92
Soviet Union: capitalism 75-6; social class 48

state 47, 60–4: agents 85; autonomy 65, 73–4, 84–5, 121; changing role 216; class oppression 87; economic development 66; national state 73, 77–8, 82; policy 112; private economy 107–8; profit 99; revolution 88
state corporatism 104
syndicalists 106, 109

technocracy 117
technological innovation 99

technostructure 47–8
Town and Country Planning Act 1947 138, 149
Town and Country Planning Act 1968 193

underconsumption 70
urban economies 51–2, 54
Use Classes Order 219

Westgate Shopping Centre 263–5
Whitehall 117

GPSR Compliance
The European Union's (EU) General Product Safety Regulation (GPSR) is a set of rules that requires consumer products to be safe and our obligations to ensure this.

If you have any concerns about our products, you can contact us on

ProductSafety@springernature.com

In case Publisher is established outside the EU, the EU authorized representative is:

Springer Nature Customer Service Center GmbH
Europaplatz 3
69115 Heidelberg, Germany